Psyche & Spirit

Psyche & Spirit

HOW A PSYCHIATRIST FOUND DIVINITY
THROUGH HER LIFELONG QUEST FOR TRUTH
AND HER DAUGHTER'S AUTISM

MELINDA EDWARDS, MD

ADVANCE PRAISE

This fascinating, courageous, and keenly observed memoir moved and inspired me. Patient, doctor, mother, Edwards details her remarkable journey from the mountains of Guatemala to the storied halls of Stanford University and beyond. She describes a lifetime of spiritual longing that culminates with an awakening to the wonders of ordinary life, made possible in no small part by a not-so-ordinary little girl, her daughter Saachi. A captivating read and a triumph of the spirit.

> —ANNA LEMBKE, MD, *New York Times* bestselling author of
> *Dopamine Nation: Finding Balance in the Age of Indulgence*

Filled with search, struggle, discovery and compassion, Psyche & Spirit is a vulnerable telling of her ability to grow, shine and finally be an advocate for herself and her daughter.

> —SHARON SALZBERG, *New York Times* bestselling author of
> *Lovingkindness* and *Real Change*

In *Psyche & Spirit*, Mindy shares her journey, a journey from Love to Love. She is an example for us of someone who has taken the teachings of Neem Karoli Baba (Maharajji) to heart: "Love everyone, serve everyone, remember God." With great determination and dedication she is manifesting them in her life, here, in THIS world. Her compelling story is a powerful reminder of the force of spirit as it seeks balance with the human mind.

> —KRISHNA DAS, bestselling chant artist of all time;
> Grammy nominee; and author of *Chants of a Lifetime*

I bow in admiration of the way Melinda has lived through and overcome so much and managed to change challenges into gifts.

> —ROGER WALSH, MD, PhD, author of *Paths Beyond Ego*
> and *Essential Spirituality: the Seven Central Practices;*
> professor at University of California at Irvine

I have found Melinda to be one of those very rare people who takes what life brings her with acceptance and grateful joy—turning what others would consider a burden into an opportunity to learn and evolve. Her understanding of autism is a prime example of this. Rather than dismissing it as a problem or an impairment, she truly understands the beauty of the autistic condition, and how, if we're willing to listen, it points to a way forward for us all. Her compassionate and insightful wisdom shine through, and it's a great honor to be associated with her and with her mission of shining a light for the benefit of us all.

—GUY SHAHAR, author of Transforming Autism and
Founder and CEO of The Transforming Autism Project

Melinda Edwards' memoir *Psyche & Spirit* offers a frank and compelling glimpse into her lifelong spiritual quest for truth. From childhood memories of Mayans grinding corn deep in the Guatemalan mountains to the grueling rights of passage compulsory for medical school, this search culminates in unexpected sorrows and delights of single parenthood where the author ultimately finds her truth in the least likely of places as she questions her preconceived ideas about her daughter's autism.

—TONI BOUCHER, speaker, consultant and author of Autism Translated

Dr. Edwards is a powerful speaker, a gifted writer, and a genuinely compassionate physician. Her wisdom and compassion are born of her own journey. As a speaker, she has a way of fully engaging not only the mind, but also the heart and spirit, making her presentations an opportunity for a deep opening for attendees. Her book *Psyche & Spirit* kept me up all night; I literally could not put it down. How rare it is for someone to share her journey and her insights along the way in such an open, intimate and engaging way! I have referred many patients to her and have seen first-hand the transformation they undergo when she works with them. Dr. Edwards is a brilliant soul who makes this world a brighter place.

—CHRISTY CONE, MD, Founder and Medical Director, Aesthetispa

I so enjoyed this fascinating page-turner. What a touching, open hearted revelation of how this transformation has unfolded. Many thanks to this brilliant being for candidly sharing her devotion to and quest for Truth so courageously.
　　—AMITA CLARK, Nurse Anesthetist

This book/journey will take you through the full gamut of human emotions. I found myself laughing in one chapter and then sometimes crying in the next and then being on the edge of my seat in the next. Rarely does one read such a personal display of vulnerabilities and pure naked honesty all of which make her book a must read. The author's heart is exposed for your view from start to end. She left no stone unturned in her lifelong search for Truth, following her heart throughout her journey. She takes readers with her, into their hearts.
　　—ED WALLACE, Entrepreneur

To Saachi
my heart whisperer

TABLE OF CONTENTS

PART I
Hell Fire and Damnation

PART II
Psyche

The Guest House

This being human is a guest house.
Every morning a new arrival.

A joy, a depression, a meanness,
some momentary awareness comes
as an unexpected visitor.

Welcome and entertain them all!
Even if they're a crowd of sorrows,
who violently sweep your house
empty of its furniture,
still, treat each guest honorably.
He may be clearing you out
for some new delight.

The dark thought, the shame, the malice,
meet them at the door laughing,
and invite them in.

Be grateful for whoever comes,
because each has been sent
as a guide from beyond.

—Rumi

From *Selected Poems* by Rumi
Translated by Coleman Barks (Penguin Classics, 2004)

Introduction

The miracle and opportunity of being born a human being lies in the potential of every individual experience to serve as a doorway Home, a path back to the Love that we all are. Each experience is a harkening from our deepest essence—a clarion call from Love Itself. In this book, I share my extraordinary journey growing up in a Mayan Indian village in Guatemala with fundamentalist evangelical Christian parents. I recount my teen struggles with anorexia and bulimia nervosa and the challenges of medical school and residency. And I share my transformative journey with my daughter, who is on the autism spectrum. My path has included meditation retreats, spiritual teachers, travel to India, and living in spiritual communities.

Although my life has been quite colorful, the human experiences of suffering, pain, and longing are universal. On my journey, I found strength and support in the realness, openness, and vulnerability of others. The specifics of their experiences weren't nearly as relevant or helpful as their genuine sharing. Their open hearts brought me more into my own, and became a healing balm, guiding me to move through my defenses, pain, and trauma and into a freedom of heart and spirit.

The Evolution of Consciousness

Each of us is on a spiritual journey, whether we realize it or not. Our inner and outer experiences offer us opportunities to become increasingly aware of the Love that resides within us, beyond the veil of reactions, personality, and circumstances. My spiritual journey has progressed through various stages: from Suffering, to Seeking, to Longing, through Aloneness/Emptiness, and into All-Oneness. But my progression on my spiritual journey has not been linear; I have often been deep into one stage of the journey only to shift to another stage. And I typically experience elements of more than one stage at a time.

We are taught that evolution involves refinement of body and intelligence, but our consciousness, or what we are aware of, also evolves. The evolution of human consciousness occurs both individually and collectively and progresses through increasingly subtle aspects of existence—from awareness of concrete physicality to the more nuanced psyche or psychological realm, which includes awareness of emotions, thoughts, and tendencies of personality, and then to a very subtle spiritual awareness of our profound connection to the greater whole.

As our consciousness evolves, we become more attuned to the subtler dimensions of being and our interconnectedness with everything. Ultimately, individual consciousness merges with the Oneness that underpins all of existence, where there is no separation at all—no "me," no "you," no other. Oneness is the fundamental fabric of all existence, the essence of what we all Are.

Oneness

Oneness is the foundation of all religions. It is the essence transmitted by religious mystics and described by quantum physicists. The great mystics are those who dive in deep to experience what their religion points to. They are pulled beyond mental exercises of philosophizing and theologizing about their religion and enter a profound knowing, which they may call Oneness, Love, Truth, God, the Tao, Enlightenment, Awareness, The Absolute, The Infinite, Emptiness, the Oversoul, the Self, or any term that signifies That. Quantum physicists have come to the same realization as the mystics—Oneness is at the core of existence and is at the core of what we all are.

Following are just a few quotes from mystics giving voice to their wisdom:

- "There is no need to look for God here or there. He is no farther away than the door of your own heart…Isness is God."—Meister Eckhart, Christian mystic
- "You are not a drop in the ocean. You are the entire ocean in a drop…Your task is not to seek for love, but merely to seek and find all the barriers within yourself that you have built against it."—Rumi, Sufi mystic
- "When you know yourself, your 'I-ness' vanishes and you know that you and God are one and the same."—Ibn 'Arabî, Islamic mystic
- "God is unified oneness—one without two. Divine existence is indivisible." —Daniel C. Matt, *The Essential Kabbalah*
- "Whether you worship Christ, Krishna, Kali or Allah, you actually worship the one Light that is also in you, since it pervades all things… One of God's names is Love. He himself resides within all, at every moment, everywhere." —Anandamayi Ma, Hindu saint
- "Each separate being in the universe returns to the common source…If you want to know me, look inside your heart." —Lao Tzu, Taoist mystic
- "You are awareness, disguised as a person."—Eckhart Tolle, modern-day mystic
- "You are the doorway to the Infinite."—Adyashanti, Buddhist modern-day mystic

Quantum physicists have come to the same conclusion:

- "Concerning matter, we have been all wrong. What we have called matter is Energy, whose vibration has been so lowered as to be perceptible to the senses. There is no matter…. Our separation from each other is an optical illusion." —Albert Einstein
- "Ultimately, the entire universe (with all its particles, including those constituting human beings…) has to be understood as a single undivided whole, in which analysis

into separately and independently existent parts has no fundamental status."—David Bohm

The realization of what we are at our core is not limited to the great spiritual mystics or quantum physicists. Many of us have had glimpses of Oneness, moments when the clouds part and our individual self dissolves, perhaps while witnessing the exquisite beauty of a sunrise, while surfing, while meditating, or in the midst of imminent danger. And we have everyday experiences of our connection: an ache in the heart for another's suffering, intuition or premonitions, consciousness of the silence between thoughts. As our defenses and contractions dissolve, our identification with the individual "me" fades, and our hearts open. We become more and more aware of our connectedness—of the Love that we all are.

All suffering is the recognition that something is not in alignment with the Truth of what we are. We are not our stories, and yet our stories and individual experiences are doorways back Home. The desire to be free of suffering arises from the place in us that is already free—the place that recognizes suffering as a spectacular show but not what we truly Are. Even as we identify with the individual "me" and move outward, the Beacon of Truth, the Beacon of what we Are, calls all aspects of us home. It calls us because it *is* what we Are. Our suffering is the path Home to what we Are. Life continually reveals and points to the aspects that are not aligned with what we truly are—to the untruths, the contractions in our system. As these defenses and walls of separation dissolve, we become more porous and less identified with the individual "me." The movement between residing as the Oneness that we all are and engaging as an individual in the world becomes more fluid. The light of the Truth of our being shines through our individual experiences and circumstances, and life becomes a dance.

As Nisargadatta Maharaj, an Indian teacher of nondualism said, "Wisdom is knowing I am nothing. Love is knowing I am everything. Between the two, my life flows."

In this book

My intention in sharing my story with openness and vulnerability is to pass forward the gifts I was given. I offer my heart as a touchpoint for yours. When our hearts open, the defenses we have each developed throughout our life begin to dissolve, as does our suffering. Even though you may not have experienced my specific circumstances, opening your mind and heart to another's takes us all to the same place: the Heart of all hearts, where we are not separate.

This deepening into Love isn't limited to you, the individual. Your opening, deep listening and receiving create a field of compassion and healing for all, including those who have had similar experiences as those shared in this book. Your awareness of others' pain, of their challenges, fosters a collective deepening and healing.

For instance, I have been asked by others with autism in their lives to include details of my daily life with Saachi in addition to my internal journey. This inclusion serves as a bridge, with the intention of reducing the perceived divide between the world of autism and the rest of society. And so, in addition to sharing my spiritual deepening, I offer descriptions of my life with my daughter Saachi as an opportunity to bring our worlds and our hearts closer together, providing nourishment to those who feel isolated and alone on their journeys with autism. Please know that your willingness to listen with an open heart as you read is a gift to those who live with autism.

I invite you to take my hand, to allow your heart to soften and open, and to allow any darkness that blocks your awareness of the light of your essence to dissolve so that the radiance of your being may shine forth.

Ram Dass said, "We're all just walking each other home."

Let's walk home together.

Preface

The Mayan Indians in our small town of Nahualá, Guatemala were crowded onto the concrete patio that joined our house and my parents' medical clinic. The musky scent of body odor—mingled with the smell of corn tortillas that clung to their skin, their thick black hair, and homespun clothing—was familiar and comforting to me. My missionary parents, both doctors, were about to show a film. The Indians had never seen a film or television. They talked in low voices among themselves, looking over expectantly once in a while at the white bedsheet that dangled from the side of our house, which served as our movie screen.

Dressed in my usual ill-fitted, high-water pants with a dress on top, I wrapped my scratchy sweater tighter around my skinny seven-year-old frame against the chill of the late evening. Tilting my head back, I looked up into the vast eternal darkness, with thousands of stars twinkling in the clear crisp air . . . searching. I didn't have words for what I was seeking, but I felt engulfed in spaciousness and deep peace, swept up in a sense of awe, of wonder at the mystery of existence.

A hush came over the crowd as the first flickering lights of the movie hit the makeshift screen. Suddenly sharp tongues of flames rose up from the bottom of the screen, while the words THE BURNING HELL descended in bright red block capital letters from the top of the sheet down through the flames. With a sharp intake of breath, I watched images of men engulfed by flames, crying out, screaming, running frantically, their skin and hair on fire. Jolted out of spaciousness into panic and contraction, my heart raced as I wiped sweat from my hands, then clenched the skirt of my dress in my fist.

I couldn't take my eyes off the very hell that I knew awaited me.

With Mt. Sinai as a backdrop, Reverend Estus Pirkle appeared on the screen and in his best hell-and-damnation voice quoted Matthew 10:28: "Jesus said, 'And fear not them which kill the body but after that have nothing more that they can do, but rather fear him who is able to destroy both soul and body in hell fire.'" He preached on. "Jesus was talking about a place . . . called hell . . . a literal hell where sinners burn forever and ever . . . where they spend eternity. *Unless you are saved, that's where you are headed.*"

The screen again flashed fire as a clap of thunder split the ground open and animated characters fell into a fiery abyss. The Reverend boomed out Revelations 20:15: "And whosoever was not written in the book of life was cast into the lake of fire."

The film then told a story of two men who had rejected the pastor's teachings. They went on a motorcycle ride and one of them was killed. The other man returned to the pastor in his grief and asked the pastor if his friend had gone to hell. The pastor said that he had indeed gone to hell, and that there was "no such thing as friendship in hell . . . All will be one long night of sorrow, regret, and remorse forever and ever."

Until then I had only imagined how terrible hell would be, but what I saw that night in *The Burning Hell* was worse than anything I had ever dared to think. An eternity later, when the movie finally ended, I looked back up at the sky, desperate to recapture the peace and awe I had experienced earlier. Instead, my terror billowed out into the expanse, projected into the vastness of the unknown. I didn't close my eyes the whole night, terrified that if I slept I would die; I would surely wake up in hell, all alone, burning up in flames.

I was certain I was destined for that burning hellfire, but in great shame I kept this monumental secret to myself. My conviction that I was doomed was certainly not due to lack of effort. I tried countless times to be saved, to accept the Lord into my heart. I'd lie in bed or sit on the dirt floor of the church and silently beg, plead, cry for Jesus to come into my heart. With each fervent prayer, I desperately hoped to feel differently, to somehow know I was saved, to feel Jesus' presence in my heart, but I never did. I assumed that he did not want to come into my heart, that there was something wrong with me. I resigned myself to the unbearable fact that I was unsavable.

Jesus would come back to earth and take my parents, my sister, and my two brothers to heaven. He'd take my entire family . . . except me.

PART I

Hell Fire and Damnation

Jesus said, "I have cast fire upon the world,
and see, I am guarding it until it blazes."
—Gospel of Thomas

CHAPTER 1

Nahualá

Be certain that in the religion of Love
there are no believers and unbelievers.
Love embraces all.
—Rumi

In Nahualá: Al'taleen, (Unknown), Baltazaar, Juana weaving,
Mom, Kathy and Mindy. Our trailer is in the background.

A sense of timelessness permeated the village of Nahualá in the decade I lived there, from 1971-1981. Ancient grinding stones found in the area dated back to 500 BCE, and were still being made from volcanic rock to grind corn by hand. Nestled high in the mountains of western Guatemala at 8,000 feet above sea level, Nahuala's climate was cooler than much of the rest of the country. During the rainy season it rained incessantly and fog covered everything in sight, while the dry season brought endless dust. Mayan Indians, who spoke the Quiché language, made up nearly the entire population. My parents' intention was to build a medical clinic and a church, with the primary goal of converting the Indians to Christianity so that they, too, would go to heaven and avoid an eternity in hell.

In Guatemala, a villager's town could be identified by the *traje* (outfit) he or she wore. Women from Nahualá wore long, dark blue handwoven skirts called *cortes,* with one thin embroidered multicolored line running horizontally and another down the side of the corte, and square-cut tunics called *huipiles,* traditional loose-fitting white tops with an occasional colorful design. Women who wore huipiles with colorful designs were considered wealthy as they could afford to buy the colorful string. Most Nahualeño men wore traditional brown plaid wool kilts that came to the knee instead of *pantalones.*

Running water and electricity were unknown to these gentle, simple people. Women and girls walked several miles down the mountain to wash clothes on the river rocks. On the return trip they carried water to their homes in *tinajas.* They balanced these large water jugs on twisted cloths that rested on top of their heads, and walked with straight backs, chins held horizontal and steady, often simultaneously carrying babies tied tightly to their backs with a woven cloth. They walked with a graceful, fluid balance learned from childhood and passed down through generations.

By Nahualá standards my family was very wealthy. The three small split-level rooms we rented from the town mayor were perched side-by-side on the mountain slope. "Upstairs"—the upper level of the rooms—held the living room, kitchen, and dining room. "Downstairs" contained my parents' bedroom, dad's desk, a tiny couch, and a small area partitioned off by thin plywood that held a shower, a sink, and a port-a-potty. Then there was "Down-Downstairs"—aka the Dungeon—a dark dank room where we four children slept in two bunk beds.

My dad had constructed our rudimentary bathroom himself. He made the shower out of concrete and rustic tiles, and the tiny rough, rippled sink simply out of concrete. The port-a-potty was just for the girls for nighttime emergencies; the boys always peed outside, aiming into a makeshift drain made of upside-down terra cotta roof tiles that ran downhill alongside our house. Kitty-corner to the clinic and upstairs, we had an outhouse, another mark of our wealth in the village.

Other than ours, there were no bathrooms in Nahualá. The Indians took a sweat bath about once a month in a *tuj*, a tiny space with a fire pit, adobe walls, and a blanket for a door. They would beat themselves with banana leaves as they sat by the fire, drenched in sweat. The ground outside served as a toilet. Men simply turned their backs and lifted their kilts to urinate wherever they were. Women squatted when they felt nature's call, hoisting their long skirts above the earth. Bowel movements required a walk up the mountain or to a ditch, with corn husks used for wiping.

Our stinky outhouse was the only thing that might have rivaled my fear of hell. Each time I stepped inside, I gagged, then held my breath to avoid breathing in the stench as I waved flies away from the concrete toilet seat. I never thought to question why the outhouse had an outside lock, which my brothers used to lock one another inside, or why our coveted commode was home to Polly the Parrot, who would often startle visitors by whistling at them from her caged perch. Even with Polly for company, I dreaded trips to the outhouse, fearful the concrete floor slab would break and I would fall into the dreadful slosh far below.

On holidays such as *Día de los Muertos* (Day of the Dead) and *Semana Santa* (Holy Week), I joined the women and children lining the street that ran up the mountain next to our three rooms. Its cobblestones were smooth and rounded by centuries of foot traffic. We watched as pairs of men walked sideways down the street carrying heavy *marimbas,* the players tapping the instrument rhythmically with their mallets. Other men blew on *chirimías* (woodwind instruments similar to oboes), shook *chinchines* (black rattles made of gourds), and beat drums. Dancers swirled by, wearing the masks of other-worldly beasts. Others joined the ritual procession swinging small tin containers of incense, and wavy streamers of smoke rose up through the air, the aromatic offerings mixing with the sharp tang of alcohol.

• • •

Although we settled in Nahualá in 1971, the circumstances leading to our move there had been set in motion decades before. My maternal great-grandmother Mary came to the U.S. alone from Czechoslovakia, having sold a cow to pay for her boat fare, and settled in the Czech community in Nebraska. My grandmother Helen was the fifth of Mary's eleven children who grew up together on the Knoflicek family farm with no running water, a big tin tub in which they bathed one after the other, and one bed where five of them slept at night. Like her siblings, when old enough Helen moved to Chicago in order to make a living; she worked the switchboard at Westinghouse, where she met her future husband, Speed.

My mother was the oldest of two children born to Helen and Speed Martin. Even as a child, mom was a "helper," bringing home friends from school who needed clothing or food. When she was twelve years old, mom got very sick and thought she would die. In the middle of the night, feverish and sleepless, she had the spiritual experience that shaped the rest of her life. As she later said, "God told me I was supposed to be a missionary doctor." This *knowing* formed the quiet inner strength that always guided her. Her religious conviction was not compartmentalized into her church-going or prayer time, rather it informed every aspect of her life—her thoughts, her judgments, her actions, and her life choices.

Dad and Mom at their medical school graduation

Mom met dad at Ohio State University in a physiology lab when they were assigned the dissection of a dog together. He had a quirky, understated, and dry sense of humor and a sharp intelligence, but was awkward socially and lived to the beat of his own drum.

That first day, Dad was inadvertently wearing his lab coat inside out, a doughnut wrapped in a napkin poking out from a pocket. Curious about this odd person, Mom told him gently he really wasn't supposed to have food in the lab. Dad took the doughnut out of his pocket, ate it in his slow, unselfconscious and methodical way, then said, "Glad we got that taken care of." He then looked to the dog cadaver on the table between them and said, "I don't think this dog is gonna make it." Mom fell in love with him, quirks and all. She told him that God had guided her to be a medical missionary and he agreed to share her vision. They married before they started medical school. Although mom was one of the only women in her class at med school, she was not in any way a women's libber or trying to make a statement; she was simply following her calling.

During their fourth year of medical school, mom became pregnant and dropped out of school. In the delivery room, a medical resident attempted to give her a caudal epidural. As she bluntly put it, "The baby's head was down low, and the needle went into the baby's head and killed it. I turned it over to the Lord. I thought, *God's in charge.* I figured I was supposed go back to med school, finish my training, and become a missionary doctor." Her faith allowed Mom to deal with challenges and difficult emotions by putting them in God's hands. It gave her the ability to surrender to what arises in life without resistance, but also served as a means to sidestep or avoid difficult emotions.

My parents were interning in Charleston, South Carolina when my brother Kevin was born. Mom withdrew from her training to care for him, as the intern year was not a requirement to practice medicine. My siblings Scott and Kathy also preceded my entrance into the world. When I was born in November of 1967, my father was in the Air Force, having been drafted during the Vietnam War. At church, my parents heard about and joined the Central American Mission in order to pursue their calling as missionary doctors. Assigned to serve in Guatemala, they began to speak at different churches in the U.S. to raise the money necessary for their mission. By the time I was a year old, their fundraising had succeeded and we moved to Guadalajara, Mexico, where they attended language school for a year to learn Spanish. We then moved to Guatemala City, where my dad completed a one-year residency that allowed him to practice medicine in Guatemala. After our time in Guatemala City, we moved to a large town in the western highlands, Quetzaltenango. Mom found a Spanish-speaking Indian to teach her Quiché, one of the Mayan Indian dialects spoken in the region, while we awaited word from village elders about our final destination—Nahualá.

At Halloween that year we trick-or-treated at the homes of other missionaries. Kathy got to dress as a Mayan Indian girl, while I had to be a ghost. I was furious! Kathy got a beautiful, colorful outfit while I had to wear a sheet. I stubbornly refused to smile as we made the rounds. At one house, mom told the missionary, "She's having a t-a-n-t-r-u-m." I knew she was talking about me. I memorized the letters she had spelled, sounded them out in my head, and figured out what she had said. I was two years old.

The village elders of Nahualá finally gave my parents permission to settle there. Our little trailer got hauled up the mountains east of Quezaltenango to Nahualá, and the six of us lived in it for another year while dad worked on our rented rooms. He installed running water and the village's first electricity, covered the dirt floors with tiles and concrete, and built our simple bathroom. He also rented an adobe building several yards up the mountain from our house, put up plywood walls to create rooms, and so established the new medical clinic. The clinic waiting room was used for church services in the early years, and the church and clinic were the center of our lives.

• • •

The clinic was usually crowded and chaotic with the sound of babies crying and dogs and chickens wandering in and out between the Indians. Dad had cemented a patio between the house and the clinic, and patients would come to our door at all hours. They came during meals, they came at night, and my siblings and I resented them taking our parents' time and attention away from us. We were too young to understand that many of them had walked for hours from other towns to reach the clinic.

We struggled with the lack of privacy. The Indians had no concept of privacy or sense of boundaries; most of their adobe homes didn't even have doors. When we lived in the trailer, they would peek curiously through the curtains. When we moved into our home, some would walk in without knocking. Even dealing with this sense of intrusion, I did eventually come to understand why the Indians came. My siblings and I wandered freely in and out of the clinic; we talked with patients, clinic workers, and our parents. We watched as patients were treated for a variety of illnesses and wounds, and saw many healed, but others die.

Babies seemed to be everywhere in Nahualá. Mothers and older children carried babies tied to their backs or chests in handwoven *tzutes* (cloths) that served as both swaddling and diapers. Mothers would slide the tzute and baby around from back to front to nurse or to sit more comfortably. Tzutes were often wet or damp with baby urine, so that sweet scent was everywhere. It was a natural part of life in Nahualá—there was no aversion to it. When Kathy and I carried babies this way, we would frequently feel a warm dampness on our skin that crept through our clothing. Babies often slept while being carried, their heads covered with a cloth. Their mothers carried them as they went about their daily business—cooking, washing clothes in the river, carrying large tinajas of water on their heads, and working in the field.

In front of the clinic: Indian lady, her children, and Mindy carrying babies on their backs

Children came into the clinic with large swollen abdomens, skin tight over their bony limbs, sick with intestinal worms and malnourished from a diet that consisted mostly of corn and beans and coffee. Day and night my parents treated common illnesses—diarrhea due to bacterial infection and amoebas, malnourishment, machete injuries that needed sutures, pneumonia. The Indians thought an injection would cure anything and often asked for them in the clinic. By the time my sister and I were eight and ten years old, mom had us giving vitamin injections. Patients offered food or a chicken in exchange for treatment, or paid pennies. Incaparina, a high protein food supplement fortified with vitamins and minerals, was given to those in need. No one was turned away.

On Sundays in the early years, the clinic waiting room served as the church sanctuary. Indians filled the room, overflowing to the patio outside to hear the preaching of Don Julian, a pastor from another town. Later, a church that better accommodated the crowd was built on a nearby hill.

My parents' priority was their Christian work and their faith, which was nondenominational and very conservative. But aside from instilling their unquestioned religious convictions in their children, they had a hands-off approach to parenting. I don't remember ever having to tell mom or dad where I was going. My parents went to work in the clinic and we kids were free to live our lives. We ran around the village playing and visiting friends in their homes. I waded in the cold river with my pants rolled up, took a sweat bath with Kathy in our neighbors' tuj, played jacks with my friend Lulú, and ran from loose dogs. That was no small thing as many dogs had rabies; if we wandered far from home or were walking at dusk, we knew to take a stick in case we had to fight off an attacking dog.

Dogs in Nahualá had their own lives, hunting for food and running loose through the village day and night. We had many of our own dogs over the years, each of whom generously shared their fleas with us. Mom took to sprinkling dog flea powder down our shirts and pants each day. We continued this practice on our own as we got older; our bedtime routine included sprinkling the powder down our pajamas.

Our neighbor Baltazaar and his family made bootleg whiskey; Indians trickled into their house throughout the day to buy alcohol, often drinking themselves into loud rants or into oblivion. We knew to avoid that house when we heard loud laughter or yelling. As we ran about the village, we often saw men passed out, lying in the street or in the alley behind our house.

Market days on Thursdays and Sundays were the busiest days at the clinic, as Indians from surrounding villages came on those days to sell their crops in the open market. They'd sit in the dirt and lay their wares on a handwoven cloth on the ground in front of them. When things weren't busy, they'd go to the clinic. On market days, we kids would make our way to the market and bargain with the Indians for a mango or a piece of sugar cane. Mom got mad when we bargained a mango down from three cents to two cents, knowing the Indians needed every penny they got, but my frugal dad encouraged bargaining, a skill I enjoy to this day.

Left to right: Dad, Kevin, Scott, Mom, Mindy on lap, Kathy

Every night before heading off to the Down-Downstairs for bed, we had family devotions. We children sat crowded on the small blue vinyl couch, dressed in our pajamas with our teeth freshly brushed. If it was a Saturday, our hair would be damp from our weekly washing. My hair often began to singe and burn as I tried to dry it in front of the gas space heater. I'd grab a blanket to smother the fire and the smell of burnt hair would fill the cool air in the room. During family devotions, Mom or Dad sat in a chair in front of us, bible in hand. After reading a passage, they asked us a few questions about what they had read, prayed with us, and then tucked us into bed.

One night, all four of us kids got the giggles. Dad was giving devotions that night. He lost his temper—a frequent occurrence—and started yelling. By that time, in spite of our attempts to smother our laughter, we were too far gone and couldn't control it. Dad reached into the makeshift closet and pulled out his belt, shouting at us to line up for a spanking. I was last in line. Dad proceeded to spank everyone . . . except me. When he got to me, he stopped and told all of us to go to bed. The fact that I was spared was not lost on my siblings. They were envious and irritated that I was Dad's favorite.

Dad was often critical of my brothers and my sister and prone to frequent out-of-control rages directed at them that terrified me. I was always on high alert, sensing into his mood, never sure when he would blow up. He would often yell at Scott, and at times would chase my brothers around, beating them with a stick when he caught up to them. I was terrified that he would kill them. Finally, when Scott was big enough, my dad tried to beat him with a stick one last time. Scott grabbed the stick from my dad, broke it over his knee and, gritting his teeth, said, "Don't EVER do that again." My dad never beat my brothers again, but he continued his critical outbursts.

Dad suffered with loud noises, holding his hands to his ears when we kids were boisterous or when there were sudden surprising sounds in the environment. He avoided being around crowds, including those in the clinic, whenever he could. Later, when we were back in the States, he actually hid in his room when company came over. He seemed unaware of social norms, and wasn't influenced by what others thought. He took his time with everything. Standing in line at a restaurant, he dallied over the menu board, unbothered by the impatient people behind him in line. He also developed a hoarding compulsion during that time, starting with his papers piling up on the dining room table. As this tendency got worse, the house became so overrun with boxes, papers, and sale items he had purchased that even navigating around the house became a challenge. He loved classical music; later, when we were back in the States, our living room filled up with hundreds of classical music CD's covering the floor and stacked high. He had a remarkable memory for details about sports, recalling scores and specific plays of college or professional games played even decades before. In retrospect, many of his "quirks" were consistent with Asperger's syndrome, now known as high-functioning autism.

Dad was born and raised in Marietta, Georgia, and had one younger sister, Betty. His grandfather Edwards was a physician who made house calls on horseback. His kind and gentle father, Grant Edwards, was formal, always dressed up in a suit and tie; he owned and ran a gas station. His mother, Gabrielle, was mean-spirited and critical of her children and everyone else, including her mother, who was a gentle and loving soul. Unlike her husband, Gabrielle had gotten a college degree, which was very unusual in those days. She bought and sold properties and hid her financial shenanigans from the Internal Revenue Service, which eventually got her in trouble.

Dad, despite his difficult upbringing and his harshness with my siblings, was always kind to me. He enjoyed all things mechanical and liked to explain to me how things worked. He often took me into his "workshop"—a closet-sized storage room just off the Upstairs room where he kept his tools. I sat on his lap at his workbench while he showed me how to use the tools as he attempted to fix various household items. I feigned interest because, at some level, I recognized my dad's loneliness and the pain beneath his rages. I felt his sadness and wanted to be there for him despite my fear of his rage. Dad's temper cast a heavy cloud over the family, leaving no room for peace or pure and simple joy. Happy times were always tinged with unease and the prospect of what would set him off next.

Being dad's favorite alienated me from the rest of the family. Mom was busy protecting my siblings from him; she assumed I was safe and did not need her attention. My siblings were jealous of my immunity to his rage and resentful of my special position. My sense of aloneness—already profound because of the shame of believing Jesus wouldn't save me—deepened.

. . .

One afternoon, I stood alone under the roof that hung over our front door, watching the downpour of rain, feeling a cool dampness on my legs as the heavy raindrops smacked into the concrete patio in front of me and splashed up onto my pants. My body was still; I was mesmerized by the sound of the rain pounding on the tin roof, the rivulets of water flooding down the small drain that ran alongside our house, and the smell of wet rain engulfing me. I looked up at the dark sky and stepped forward onto the patio, opening my mouth and raising my palms, welcoming and absorbing the rain into myself.

Suddenly, a brilliant flash of yellow light came down from the sky and struck my chest with a loud *Boom!*, jolting and reverberating down through my whole system. The shock paralyzed my body and glued my feet to the ground. My eyes were blinded by the light. When finally I was able to move, I heard a piercing scream coming from deep in my throat. Mom rushed out of the house, picked me up, and carried me inside, doing her best to calm me. I kept screaming, my body buzzing, my ears ringing, and my hair standing on end. I didn't know what had happened, and neither did Mom. I only knew that light had hit my body. Not until later did I realize I had been struck by lightning. My child's mind though, already trained to judge experiences in terms of good and evil, chalked up the lightning strike as yet more proof of how bad I really was at my core. God had struck me from the sky, warning me loudly that if I didn't get saved, I was going to hell.

But for me there was no getting saved, no matter how hard I tried.

• • •

"Good night, I love you, have a nice sleep and sweet dreams and don't forget to say your prayers!" My sister Kathy and I lay in our beds going through our nightly ritual chant, racing to see who could say it the fastest. We were in the bedroom we shared with our two brothers, that dark cold room—the Down-Downstairs—with the perpetual smell of damp concrete. I was five years old. Kathy's bed was a few feet away from mine; she slept on the upper bunk of one bed while I slept on the lower bunk of the other. It wasn't yet bedtime for Kevin and Scott, so Kathy and I had the room to ourselves. We each snuggled under our blankets, giggling and chatting as we resisted the pull to sleep. "I won! I said it faster! One more time! On your mark, get set, GO!"

"Nightloveyousleepsweetdreams!" We speed-talked through the words, each claiming to have said them faster. Eventually, our chatter and giggles faded and we slept.

Sometime later in the night I awoke suddenly to a piercing, deafening silence in the room that filled my body with terror. The Silence was so loud, so overwhelmingly present, that it penetrated the entire pitch black room and jolted me out of sleep. At first I could hear Kevin in his bunk bed above me, breathing steadily in his deep sleep. Then the deafening Silence became louder, swallowing up Kevin's breathing, swallowing up everything around me.

I clung to my mattress, paralyzed, unable to scream, unable to breathe. Louder . . . LOUDER . . . the Silence engulfed me. This presence wasn't only loud to my ears; its profound realness roared throughout my whole being, permeating every cell of my body. Now it began swallowing me up . . . swallowing my thoughts . . . swallowing my ability to think . . . swallowing my sense of *me*, any remnant of an idea of a *me*. I was disappearing, dissolving. Frantic, I felt like I was drowning, kicking and fighting for survival although I couldn't move. Then there was nothing left but this Presence. No me, no objects, no struggle, no nothing except for *This*.

With monumental effort, I forced a thought: *I'm here. I'm here. I'm here*—a mantra I clung to, desperately fighting against this death of "me."

Eventually, the roaring silence that had swallowed me up began to recede. I became aware of a body within the vast silence. I WAS the silence, inside the body, outside the body, everywhere. Gradually, I became more aware of the body that lay on its back, arms outstretched, hands clinging to the mattress. I felt the rapid thud-thud, thud-thud in my chest, and recognized a heartbeat. I heard the rhythmic whisper of breath, in-out, in-out, and I pulled into that body with all my might, with all my mind. I looked through its eyes, frantically searching for objects my mind could name. My eyes noticed a pinpoint of soft orange light to my right, hanging from the wooden post of the bunk bed—the control for the electric blanket. My mind came alive, labeling, defining the objects I could make out in the dim orange glow. In the distance I heard a repeated *arf, arf,* and my mind recognized the distant barking of a dog. I found myself more and more in this body, and with tremendous relief I very intentionally moved a hand up close to my face, opening and closing the fingers. *I'm here. I'm here. I'm here. This is my hand, my arm, my body.*

Although the silence diminished and bodily awareness returned, the terror remained. I had no way of knowing or understanding that through some unfathomable grace a crack had opened in my normal consciousness and given me a glimpse of what we all are at our core, beyond our human bodies, our human personalities, our human thoughts and minds. I was given a glimpse of *that* which exists prior to thought, individuals, or objects—*that* which gave birth to the universe. But I couldn't grasp any of this as a young child. I was left with the utter panic brought on by the threat of the death of "me." It shook me to my core and added to the terror that had become the very fabric of my childhood.

By the next morning, unable to withstand the immense weight of the encounter with the "Great Silence," my terror shifted into shame: once again, I knew something had to be terribly wrong with me for this to have happened. I told no one about this experience and blocked it from my memory for a long long time.

A few years later, the silence revisited, this time while I played quietly one day in our bedroom. Again, the silence was so real—more real than anything I had ever encountered or imagined—and so loud it swallowed me up. The only vestige of "me" was terror. I again fought back desperately and eventually the silence subsided. This time, with shame and religious beliefs more firmly in place, I knew God was punishing me because I was bad, I was evil, and I was far beyond saving. I again blocked this from my memory. The remembrance would return years later during a meditation retreat.

I couldn't know then that this glimpse of Truth, of Source, would pull me in more and more fiercely, with more force than a black hole, ultimately dissolving me completely. I couldn't know then that in spite of the terror, in spite of the shame, in spite of all of the suffering that was to come, that which is deeper, truer, and more real than anything in this realm would pull me into Itself with an omnipotent force—and would give birth to the dance of Life, the dance of Love. Indeed, the terror, the very suffering itself would serve as my doorway to Truth.

CHAPTER 2

Huehue Academy

I wish I could show you when you are lonely or in darkness
the astonishing light of your own being.
—Hafiz

Inside the trailer, left to right: Mindy, Kathy, Mom, Scott, Kevin.
The couch folded into a bed each night, as did the table.

When we were in Quezaltenango, Mom began teaching my four-year-old sister kindergarten lessons. Kathy was very social and preferred running through the village visiting old friends and making new ones to boring book work. I was only two, but sat with them during lessons and innocently blurted out answers to my mom's questions, adding to my sister's frustration with academics. Mom again home-schooled Kathy in Nahualá for first grade. Kevin taught me to read that year when I was four.

Just as when mom had taught Kathy kindergarten in Quezaltenango, I sat with mom and Kathy at the dining table in our tiny trailer and often answered mom's questions before Kathy had a chance to respond. The next year, Kathy was sent to a boarding school along with my brothers, and mom taught me first grade at home. I enjoyed the lessons, but I missed Kathy terribly. The next year, six years old and a second grader, I joined my siblings at Huehue Academy, a Christian boarding school for missionary children in Huehuetenango, Guatemala. The school accommodated seventy students for the first through ninth grades. Kathy and I lived in the Little Girls' Dorm—a long hallway of bedrooms and a living room area with a fireplace, chairs, and a ping pong table. Our dorm parents, Aunt Louise and Aunt Peg (we addressed all our teachers as "Aunt" and "Uncle"), lived in a small apartment on the other side of the living room.

My first day at Huehue, Aunt Louise walked with me through the dorm to show me my room. The hallway seemed so long—lined with so many rooms—that I was worried I wouldn't remember which room was mine. Shy and sensitive, I was overwhelmed by all the new sights, sounds, and smells. I was introduced to my two roommates, who were busy unpacking their clothes and placing them in the rickety dressers and cubicles. Alice, a roommate who was a few years older than me, helped me put my clothes in the dresser and make my bed. I placed my brightly-colored patchwork quilt on my bed and at first was comforted by its familiarity, but then was reminded of all I had left behind. Alice climbed up on the dresser, asked me to hand her my suitcase, and hoisted it into the opening above the closet. She looked down at me and saw tears spilling down my face. She jumped off the dresser, took me by the hand, and said, "Come on, I'll show you around, Mindy. It will be okay, I promise!" Alice took me under her wing that first year, telling me how things worked at Huehue, showing me how to do my chores, and giving me important information about different teachers and how to avoid getting in trouble.

That first night, toothbrush in hand, I followed the other girls down the long hallway to our dorm mothers' apartment, where Aunt Louise put toothpaste on our toothbrushes. I was silent, the newness of everything a shock to my system. I felt a sense of expansion, as if I extended out beyond the confines of my body. As I walked quietly back down the hallway towards the bathroom to brush my teeth, carefully holding my toothbrush with its freshly applied paste and listening to the sound of my onesie's pajama feet scraping rhythmically along the cool tile floor, I heard Aunt Louise say to Aunt Peg, "Isn't she just so cute!" For the first time, I experienced self-consciousness—awareness of someone else's perception of me. I didn't understand it at the time, but this self-awareness marked the beginning of my loss of childhood innocence.

Huehue accommodated kids from a variety of Christian missions, all equally conservative. Classes were taught in English, although everyone also took Spanish classes. The Spanish classes were advanced, as we all spoke it fluently, having grown up with friends in our villages who spoke Spanish. The boys and girls were together throughout the day in classes and activities, such as sports, games, free time, and hikes, but we slept in separate dorms. Although I wasn't ever allowed to room with my sister, I saw her throughout the day when our paths crossed during activities, as she was just one grade ahead of me. I saw my brothers at meals, but didn't have much interaction with them as they were older and involved in different activities.

Before meals, we all stood in line in the hallway outside of the dining room. While in line, I sometimes found myself gagging at the smell of cooked cauliflower or liver, knowing I would have to eat whatever was served on my plate. Between meals, we were often hungry. In an attempt to dampen our hunger, my best friend Amy and I would sometimes sneak into the dining room, grab salt and pepper shakers from the nearest table, shake some of each into our palms and lick it up. Although a good distraction, it didn't do much to satisfy hunger.

Every day while we ate lunch, the principal of the school, Uncle Harold, stood behind an empty table with a stack of envelopes in his hands. Needless to say, no one living in the villages of Guatemala had telephones, and telegrams were used primarily for emergencies. Our only form of communication with our parents while we were at Huehue was through letters. We all listened with hopeful anticipation as Uncle Harold called out the names of the addressees, then placed their letters from home on the table. The lucky ones rushed through lunch, eating everything on their plates as required, quickly walked their dishes to the kitchen window, then speed walked to the mail table in search of their precious missives. My brothers, sister, and I were often among the recipients. We could each count on a weekly handwritten letter from mom—a steady and dependable fact of our lives, an unconscious bulwark against loneliness and a reliable, concrete manifestation of our parents' presence in our lives. In retrospect, I can imagine my mom staying up late after working long hours at the clinic fulfilling her life's mission, but steadfast in her determination to be there for us as best as she could.

Each Friday, all students wrote letters home, except the students that were going home for the weekend. When my older brothers first began attending Huehue Academy before Kathy and I did, students were required to remain at school all year, returning home only for Christmas break. My mom felt Scott was too young for this long separation and pulled him out of school his first year. She wrote to the head of the mission in the U.S., telling him that separating children from their parents for that long was wrong—children needed to be allowed to return home for weekends whenever parents could bring them home. Not long after she wrote the letter, the policy was changed. By the time Kathy and I began attending Huehue, students were allowed to visit home. We were one of the very fortunate families going home every other weekend; most of our friends went home much less frequently.

Kathy and Mindy

When we took the bus home from school every other Friday, Kathy would watch anxiously out the window so we didn't miss our stop. Sweet, innocent, and naive Kathy worried about everything. I had to reassure her often, especially when Kevin picked on her or Dad called her "dumb."

Today Kathy is a very bright and gifted teacher, but overcoming what she was told about herself as a child and her own childhood fears about salvation and hell was not an easy journey. Christianity was central to my parents' lives, and our family's life. Each word in the Bible was taken as the literal word of God, and the focus was on fear of—and salvation from—hell. There was a simple solution. Just receive Jesus into your heart and you would be saved, avoid hell, and be taken to heaven when the Lord came back for the second coming of Jesus. As an adult, I found out that I wasn't the only kid in our family terrified of going to hell. Kathy told me that she, too, lived with that fear. She had asked Jesus into her heart over and over again until she was eight, when she finally felt she was saved. "But even when I was older," she shared, "I doubted myself. Mom took me aside when I was fifteen and told me that based on what I told her about having asked Jesus into my heart, I *was* saved. She showed me bible verses that gave me peace. I worried about everything. When Mom told me that God was in charge, it settled my heart and helped with my worrying and anxiety." I never had a conversation like this, or any reassurance from Mom about the status of my soul. The trauma of *The Burning Hell* and the fear-based Christianity that I grew up with was not addressed or healed in my childhood.

I dreaded Sundays when, after our weekend at home, one or both of my parents drove us back to Huehue. They typically stayed only a few minutes after dropping us off. My sadness and grief were profound, but I always stifled the overwhelming urge to weep my heart out. I fought back my tears because sadness was taboo at Huehue. There was an unspoken rule that we weren't supposed to cry when our parents brought us back to school. Those who couldn't control their sadness and cried were embarrassed and ashamed. I would sometimes rush into the bathroom stall to hide the few tears that slipped out, trying my best to hold back the floodgates. The heaviness and heartache stayed with me Sunday night and the next day during my classes. I did my best to shake it off, bringing all my attention to whatever activity I was engaged in. Eventually, the heaviness would fade, but a residue always lingered. Until I was in my twenties, Sundays and Mondays were heavy days for me.

One Sunday, Mom and Dad stayed at school longer than usual, even joining us for supper. As I hugged them goodbye I felt the familiar ache and fought back tears, but I pretended to be okay. After going to bed I was fully aware that my parents had not left the school grounds yet, as I had been listening intently for the sound of their car starting up. I assumed they must be with Kevin and Scott in the boys' dorm. I lay in bed, my heart aching, weeping silently into my pillow, careful not to let my roommates hear.

That night my heart could no longer bear the immensity of the ache. I found myself sneaking to the front door of the dorm, terrified of being caught yet unable to stop myself. I planned to get into the back of the car and hide, without my parents knowing I was there until we arrived in Nahualá. Reaching the front door, I realized the futility of my plan. Even if I managed to get to Nahualá without being caught, my parents would bring me back to Huehue, and I would ultimately end up right back here. Feeling helpless, I dropped to the floor, quietly sobbing, then crept back to bed, the front of my nightgown wet with tears. I lay awake for hours. The next morning, my roommate asked why my eyes were swollen. I lied, saying I slept on them the wrong way.

In third grade, a new girl joined our class. Amy and I became best friends the moment we met. I was mischievous, often getting into trouble with my antics and frequently roping Amy into adventures. Schoolwork was where I excelled, but I hid my grades from Amy, knowing she didn't do as well. One time she saw I had gotten an A on a test and teased me about it. On the next few tests I intentionally wrote incorrect answers and made sure she saw my grade, not wanting her to be upset with me. Amy, however, was much more athletic than I was, beating me in track and other sports and always chosen first by other kids in team sports.

In spite of our academic and athletic differences, Amy and I were inseparable comrades in mischief. At one point during the third grade, we concocted an elaborate plan to run away from school. For weeks we snuck bread in our pockets at meals, later wrapping the bread in a cloth and hiding it in a trunk. We pocketed old bars of soap and coins that we were supposed to have placed in the church offering plate, which we also wrapped in cloth and placed with the bread. We spent hours discussing the best time for our escape and decided to leave right before Sunday Night Sing, when the entire school gathered to sing Christian songs. We hoped we wouldn't be missed in the large gathering.

As soon as we heard the first warning bell for Sing, we rushed to the dorm bathroom to hide, standing on the toilets in separate stalls so that no one could see our feet under the stall doors. After the second bell we gathered our loot from the bottom of the trunk, tiptoed out the front door, and headed for the barbed wire fence behind the Big Boys' Dorm. We crouched through the barbed wires and ran down the dirt road, giddy and nervous. Dusk was quickly turning into night. Out of breath, we slowed to a walk. I turned on my flashlight. Trees and brush on either side of the road cast ominous shadows that jumped and swayed with each step. Our glee shifted to nervous chatter, although I feigned fearlessness. I pulled out a hunk of bread from my bag and gave Amy a piece. The bread was hard and stale and tasted of soap. I spit the bread out and rinsed my mouth with water from my tin thermos. We walked on at a slower pace, beginning to realize we hadn't planned past the moment of our escape.

"*Shhhh!* Mindy, what's that sound?" I stopped and listened; I heard a dog barking in the distance. A sudden rustle in a bush to my right made my heart race. "Chata!" Amy used her nickname for me, reserved for special circumstances. "Maybe we should go back! What if there's a wolf in the bush?" She gave voice to her fears, fanning my own. I felt terror climbing up my throat. Simultaneously, we turned around and ran full speed back down the dirt road. As we scrambled through the barbed wire, a barb caught on my sleeve and ripped my jacket and my skin. Fueled by fear, I barely felt it. We rushed back to the dorm and threw our bags into the trunk just as our roommates began returning from Sing. That was the end of our escape dreams.

Occasionally, missionary speakers would come to Huehue to give a sermon. One weekend, a couple, Aunt Yvette and Uncle John (we addressed all missionaries, including the parents of other students, the same way we addressed the teachers), came from Guatemala City. They were different from others who had come—they were young, well-dressed, and well put-together. Aunt Yvette seemed kind, and even wore a bit of makeup! When Aunt Yvette and Uncle John spoke to us, they spoke about God's love, not about hell, and their words were infused with kindness. By this time I was having difficulty bearing the weight of my terror—the knowledge that I was unsaved and doomed to hell. Although I briefly forgot the terror when I lost myself in activities, it would inevitably slam back into my awareness the moment activity slowed. I often found myself near tears, alone with this terrible fate. Desperate for relief from holding the weight of my secret for so long, I decided to talk to Aunt Yvette. We set up a time to meet.

The next day my body quaked as I walked over to the Teachers' Dorm where Aunt Yvette was staying. Hands clammy and heart filled with intense emotion, I burst into tears as she invited me in. She sat beside me on the bed and asked what was troubling me. As I cried, she seemed distant and I wondered if I had made a grave mistake in bringing this to her. Nevertheless, I had come this far and so I plunged in. "Aunt Yvette, I don't think I'm saved," I said, between sobs. To my dismay, the floodgates opened and I wept harder, heaving with all that I had held in, unable to hold back any more.

Aunt Yvette was in over her head. She sat beside me silently as I wept. Eventually, when my cries quieted, she calmly said that all I had to do was to receive Jesus into my heart and I would be saved. My heart sank to the floor. She didn't get it. I had tried that so many, many times and it didn't work! Numb now, with an utter hopelessness settling in, I went through the motions, getting down on my knees as she instructed, repeating the words after her, "Dear Jesus, Please come into my heart. In Jesus' name, Amen."

"See honey, that's all it takes. It's all better now." She smiled, reserved and detached, as she gave my back three brief pats. I nodded, filled with shame for having shared my terror, for having revealed to this stranger my deepest secret, the depth of my anguish, my horror about being unsavable. I resigned myself to the hopelessness of knowing that I would have to continue to bear this burden alone, and then burn alone in hell forever. Neither Aunt Yvette nor I understood that what my aching heart needed was to be met fully and completely with love.

• • •

We spent Christmas break and summers in Nahualá. Occasionally, we took family vacations. We visited the Mayan ruins of Tikal in Belize a number of times, climbing up the steep, giant ruins. Some were so tall that we were perched above the trees by the time we made it to the top. We also vacationed at Likin, in Puerto Quetzal, a town on the Pacific coast of Guatemala where the ocean is lined with a sandy beach black from volcanic ash. The ocean at Likin is now famous for its dangerous riptides; these days no one actually swims there. When we were there, staying in a small cabin, we didn't know that. We swam in the ocean, jumped waves, and walked along the beach, suffused with the happy, relaxed energy of the rhythmic crashing of ocean waves and the soft, salty ocean air.

One morning, while Mom and Scott sat on the hot beach, Kathy, Dad, and I jumped waves in the ocean, only a few yards out from shore. Between waves, the water came up to my waist. As a big wave approached us, I reached for my dad's hand, as did Kathy. Suddenly, I found myself treading water, unable to reach the bottom with my feet. I turned towards my dad, but he had disappeared. I saw Kathy doggy-paddling nearby, and saw a wave crash over her head. Then I was being sucked under the water. Panicked, I paddled my arms and legs as fast as I could as the current and the waves pulled and tumbled my body. My lungs burned. Unable to hold my breath any longer, I gasped and choked on water.

At some point my head resurfaced. Waves crashed over me as I paddled and choked, coughing up salt water from my lungs. I heard Kathy calling out, "Lord save us!" My panic intensified, knowing that I would go to hell if I died. I couldn't cry out to God for help because He had already rejected me: I was unsaveable. Between waves, I glimpsed Dad off in the distance—my strong dad, who kept us safe and took care of everything—struggling to keep his own head above water. In a flash I remembered having read about swimming parallel to the beach instead of trying to get to shore. I tried to turn my body, but was unable to turn against the force of the riptide. I was only able to keep paddling and to thrust my head above water when I could to get a breath before another wave crashed over my head. I was losing strength. I was desperately trying to breathe through the water in my lungs, and my lungs could not keep up. My whole body, my lungs, my muscles, my heart, my cells were all crying out for air, for oxygen.

Abruptly, the waves disappeared. The surface of the ocean stilled.

I swam frantically for shore, coughing up water and gulping in air. Even in the midst of my panic, the stillness of the ocean held me in a surreal silence. As if in a bubble, I again heard my sister crying out in prayer. She was close, but inside the stillness, her cries sounded far away. We were only a few yards from shore, but we couldn't get there; the residual undertow from the rip tide kept us from reaching safety. Scott ran up to the pool, got a raft and raced back to us. Plunging into the water, he thrust the raft at us. Kathy and I grabbed it and held on for dear life as he pulled us to shore. Dad, pasty white, followed. Mom got us up to our cabin, weeping and praying the whole time, thanking God for saving us. She helped Dad into a chair, where he sat all afternoon—rigid, eyes closed, white as a sheet, and sweating profusely. We left Likin the next day, never to return. We hardly spoke of this traumatic event for years.

I pushed the memory and emotions of this trauma down as best as I could, just as I had with another near-drowning I experienced when I was only three years old. We had gone on a day trip to Escuintla in south central Guatemala, where we could swim in a pool all day. After the three-hour trip, we children were eager to spend as much time as possible in the pool. Mom put me in a blow-up vest and asked Dad to watch all four of us while she went to change into her bathing suit. When she returned a few minutes later, she found me floating in the water, face down. The other kids were playing in the pool and Dad's attention was elsewhere. Horrified, she pulled me out of the water and did CPR.

• • •

At times when we were home from school, Kathy or I would accompany mom on a house call to see a sick patient who couldn't get to the clinic. House calls were usually in another village—Xepatuj, Patzité, Patzij—on the other side of our mountain or on another mountain, a few hours' hike away. We'd enter a dark, damp, windowless, single-room, adobe hut with its hardened dirt floor, home to an entire extended family. A fire always burned in the center, over which the women heated coffee in battered tin pots and tossed thin tortillas—made from fresh ground corn clapped flat between their hands—onto *comales*, the flat griddles on which the tortillas sizzled and popped. We'd be served lukewarm sugary coffee, and occasionally I'd have to gag down some soup with a small piece of gristle (a special treat!) that Mom said I had to eat.

These villages had never allowed white people in, except for Catholic nuns, but had granted permission to my parents because of the clinic and medical care they provided. Most of the Indians had never seen pale skin or light-colored hair before. Without any other context for us, some believed we were gods and goddesses from another realm. Since there was a chance we might be gods, we were always treated with great respect. Completely fascinated by our hair, the Indians often reached out to touch it, and at times we'd be surprised by a comb running through our hair. When Kathy was three years old, she began rubbing her head, saying, "Mommy, my head hurts!" Mom looked through her hair and screamed. She had never seen head lice before. After ridding us all of lice, she told us not to allow anyone else to comb our hair, but this was easier said than done. We had to have quite a few more treatments with lice shampoo over the years.

When I was seven years old, Mom and I walked for an hour with a patient's wife who had come to fetch us to their hut. When we arrived, my tall mother had to duck down to get through the door. I felt the usual sting in my eyes from the thick smoke coming from the fireplace. The familiar smell of sweet coffee, corn tortillas, and smoke filled my nostrils; the smoke burned my lungs and I did my best to stifle a cough. Only a stretched-out rectangle of light, let in by the open doorway, kept the room from being completely dark. Mom went to the figure lying in the corner under a blanket. Between his hacking coughs, I heard his labored breathing. There was a hush in the room as Mom spoke quietly in Quiché to the man.

His young daughter lifted a tin pot from the fire, poured some of the tan liquid into a dirty tin cup, and gently handed it to me.

"*Maltiox, na'an,*" I said as I reached for the cup. I knew better than to refuse anything from the Indians. Mom had told us many times that we must accept whatever they offered, even if we didn't want it, as to refuse went against custom and would hurt them deeply. Kneeling by the fire, I held the syrupy coffee, occasionally pretending to take a sip. Mom put a thermometer in the man's mouth and her fingers on his wrist, taking his pulse. Next, she pulled her stethoscope from her purple-and-green *morral* (woven bag). As family members helped him sit up, his coughing intensified. I watched as he covered his mouth with a blood-stained cloth. When the physical exam was complete, mom pulled out a bible from her bag and read some scripture in Quiché to the man. She then closed her eyes and prayed in Quiché. Finally, she reached in her bag and pulled out a bottle of medicine. "*Jun cuchará oxmul jun 'ij.*" Take one teaspoon three times each day. As we said goodbye, we were given hot tortillas wrapped in a dirty handwoven cloth.

Sometime after this visit, I quit eating. I wanted to pretend to be sick to get attention. When we kids were sick, mom put a blanket on the hard wooden bench in our living room and let us lie there while she worked; she'd come from the clinic to the house to check in on us throughout the day. I was determined to get attention, so I also quit drinking, even water. After a few days, Mom began to worry. By this time, I was afraid the pretending had gotten the best of me and I didn't know how to pretend to get well. I didn't have a fever, but I was growing weaker. After a week of eating and drinking very little, my parents took me to a doctor in Quetzaltenango, a town forty-five minutes away. The clinic there had more modern medical care, with an x-ray machine and the ability to draw blood for lab samples. Dr. Cohen admitted me to the hospital for tests.

As I shivered in my hospital gown, the X-ray technician nudged me closer to the cold metal plate, instructing me in Spanish to lean against it. He placed my arms above my head, hands cupping my head. The technician disappeared to another room and I heard his instruction to take a deep breath in and hold it, hold it, hold it. A loud click, then "*Ya puedes respirar.*" I exhaled, dizzy from holding my breath. He adjusted my body a few more times for more X-rays before wheeling me off to my hospital room, where my mom waited. Soon a cheerful nurse entered the room, pushing an IV pole with a bag of fluid hanging from a hook. I saw the ominous-looking needle in her hand. I turned my head and pinched my leg hard to distract myself from the prick of pain. (It's still a habit whenever I'm jabbed by a needle.) The nurse connected the long, thin tube from the bag of fluid to the needle in my arm. I felt a cold rush into my vein as the bag began its drip-drip-drip.

A few hours later, Dr. Cohen arrived. He chatted with me briefly before turning to my mom. "I've looked at the X-rays, and it looks like she has a Ghon lesion in her right upper lobe." I didn't know what they were talking about, but was relieved that *something* was wrong, that I wouldn't get found out for what I thought was faking being sick. After Dr. Cohen had left the room, Mom explained to me that I had tuberculosis, or "T.B."—a bacteria had gotten into my lungs but it could be treated with antibiotics. She said I had probably caught it from her patient at the house call we had made a few months earlier.

The next morning, fully hydrated and having eaten breakfast, I felt some strength return. I asked mom for pen and paper so I could write a letter to my grandma in the States. I wanted to let her know I was in the hospital and had tuberculosis, but was still okay. Mom was visibly relieved that I was feeling better. She smiled as she read the finished letter, saying, "Grandma will love getting this, Mindy." When Dr. Cohen came by to make his rounds, I heard him and Mom both laughing. I looked up from my Nancy Drew book; to my dismay I saw that Dr. Cohen had read the letter to my grandma. I had no idea what was so funny. I was so mad I wouldn't speak to either of them. Years later, my mom and I had a good belly laugh over what I had written to my grandma: "I am in the hospital because I have T.V. but I am doing good."

I was completely surprised and relieved in the way only a child could be about having a serious diagnosis. It kept me from getting into trouble for pretending to be sick. To this day, I don't know if I lost my appetite because I was coming down with tuberculosis or if I quit eating to get attention. The upside was that I was diagnosed before the symptoms were severe and placed on triple antibiotics. This was the gold standard treatment at that time, and included streptomycin injections and daily oral antibiotics (rifampin and INH), which I took for two years. My parents taught my dorm parents how to administer the injections. Three times each week Aunt Peggy would wake me up before the other girls and I'd walk down the long hall to their apartment, half asleep, to get stung. For several years I looked forward to my regular appointments with Dr. Cohen in his outpatient clinic in Quetzaltenango. He had a kind, gentle spirit and a twinkle in his eye. He listened to my lungs with his cold stethoscope and took X-rays to ensure the encapsulated Ghon lesion had not spread.

But no matter what was going on at home or in school, I was always aware that I would be left behind and sent to hell when the end time arrived. At home, knowing this could happen at any moment, I frequently checked to make sure family members were around, that Jesus had not yet come back and taken them from me. Once, curled up in a chair reading and caught up in the story, I suddenly noticed that nobody else was in the room. Panic ripped through me. I raced outside, desperate to lay eyes on any member of my family. A chicken clucked on the patio as an Indian lady walked by, carrying a basket on her head, her baby tied to her back with a cloth. Our dog Thurman lounged in the sun, deceptively relaxed; he was always ready to jump into action and chase away any dog that dared to intrude on his territory.

I sprinted across the patio and into the clinic's waiting room. Don Manuel stood behind a table, checking in a mother who held a pale, coughing baby. I pushed through the crowd as he handed her a piece of cardboard with a number on it. Suddenly I heard the sound of my mom's voice on the other side of the thin plywood wall, explaining to a patient how to take her medication. My relief was profound. Mom was still here. Jesus had not come back and taken my family away to heaven. I stood still, my breath rapid, my heart pounding. I looked around. The crowded, normally noisy waiting room had fallen silent, all eyes on me. I pulled myself together and smiled weakly, desperate not to expose my panic and the secret that I wasn't saved. Doing my best to pretend everything was normal, I turned to Don Manuel and greeted him weakly, "*Como está?*"

"*Bien, bien. Estás bien, Mendy?*"

I ran out of the waiting room and back to the privacy of our home, shaken and sweaty with the residue of the terror that seemed to follow me everywhere I went.

• • •

Reflections on trauma

Just as children lack the ability to care fully for themselves physically, they are not yet developmentally able to care fully for themselves emotionally. Children need an external source of love, kindness, and openness in order to remain open to their own pain—whether their pain comes from trauma or simply from the uncomfortable feelings that are a natural part of daily life. The degree of love that we have access to as children has a tremendous effect on the defenses put in place to protect ourselves from pain, or conversely, the degree to which our hearts can stay open. Love and kindness directly impact the development of personality—how we navigate the world and how we respond and react to people, circumstances, and stressors throughout life.

Only someone who has allowed themselves to experience their own pain has the capacity to meet it in another. They have the intuitive knowing that what is needed is to invite full expression of feelings and to hold and meet the feelings, and the person, fully and with love. They realize that it is not helpful to submerge the painful feelings and make them "go away." Deep healing and the possibility of true wholeness come only when we completely welcome all aspects of ourselves.

Some experience emotional pain in the body and nervous system that can be traced to specific traumatic events while, for others, the pain occurs in reaction to more subtle and often repetitive traumas of the spirit. When our hearts close in response to unmet pain and trauma, defenses and patterns of personality are erected to protect us from that pain. This is the nature and dance of human experience—an initial openness of spirit and heart, the development of personality/beliefs/contractions over time, awareness of our own suffering in a variety of forms and intensities caused by resistance to pain, and seeking relief from the suffering through various pursuits or addictions—all of which eventually lead to more suffering.

Ultimately, all of existence pulls us more deeply to an understanding and unwinding of the suffering itself into the realization of Spirit at the core of our being. We are all being called Home to our hearts. In truth, the defenses and the pain themselves are an opportunity—a beckoning from Love itself—to allow the heart to open more fully. We can allow the pain to serve as the doorway to our hearts, to peel away defenses and return to Spirit. This opportunity and calling from Love remains throughout life. Indeed, it is our birthright.

We are born open, innocent, and pure. Our bodies and nervous systems are born with specific sensitivities and tendencies that contribute to the contractions that we develop over time. Our ancestry, genes, family and physical environment, and our life experiences shape the contractions that make up our personality and our tendencies of thought, emotion, and expression. These contractions separate us from Spirit, from the heart, and are the source of all suffering. This suffering is a doorway: the opportunity of all suffering is to bring us back to Source. As we heed Life's calling, allowing our defenses to dissolve and our heart's capacity to expand, we develop an intuitive wisdom. We sense into our emotions, our responses and reactions, and discern when there is further opportunity for opening and deeper healing. We know when tools, techniques and medication are being used to keep the original pain at bay, bypassing the opportunity for growth; and when they may effectively aid us in shifting or releasing habitual, ingrained patterns.

The forces orchestrating our return to Spirit are always at work, regardless of how things may appear on the surface.

CHAPTER 3

Goodbye Guatemala

The only way out is through.
—Robert Frost

February 3, 1976 was a regular Wednesday at Huehue. We awakened at 6 a.m. to Aunt Peggy's "Rise and shine!"—repeated cheerfully as she walked down the corridor, her brown polyester bell bottom pant legs swishing against each other. I stretched, jumped out of bed, and rushed to dress and complete my assigned morning chore. Chores were rotated each week and included dusting, folding and separating laundry on the ping-pong table, and sweeping the hallway or sidewalks. On this day, after dressing and splashing my face with cold water, I took the push broom from the hall closet and began trotting up and down the hallway behind it. "Mindy! If you don't slow down and sweep properly, that will be a check mark."

Doggone it! Aunt Peggy had seen me running in the hallway, which was against the rules. I slowed to a walk, fearful that I would get my third check mark that week and have to miss out on Friday night treat, our weekly dessert given during Friday Night Reading, when our dorm parent read to us from a book. I knew I'd have to hurry back to finish sweeping after breakfast, as being late for break-fast wasn't an option.

At the breakfast bell I ran to the main building, breathlessly taking my spot in the hallway line. Uncle Harold stood ominously at the head of the hallway while we all stood silently until he motioned us to enter. There were nine tables in the room, each with seven students and one teacher, and I walked to my assigned spot and stood behind my chair. After a short prayer, the room was filled with the noisy screeches and echoes of seventy chairs scraping on tile as they were pulled out from under tables.

This week, Aunt Louise was at the head of my table. I passed my bowl up to her and watched as she plopped a big lump of sticky oat-meal into it, dashing my hopes for a small scoop. Ugh. But today was a special day—after we finished our oatmeal, we could have honey and butter with biscuits. We all wolfed down the oatmeal, then joined together in the Honey-and-Butter ritual. I took my knife, scooped some butter on my plate, took the glass pitcher and poured honey on top of the butter, and then began beating the honey and butter together with my knife. The clack-clack-clack of seventy other knives beating at once echoed in the dining hall, all with the goal of mak-ing our concoction as white as possible. The harder we whipped, the whiter and tastier it got.

After breakfast, I hurried back to the dorm to finish sweeping, then brushed my teeth, aware that by now only a few of us were in the dorm, the others already on their way to morning devotions. The outdoor bell rang as I was rinsing my mouth. I ran from the Little Girls' dorm across campus to the Teachers' Dorm for devotions with Aunt Julie. That day the three other girls in my class and I practiced our verses from our *Bible Memory Verse Book*, which we would recite by memory on Friday and get a grade based on how many words we missed.

And so continued our normal day at Huehue, with our schedule structured to keep us busy and out of trouble. We had class, recess, class, lunch, break, class, Cookie-and-Water, and then afternoon activities that were assigned based on age—track, soccer, volleyball, or band. Finally, the last bell of the day announced that it was time for supper. After supper, we little kids got ready for our 7:30 p.m. bedtime; the big kids had study hall until their bedtime at 9 p.m. I fell asleep quickly, my body tired from another full day.

I was awakened suddenly in the night by a violent shaking. My hands gripped my mattress in terror as my bed and everything around me shook. I heard the sound of bicycles falling to the floor in the bike room next door, crashing sounds as things fell off our dressers, and then the sound of the dresser at the foot of my bed falling over and slamming to the floor. My roommate screamed out in fear. I heard the cries of others in their rooms down the hallway. Filled with panic, my body broke out in a cold sweat, a silent scream paralyzing my lungs and my throat. I assumed that the time of reckoning had arrived. I fully expected Jesus to descend from heaven and take everyone around me to heaven, leaving me to be swallowed up into the eternal fire of hell.

When the violent shaking ended, we girls gathered in the hall bathroom, frightened, confused, and chattering nervously. We didn't know what had just happened. Soon Aunt Peggy appeared in the bathroom doorway. She told us there had been an earthquake and that we all needed to return to bed. We did as ordered, but as soon as her footsteps faded down the hall, we rushed back into the bathroom and compared notes in hushed voices—*What's an earthquake? Did you hear the bikes crashing? My lotion fell on the floor and broke, and I stepped in it when I fell off my bed!* Soon we heard Uncle Jim's footsteps and we were ordered back to bed again. And so it went that night—sneaking into the bathroom repeatedly and returning to bed when we were caught.

Although I had never heard of an earthquake and had no idea what it was, I was profoundly relieved that Jesus had not yet come back and left me behind.

In the morning, we started cleaning up. The furniture in our bedrooms had to be righted, as did all the bicycles in the bike room. The biggest mess was in the library; all the bookshelves had fallen over and books lay scattered in piles across the floor. While we stacked the books in piles, we heard teachers talking about the extensive damage throughout Guatemala, "7.5 on the Richter scale!" *What in the world was a Richter scale?* There were 23,000 dead, 77,000 injured, 1.2 million homeless—statistics we wouldn't learn until much later. The earthquake leveled most of the adobe houses around Guatemala City and many entire villages.

As we heard the teachers talk, it dawned on us that our parents had likely experienced the earthquake, too. With no telephones, all seventy-plus children anxiously awaited telegrams, which under normal circumstances took two or three days to arrive. My parents managed to send a telegram to the school several days after the earthquake, and my siblings and I were told they were alive and well. Mom and Dad had been at a conference at Lake Atitlán. After the earthquake, Dad drove around landslides to get to different villages where he set broken bones and sewed up large wounds.

A few days later, Amy came to me, eyes big and round, face chalky white. I asked her what was wrong.

She sat down on my bed, shoulders hunched over, her arms wrapped around her stomach. "Aunt Lorraine just told me that my parents are probably dead, because Joyabaj was flattened. I don't know what to do. I don't know who our parents will be now. I don't know how to reach any of my relatives in the States, and I don't really know any of them. I don't know where we will go!" I sat down next to my best friend in the world and silently wrapped my arms around her trembling shoulders as she wept. I knew there were no words of comfort that could soothe her devastation.

Apparently, Aunt Lorraine had taken Amy aside and told her this "news" (although she had not received any word from or about Amy's parents), and that was it. No words of comfort, no reassurance that Amy and her brother would be cared for, nothing. Amy's younger brother Nate was one of the kids that always cried for a long time after a weekend at home. Amy knew he wouldn't be able to handle the news that his parents were likely dead, so she didn't tell him. So on top of her own grief, Amy experienced the shock of believing that she, as the elder sister, was now responsible for her brother and needed to find them a place to live. Two weeks later her parents arrived at the school, having managed to get a flight to Huehuetenango in a small private plane. They had been unable to get word to the school via telegram and couldn't travel the roads due to landslides.

Joyabaj was indeed flattened, but as her father told Amy, an angel awakened her parents right before the shaking began. He and Amy's mother leapt out of bed and stood in the doorway as the bedroom walls fell on their bed and the remaining walls of their house collapsed around them. They were left standing in the solitary door frame. Amy recounted, "They spent the whole night digging through the rubble in the village with their hands, trying to save people who were trapped. All they could hear was screaming under the earth. Many villagers were killed, including my dad's best friend."

Although Nahualá was not hit as hard as some parts of Guatemala, many homes in Nahualá were damaged, and a few flattened. Our Down-Downstairs suffered a crooked crack about an inch wide that ran up the length of one of the adobe walls. It was never repaired, and served as an ever-present reminder of the fragility of our lives.

The frequent aftershocks went on for months, and we dove under tables or beds or sprinted to stand in door frames each time we felt them—heightening and intensifying the constant theme of terror in my life.

• • •

Tired of the regimented and harsh environment at Huehue, Amy and I decided to ask our parents if we could take correspondence school from home instead of returning to boarding school for eighth grade the next fall. Although her family's village of Joyabaj was a three-hour car trip from Nahualá, we hoped our parents could take us to visit each other for a week or two once a month. I was surprised and thrilled when my parents agreed. I didn't know it then, but my parents were also unhappy with the treatment I was getting at Huehue. When Amy told me that her parents also agreed to the plan, we jumped up and down, screaming and laughing with joy, thrilled to be leaving Huehue behind us. We would soon embark on new adventures together in our home villages.

Meanwhile, the political situation in Guatemala had been deteriorating for some time. We heard of villagers disappearing, kidnapped or killed by guerrillas. Many missionaries feared for their lives, especially those in remote villages. Several times at home we heard gunshots; we had never heard guns being fired before. None of the village Indians had guns, so we knew the shots came from the *guerrilleros*. Propaganda leaflets were thrown onto our patio at night. A sense of danger grew in the air in all of Guatemala. That summer, before Amy and I had a chance to visit each other, Amy's family found a handwritten note at their door ordering them to leave Guatemala within forty-eight hours or be killed. They packed their suitcases quickly, scrambled to say goodbye to their friends, drove to Guatemala City, and boarded the next flight for the U.S. They left nearly all of their belongings behind.

My plans collapsed. I missed Amy terribly, and my closest friend in Nahualá, Lulú, also moved away. Scott had finished up at Huehue (which only went through 9th grade); so I did my eighth grade and he did his tenth by correspondence school that year, while Kathy did her ninth grade at Huehue. Scott and I didn't need much guidance with our school work; Mom worked in the clinic while we spent a few hours each day doing schoolwork. When we finished, Scott diligently practiced magic tricks and skateboarded outside on his home-made ramp. I often felt lonely and lost myself in reading, trained my dog Henry, or played jacks with my Indian friends.

My oldest brother Kevin had graduated from Huehue a few years earlier and had been living with a pastor's family in Norfolk, Virginia, while attending a Christian high school. He was expelled after he was caught having sex with his girlfriend, and he returned to Nahualá that fall, angry and rebellious. One day, Kevin commented sharply to me that I was getting chubby. I had been unaware of my body size up to that point. I looked up to Kevin, who had always been kind to me. His criticism of my weight hurt me deeply and triggered a new source of shame.

Not long after this, I noticed I was developing breast buds. There was absolutely no talk of anything associated with sex or sexuality in my family, so when my body began to develop, my natural reaction was to fill this unmentionable void with yet another kind of shame. Always having been Dad's favorite, he now treated me differently—he was more distant, and at times he unleashed his rage at me, whereas in the past I had been immune. This shift in my relationship with my dad and the growing shame I experienced with my developing body became a tipping point. I was no longer able to hold or contain the accumulated terror, shame, and pain that had been building throughout my childhood. Kevin's comment echoed in my mind for months, and eventually I decided to cut back on what I ate in order to lose weight.

Fueled by volcanic emotions, I applied my determination, stubbornness, and perseverance to my secret task. To my surprise, I began to lose weight. My clothes were no longer tight. Soon I had to use a belt to hold up my pants. Although I constantly battled hunger, the euphoria of successful weight loss strengthened my resolve. My out-of-control emotions were subdued by the sense of control I felt over the food I did not eat and the weight that I lost. Over time I began to channel all the intense emotions I was avoiding into a single-pointed focus: food and weight.

The accumulated terror and shame of an internalized doctrine of hellfire Christianity and of my dad's uncontrolled rages; the shame of a body that was beginning to develop despite my unconscious efforts to shut it down; the absorption of the family pain because of my sponge-like sensitivity; PTSD from the earthquake and the near-drowning at Likin—all was kept at bay by my fierce fixation on food. I attempted to gain control of these uncontrollable feelings with all of my might. I cut back on portion sizes, weighed myself each morning, and took stock of how loose my pants were around my waist.

The intensity of my internal landscape was matched by external events that year. In 1981, after eleven years in Guatemala, my parents decided it was time for us to return to the United States. Their intention had been to build a clinic and a church that would ultimately be run by the Indians, and this had been accomplished. The precarious political situation in Guatemala threatened our safety. My parents also felt that moving to the U.S.—and beyond correspondence courses—would be best for our continuing education. My parents were devastated that Kevin had seemingly turned away from the Lord, and they likely blamed themselves for having sent him to the U.S. without family supervision.

I pleaded with my parents to let me take my dog Henry with us, but they insisted it wasn't possible. My heart ached at the thought of leaving him behind. Because we actually fed our dogs and they did not have to scour the streets for food, our dogs were always the largest in town, and Henry was no exception. Dirty white in color, with a brown figure 8 on his back and a patch of brown over each eye, he reveled in his position as top dog of the town. By day Henry wandered the streets and enjoyed his own adventures, occasionally returning home for a nap. At night Henry returned home to be with the family, to eat his supper and to protect us. I taught him to do tricks—to sit, beg, and bark on command—and had developed an even stronger bond with him the year I stayed home for correspondence school. He had been my only substitute for Amy and Lulú, and to leave him was another deep loss.

Our neighbors cried when we told them we were moving. Baltazaar, the smell of his homemade bootleg whiskey on his breath, wept loudly and spoke at length of his gratitude to our family. When we asked Baltazaar and his wife Juana if they would keep Henry, they agreed, assuring us they would take good care of him. They knew he would also take care of them. Henry had come to their aid on occasion when visitors to their home drank too much and got out of hand.

• • •

In spite of the difficulties of the transition, we were excited about moving to the U.S. To us, the States represented profound privilege and wealth. When I was nine years old, we had gone to the States for a one-year furlough, and from the time we arrived at the border, that year confirmed this glowing vision. That first day we sat in the hot car at the customs border crossing near McAllen, Texas, waiting for dad to navigate our entry into the U.S. It was easiest on the Mexican side; it was common knowledge that you simply had to pay a *mordida* (bribe) to the border officials if you wanted to pass through. Even so, we had waited hours on the Mexican side, and were now waiting again on the U.S. side as officials rifled through our belongings. I rested my head on my mom's lap, listless from the heat. My brothers skateboarded in the parking lot. Suddenly, Scott ran back to the car. "Look what I found!" He held up a dime and two nickels. "I found them in the parking lot!" The rest of us scrambled to the parking lot, scanning the hot pavement for a glint. Each of us found a few coins. We couldn't believe our good fortune, and excitedly spoke of nothing else the rest of the day. This experience confirmed our impression that the States was a land of abundance and prosperity. We couldn't wait to spend our money on "stateside candy." And now, in 1981, we were returning to the land of abundance—forever!

My dad was a big procrastinator and I don't remember him ever being on time. In Guatemala, this usually wasn't a problem, as Guatemalans operate on what they affectionately term *la hora Guatemalteca* (Guatemalan time). If you agreed to meet someone at noon, it was not only possible but likely that they would show up a few hours later. My dad was always late to meals, late to work, late getting home from work, late for appointments. Mom had long ago accepted this about him, and we kids didn't know any different.

Dad also procrastinated packing for trips. He was in charge of packing everything except clothing, and was responsible for loading up the car. Leaving on trips, we four kids often waited sweating in the hot car with mom for an hour or more, after he told us he was definitely ready to go. He always found more to do before we could leave. That April day in 1981 was no exception.

We were leaving Nahualá for good—taking our belongings, say-ing goodbye to the Indians and my dog Henry, saying goodbye to our childhoods. We planned to attend a missionary conference at

Huehue Academy with all our belongings in tow, and from there drive through Mexico to the U.S. True to form, Dad waited until the day before our planned departure to begin packing. He was up all night and spent the next morning packing our maroon-and-gray Suburban and the utility trailer he had painted to match the car. By the time he hitched the overloaded trailer to the Suburban, he was too exhausted to drive. Dad was notorious for falling asleep at the wheel on trips back to Nahualá from Guatemala City, allowing the car to slowly veer off the road, and terrifying us when he jerked the car back onto the road. Mom made a point of staying wide awake while he drove, especially on late night trips. Dad often joked about "taking a siesta" while driving, but this day even he knew it was unsafe for him to drive. Kevin was now seventeen years old and had some experience driving on the mountain roads. Dad handed him the keys.

We bumped down the cobblestone street for the last time, trailer in tow. Hundreds of Indians lined the patio and street, waving, many openly weeping. They brought gifts of tamales and colorful handwoven shawls and bags, which we loaded into the already-stuffed car. Kevin drove, Mom and Dad next to him in the front bench seat. Scott sat in the jump seat behind them. The bench seat beside him was down flat, piled with boxes. Kathy and I were in the last seat in the back of the car. We leaned forward and stuck our hands out of the window, waving as we called out to our friends, *"Ja' e'! Ja' e'! Cha'bej chik!"* They called out, waved, and reached out to touch our hands, some with tears running down their cheeks.

As we reached the bottom of the mountain, the Indians disappeared behind us. Kathy and I waved a while longer before sliding back into the seat. As we turned onto the dirt road, dust clouds puffing up behind the trailer, a stunned, empty silence hung in the car. We were leaving behind all that was familiar, all that we had known.

My sister and I settled into our own worlds, each of us sprawled out on opposite ends of the bench seat. I read a book, fighting nausea as the car twisted and turned down the mountain. Kathy played with a Slinky, the rhythmic sound of the metal coils bouncing back and forth fading as I became absorbed in my book. Scott read one of the volumes of his *Tarbell Course in Magic* books in the jump seat in front of us.

As the car alternately climbed and descended through the mountains, the road wet with a light rain, we encountered clouds of fog. I glanced out the window as our car hugged the cliff. Suddenly I heard my dad choke out, "NO!" I felt the car drag sideways as I saw the cliff wall outside of my window pull away from the car. I turned my head and looked out the other window. The car was sliding towards the edge of the cliff. There were no guard rails, nothing to halt the sliding. The emptiness rushed forward.

Silence descended. In front of my eyes, a movie played in slow motion. The rear trailer wheel slipped off the road and the trailer went over the edge. The car went with it. I caught a wide-eyed glimpse of a bottomless cliff as the car slipped over the *barranco,* the precipice. I slammed my eyes closed. I could feel my body tumbling and bouncing around inside the car as it rolled over, rolled over, and rolled over again. Silence, darkness, slow motion.

Everything stopped.

There was only silence. Darkness. Was I dead?

I moved my limbs, one by one. I lifted an empty cardboard box off my face. My body was behind the front seat, next to Scott, where he sat in the jump seat, right where he had been before the wreck. His right arm extended straight up, his hand on the car ceiling. None of us wore seatbelts, but Scott had held himself in place by pushing his arm up against the ceiling. I heard Kathy stirring behind me. I watched my dad climb through the hole where the windshield had been, blood on his back. Kevin was already scrambling up the side of the cliff, afraid the car would explode. I heard my mom's voice break the silence as if from a great distance: "Is everyone okay? Scott? Kathy? Mindy?"

Her question unleashed a burst of energy. Scott's face and shirt were smeared with icing from the doughnuts we had brought along. Kathy and I began to laugh hysterically. Scott, ever the jokester, wiped a finger through the icing on his face and began to lick it.

Mom began to pray aloud, praising God that we were all alive, thanking him for this miracle. We each climbed through the windshield to get out of the car.

Perched on the side of the steep cliff, I looked around in disbelief. Far below, I saw clouds and fog, but I could not see the bottom of the cliff. It seemed endless. The utility trailer had broken away from the car and cracked open. All our belongings decorated the steep slope; split-open boxes and suitcases, clothes, dishes, pots and pans, and shoes were strewn as far down the cliff as I could see. I grabbed onto shrubs and roots as I climbed through the mud up towards the road. The rain came down in earnest now, soaking my hair, clothes, and our scattered belongings.

Reaching the road, I turned around again to survey the scene. There were no trees on this cliff, except the two large trees where our car rested. These two trees, sticking out of the side of the cliff like giant arms, had somehow caught our tumbling car in mid-flight— in an upright position—and halted our fall. This did seem miraculous. In a state of shock, we waited on the side of the road in the rain for a bus to take us back to Guatemala City. A few Indians appeared out of nowhere, climbed down the cliff and began helping themselves to our belongings. When the bus came by, Dad and Kevin stayed behind, hoping to salvage some clothing and basic items to get us through the next week. When we arrived in Guatemala City, Mom called Huehue and they sent someone to pick up Dad and Kevin.

Like every other trauma we'd been through, we spoke very little about it.

CHAPTER 4

Starving in the States

He was so slim, his heart was visible.

—Hafiz

Mom and I stood in the cereal aisle of the Winn Dixie grocery store in Greenville, South Carolina. We gaped at the endless shelves of cereal, unable to move, completely overwhelmed with all the choices. A toddler with brown curly hair in a grocery cart rolled by, crying as her mom briskly pushed the cart. The mom reached between us to grab a box of Lucky Charms, which I had never heard of. I felt an overwhelming need to weep. The abundance, the wealth, the infinite choices didn't even register for others, but for us it was as if we had landed on another planet.

We were used to a simpler life, and much simpler shopping—bargaining at the outdoor market in Nahualá for an avocado or a piece of sugar cane or shopping at the small supermarket in Guatemala City where there were one or maybe two choices for cereals, not an endless array of brightly-colored packages all lined up neatly, and all vying for our attention. Even the streets and traffic in the U.S. were organized, not the loud chaos of Guatemala City buses and trucks weaving in and out of cars, spewing black fumes as their drivers honked horns in greeting and to warn of their presence. Instead of stopping on the side of a mountain to relieve ourselves behind a bush, there were actual public restrooms. And they were clean! Everything was so clean, so organized, so fancy, so modern. And so overwhelming.

My dad had taken a job as a partner with another Christian physician, Dr. Peter Watson, in Greenville. Dr. Watson rented us a home across the street from his house. Although small by U.S. standards, it felt like a mansion to us. We even had a real toilet! We attended Southside Baptist Church, a conservative church with an associated school, Southside Christian School. The values taught by the church were familiar ones: we are born sinners; the Bible is God-inspired, without error, and is the final authority on all matters; we exist to glorify God and to save the lost—teachings I had been steeped in since birth. What was new to me were the unspoken values held by the kids around me at school, who often spoke about fashion, music, cars and whatever was the latest fad. I was unable to reconcile the conservative Christian values with hearing others talk about fashion, cars, or the latest fad. Having grown up with the vastly different values of the Indians, I recognized that different cultures and individuals held diverse ideas about what was important and placed value on different things—but at the time my mind couldn't make sense of this recognition.

I was used to superficial cheerfulness and friendliness that accompanied social life in a Christian setting, and the denial of any emotion that wasn't appropriately happy. At Southside I sensed the same nonverbal agreement that nothing was to be shared other than joy or enthusiasm. I assumed that pretending everything was rosy was simply the way it was. Because so much pretending was going on, I thought that the kids my age must be feigning interest in clothes and dates and cars—as was expected of them—because I couldn't make any sense of these foreign, empty interests. Everyone was playing by the rules, so I did, too. I pretended to care about the "normal" American teenage interests, but there wasn't any juice in it for me. I had no desire for the things that were valued in western culture.

None of the outer trappings of this new culture seemed real to me—and in spite of the mental gymnastics my mind performed in trying and failing to make sense of it all, eventually I realized that others actually believed in this shared cultural illusion—they weren't just faking interest. They didn't see the emptiness that was my reality. I once again defaulted to shame: there had to be something wrong with me because I found no value in what the others prized. I labeled myself as depressed, not recognizing that this sense of emptiness was actually a deep realization of the emptiness of the "ten thousand things," the emptiness of this world. This disconnect with those around me mirrored the feelings I had about not being saved; I was afraid and completely alone. Shame was familiar and masked these intolerable feelings.

The realization that all values weren't necessarily shared, much less absolute, gave rise to a deep despair. If nothing was universally meaningful, nothing was real. What then was my compass? If nothing was real or meaningful, where could I place value? If nothing was important, if nothing gave meaning to life, what motivated me? If everything I considered important or real was just a relative value, why keep pretending that anything truly mattered? How was I to live in a world that was set up for human beings to place value on objects, when deep down I knew that none of it was real?

• • •

After arriving in the U.S., my adjustment to a whole new way of life was fueled and intensified by my one-pointed focus on losing weight. A profound heaviness hung in our home and compounded my own heaviness of heart and spirit. We were all suffering from culture shock; from PTSD related to the car accident, the near-drowning at Likin, and the earthquake; from the stifling oppression of the religious beliefs we had absorbed; and from my dad's rages.

I had long since given up all hope that Jesus would come into my heart so I could avoid an eternity in hell. I no longer secretly prayed for salvation, and felt an even bigger divide between myself and the rest of the family. I carried the heaviness of shame, aloneness, and terror, always—and I could no longer manage the intensity and weight of these emotions. All the force of my pain and fear lined up like an army with a one-pointed focus on my diet and weight as a means of channeling the immensity of the emotions that I could no longer contain. My refusal to eat became a focal point for the family's pain, and I became even more of an outcast. I was now the black sheep of the family. Without understanding it at the time, my anorexia served as a way to help the family avoid their own pain.

Before leaving Guatemala I had simply limited portion sizes, but after arriving in the U.S. I educated myself on the caloric and fat content of food. I began religiously counting every calorie I ate, limiting myself to less than a hundred calories each day. I cut out all fats, refusing to eat anything that had oil, butter, or mayonnaise. I ate only vegetables or a piece of fruit. I knew the caloric content of everything I put in my mouth. A celery stalk had six calories and a carrot contained twenty-five calories, so when social etiquette required that I eat at a gathering, I nibbled on part of a piece of celery and didn't touch the carrots. I certainly didn't touch anything else being served. When I was forced to eat a bit of rice in order to pretend I was eating a meal, I was tormented by guilt, unable to sleep, and made up for it by eating even less for several days. Each day when I weighed myself, I briefly felt a sense of relief that I had lost weight, but quickly shifted my attention from relief to planning further food restriction and weight loss.

My body grew thinner and thinner, weaker and weaker. I pressed on, continuing with daily activities, which took immense effort because of my physical weakness. Even walking down a corridor required tremendous effort. Eventually, thinking, talking, and forming words were laborious endeavors. I barely registered the stares at my emaciated body when I was out in public. Without any fat on my body for insulation, I was always freezing cold, shivering in the middle of the hot summer, a constant chill through my bones unlike any I had ever experienced. During the summer I could hardly wait to get into the searing hot car to try to warm my body up. While the hair on my scalp fell out in handfuls and thinned from malnourishment, the skin on my back and arms began to grow a soft, light-colored hair I would later learn was called *lanugo*—an emaciated body's attempt to insulate itself. There was no padding between my skin and my bones, so sitting was painful; it felt like I was seated on three spikes—my coccyx and two pelvic bones.

Although many with anorexia lose their appetite, I experienced extreme and intense hunger every waking moment. Later I would wonder at the super-human willpower it took to starve myself when food was all around. The smell of anything cooking left me feeling out of control internally. My entire body craved food, every second of every day, and the willpower and discipline I exerted in refusing to eat seems impossible to describe. But I was not only starved for food, I was also starved for kindness, for love, for deep nourishment, starved for someone to hear my pain, my terror, my anguish. My obsessive fixation on physical starvation allowed me to deny the starvation of my heart and soul.

Only one time did I feel that I lost control. My family was eating lunch at the home of a pastor and his wife. Social situations always caused me a great deal of anxiety, as I knew that in a social situation I would have to pretend to eat while fighting the immensity of my hunger and doing my best to make conversation. I served myself a small amount of food, and through the course of the meal managed to spread most of it around on my plate. I pretended to take several bites, and snuck some of it into my napkin. At the end of the meal, I felt a sense of relief that I had managed to get through the meal without ingesting any calories.

My short-lived relief was replaced by horror when I realized that we were not yet done—the pastor's wife was bringing each of us a piece of blueberry pie. She didn't ask if we wanted it, so there wasn't the option to politely or inconspicuously decline. I panicked, not knowing how I would pretend to eat a whole piece of pie. I had no room left in my napkin, as it was filled with food from the main meal. I sat paralyzed, staring at the purple berries, the crust laden with fat and sugar, brimming with calories. I fought the burning hunger that rose up in me with all of my might, in what felt like an epic battle.

Then something popped. I watched my fork as it broke the crust, dove in deeper to the berries, and scooped up a bite of pie. I watched my hand bring the fork up close, felt my mouth open and close around it. Inside, I was screaming, NO! NO! But I had crossed a threshold and there was no turning back. Salivary glands that had been inactive for months burst into action, trying to squirt liquid into my mouth so fast that my glands swelled up and screamed out in pain. I successfully fought the maniacal impulse to grab the whole piece of pie and stuff it into my mouth all at once. But I kept eating.

I ate the entire piece of pie. My GI tract had not digested anything of the sort for years, and not long after the meal I had to race to the bathroom, gripped with diarrhea. I was overwhelmed with guilt, shame, and with harsh, self-castigating thoughts. I started figuring out how much more I would have to restrict my meager food intake over the next few weeks to make up for the three hundred-calorie binge I had just succumbed to. I locked in my one-pointed determination, vowing that this would never happen again.

I heard my mom asking the pastor's wife for the pie recipe, giddy with happiness that I had at last eaten something and thinking I might eat it again. Although my parents were physicians, they believed that my weight loss was simply an act of rebellion and did not understand the depth of all that was fueling the symptoms. In her frustration, a few times mom took a spoonful of food and tried to force it into my mouth. I clenched my teeth together, horrified that the vile stuff had touched my lips. My steely, silent determination intensified.

As a requirement prior to beginning the school year at Southside, all students had to attend Wildfire Camp in Summerton, SC, about a three-hour drive from home. I was to begin ninth grade that fall. I was thirteen years old and weighed less than seventy pounds. Before we left for camp, I sensed that I was near death. Everything had been a tremendous effort for a long time—standing up, taking a step, moving my arm felt like climbing a mountain. Even breathing took concentrated willpower. My ankles were swollen, a symptom of heart failure. The morning I was to leave for camp, I broke down in tears, telling my parents I could barely get up each morning, dreading having to reach up to open the blinds because it took so much effort. They promised that if I went to camp, I could come back any time. Much later Mom told me she was afraid for me, but as she always did, she had put my well-being in God's hands. So I went.

My cabin mates giggled and chattered as we unpacked and changed into our camp uniforms. When I took off my shirt, I could hear the other girls draw in sharp breaths in the sudden dead silence. They could see that I was literally nothing more than skin and bones. By now, I was experiencing everything in slow motion, and from a distance, as if only part of me remained in my body. That night, I knew that if I went to sleep, I would die. All night, I willed myself to stay awake, willed myself to breathe, willed myself to remain alive.

The next morning, I found my sister and begged for help. "Kathy," I said weakly, "I'm really sick." Kathy was terrified. She had watched me try to play a camp game with others with a large leather ball, and was terrified that my tiny frame would get crushed by the ball. She saw my swollen ankles and legs, and went to speak with one of the adult women at the camp. I waited and waited, each minute interminable, every second moving closer to death. I waited an eternity—until finally, the woman came and spoke with me. As she approached me, I opened my mouth, pushing forward with all of my might to speak. "I need to go home," I whispered.

"Oh no, honey, " she said cheerfully, "you need to stay right here at camp!" She held my limp hand and prayed to the Lord for my comfort.

Voice cracking and devastated, I pushed out more words. "My parents said I could come home if I need to." Reluctantly she agreed to let me speak with the pastor. The minutes, the hours ticked by, and I fought to remain in my body, to stay alive. I could smell death.

That afternoon I met with the pastor. He told me I needed to eat, and quoted several Bible verses to me: "*Exodus 16:8*: Moses also said, You will know that it was the LORD when he gives you meat to eat in the evening and all the bread you want in the morning, because he has heard your grumbling against him. Who are we? You are not grumbling against us, but against the LORD; *1 Corinthians 10:31*: Whether, then, you eat or drink or whatever you do, do all to the glory of God; *Ecclesiastes 2:24*: There is nothing better for a man than to eat and drink and tell himself that his labor is good."

He had no idea that he was praying over a corpse, that I was dying in front of him, and I didn't have the strength or the words to tell him. When he finally paused, I whispered, "I need to go home." He read another Bible verse, then finally agreed to let me go home, but said it would be tomorrow. He didn't understand that my soul was slipping away, that I could barely hold on. It was a monumental task to remain tethered to what was left of my body, second by second. I gathered all of my strength and looked up at him. "I have to go now," I whispered.

Eventually, the woman who had met with me earlier took me to her car. As we drove down the dirt road away from camp, dust rising in clouds behind the car, the crunching sound of gravel under the wheels, she chatted in a cheerful, superficial voice, seemingly unaware of death in the car. No longer able to hold my head up, I watched as it fell between the head rest and the window. My head stayed there the rest of the trip, as I clung to my body.

When I finally reached home, my parents at last saw my condition. They took me to see Dr. Watson, dad's partner, who did a physical exam and admitted me to St. Francis Hospital in Greenville. Initially I was only given IV and oral fluids, as Dr. Watson was uncertain if my GI tract would tolerate anything else. After a few days of rehydration, he came in the room with a long, thin plastic tube in hand. Dr. Watson walked to the sink, filled a styrofoam cup with water and added a straw, elevated my bed so I was sitting up, and handed the cup to me. I was still weak, and felt dizzy.

"Okay, here we go," he said. "After I put this tube in your nose, I want you to take sips of water and swallow." I jerked as he inserted the tube in my nostril, feeling the scrape of the tube along the floor of my nose. When the tube hit the back of my nasopharynx, Dr. Watson told me to swallow. Weakly, I sipped the water, and swallowed . . . swallowed . . . swallowed as he nudged the tube further down my esophagus and into my stomach. "Very good, Mindy, we are finished. A nurse will be in soon to start the feeding. We'll start with milk to see how you tolerate it, and if that goes well we'll move to Ensure, which has more nutrients and calories."

Dr. Watson did not believe in psychological illness and attributed my weight loss to hypothyroidism. Lab tests had revealed that my thyroid function was slightly low. He said that it could be easily fixed with medication, that all we needed to do now was feed my body and re-nourish it. He mentioned heart failure, but said that with re-nourishment my heart would be fine. Years later when I studied hypothyroidism in medical school, I realized how bizarre Dr. Watson's diagnosis had been. Although I'm sure my thyroid function tests indicated hypothyroidism, a low-functioning thyroid typically slows down metabolism and thus causes weight gain. Anorexia and starvation can cause hypothyroidism, but hypothyroidism does not cause anorexia.

I didn't understand the cause of the anorexia but I genuinely wanted to get better. I had taken on my parents' belief that I was somehow bad or evil for obsessing about my weight and starving myself, but I hadn't known how to stop those forces inside of me. By now I was so weak, and so relieved to still be alive, that I didn't fight the tube feeds and all of the calories that were entering my body. Because my whole GI tract had barely functioned for months, I experienced terrible cramps, diarrhea, and loud noises from my abdomen as my stomach and intestines reawakened. I would grab onto the cold IV pole and stumble to the bathroom, trying to make it to the toilet in time.

With adequate nutrition my brain began to wake up, and I found that thinking was no longer an effort. Soon speaking came easily, although I was mostly quiet and passive. Without any fat left to use, my body had literally eaten up my muscles and now I watched in awe as the contours of muscles began to appear under my skin. Relieved to feel some physical strength returning, and relieved that I was no longer condemned as evil or sinful since I was cooperating with the tube feeding, I agreed to begin to eat food. Unlike many others with anorexia, my appetite had never disappeared, and it was a relief to respond to it. However, the intense sense of hunger did not recede for several years, even when my stomach was full of food.

After nine days in the hospital, I was discharged. Before going home, a dietician reviewed in detail my new schedule of meals and snacks for home and school. I signed a contract and followed the diet immaculately for several weeks, but to my great dismay I found that the compulsion to starve myself and lose weight remained. I truly wanted to get better, so I fought the compulsion to restrict the food I put into my body and was able to continue to gain some weight. But only the physical symptoms of anorexia had been treated; none of the underlying causes, forces, family dynamics or emotions had been addressed . . . or even mentioned.

In time I was no longer able to overcome the forces driving the compulsion to starve myself. At school I was required to visit the nurse each day for a supervised snack. I began to secretly rip the crust off the bread, decreasing my caloric intake whenever I could without being noticed. I despaired as my weight dropped, but was unable to control the "sinful" forces within me.

Within a few months, my body dropped back to seventy pounds. I was again hospitalized at St. Francis Hospital. After my strictly "medical" treatment the first time, this time a man named Jay Broadwell from the Christian Counseling Center visited me. When Jay entered my room, it was like a gentle light had walked in. He was easy-going and unassuming, and spoke slowly, with a southern accent, as if he had all the time in the world. I sensed that he had no agenda; he wasn't trying to get me to eat, he wasn't judging me or trying to save me. He didn't read Bible verses or talk religion. He didn't bypass my pain and my soul. He was present, open, and kind. I hadn't experienced anything like this in another person in my entire life. At the time, I needed more help than was available at St. Francis, but Jay's kindness touched my heart and imprinted a sense of hope on my spirit.

After I was medically stabilized, I was transferred to the teenage inpatient psychiatric unit at Duke University Hospital. Dr. Jones was the psychiatrist in charge of the ward—a kind, elderly man, he wore a long white lab coat and smoked a cigar during sessions. He listened quietly during my sessions with him, occasionally reflecting back to me what I shared, or asking questions about my feelings. With Dr. Jones, I felt I was learning a whole new language. I had never before thought about or bothered to identify my feelings, and this was the first time that anyone had ever shown interest in how I felt.

The second week I was at Duke, a tall, handsome teenage boy was admitted to the unit. Mike had been caught stealing and his parents had him admitted. I was fully occupied with this new world of emotions that was opening up to me and had no interest in boys. Although I engaged socially with the other kids on the unit, I was much more interested in the inner landscape I was beginning to traverse. I was a bit clueless about boys anyway and had no idea that Mike was pursuing me, until one of my roommates—one of the older girls—sat me down and said, "Mindy, do you realize that Mike likes you? He keeps trying to talk with you and you hardly give him any time. He is really hot, Mindy. If I were your age I'd be all over him."

I was still acutely aware that I felt different from others my age—that all the things they were interested in and valued meant nothing to me. However, Mike was intent on winning me over and I began to sit and talk with him. He wrote love notes, held my hand under the table, and tried to kiss me. Even when I backed away from the kiss, he wasn't discouraged. His persistence eventually paid off and I agreed to be his girlfriend. We lost touch sometime after I was discharged from Duke, but later got back together in college for a long distance relationship.

After I reached my target weight at Duke I was sent home for a few weekends as a trial, but I lost weight each time. Our health insurance did not cover mental health treatment, and having spent $30,000 on my four week stay at Duke, my parents met with Dr. Jones to discuss other less costly options. He told them I was not ready to go home; although I was making progress identifying and sharing my emotions, if I left inpatient treatment now I would develop anorexia again. He suggested an adolescent unit at the state mental hospital, which would be much cheaper.

The state hospital was nothing like the supportive and therapeutic environment at Duke. The unit was filled with rough kids from rough backgrounds, all of whom were there for behavioral issues, and many who were sent there as part of the juvenile justice system. I had never been exposed to anything like this—the rough language, the fighting, the violence. I didn't feel safe physically and constantly had to watch my back. One older teenager on the unit, Dave, had been admitted after stealing a car. He was angry and rebellious, and always seemed to be wearing a confederate flag tank top. Dave alternately tried to flirt with me and demean me. I was careful never to be in a room alone with him. During group therapy one day, Dave jumped up from his chair, walked across the group circle to me, and slapped my face as hard as he could. The therapist, who was a student intern, clearly did not know how to handle this and asked me how getting slapped made me feel. Angry and humiliated, I refused to answer.

I had different roommates during my time at the state hospital and although I tried to be friendly, I kept all of my interactions to a minimum. One roommate lied to the staff and told them I was vomiting. They believed her and added restrictions to my day, including staying out in the day room for observation for an hour after each meal. I was always on my best behavior so I could get discharged and was stunned and angry that this girl would lie just to make things harder for me. The constant heavy energy that permeated the ward scared me, and I missed the kindness and friendship at Duke. I stayed focused, maintained my weight and went through the motions so I could get out of that hell hole.

I did get out, and went from the frying pan into the fire.

. . .

Reflections on Emptiness, Love, and Truth

Ultimately, seeing that nothing in the world was real, the emptiness and despair that came out of this realization led me to seek that which *is* real and true. My disillusionment and despair were in fact a clarion call from Truth Itself.

Love and Truth are two sides of the same coin—at their core, they are the same. At our core, we are *that*. The inner call of love and truth from our very being acts as a powerful magnet, pulling us deeper and deeper into *that* which we are, into *that* which gave birth to us. Our individual lives are perfectly orchestrated to pull us more and more deeply into truth and love by means of the illusion of separation we each carry. Dissatisfaction and suffering arise when we believe that we are separate individuals, separate from each other and separate from Source—from Spirit. The suffering created by this illusion is a doorway that invites us to the reality of our true nature.

When we believe we are separate, we suffer. To escape this suffering we seek pleasure or at least relief: chasing after shiny objects—a new car, a new partner, faster electronics, nicer clothes—or pursuing success, power, or connections through work, sports, games, social media or hobbies. We may try to find relief by changing things up — finding new jobs, homes, or partners—or through addictive behaviors like anorexia or alcoholism. We avoid pain, and embrace distraction. When we do get what we want, there is a brief happiness, then suffering sets in again and a new desire or fear comes in to fill the void. The cycle keeps repeating—suffer / seek relief from suffering / get a little relief / become disillusioned / plunge back into suffering—until we burn out.

Finally we recognize the emptiness and futility of all the things that tug at us from the outer world. This is a pivotal point: when we give up and stop seeking external fulfillment because nothing "out there" is going to do it. This utter disillusionment with the world and with all our efforts and pursuits—and the impossibility of drumming up anything else to chase is sometimes called the "dark night of the soul." The objects of external pursuit are known to be empty, and even our thoughts stop feeling real. Nothing is left to get or do. The impetus to seek or resist simply collapses.

This collapse is like a "death"—the end of all interest, motivation, and the end of how we used to engage in the world—the death of the construct of *me*. For some this is a singular event, while for others it can be a series of deaths throughout a lifetime—the progressive dissolution of different aspects of the *me* that provided a solid sense of self.

But the collapse of pursuit and effort is actually a harbinger of the emergence of Truth, Love, and Life itself. Many religions teach of the need to "die to the self" in order to have life, in order to be born again. With the death of the *me*, these teachings can become a lived experience as truth and love; the God in each of us emerges from the core of our being. When we allow our pain and grief—the suffering of the separate *me*—to open us to the tenderness, purity, humility, and strength that emanate directly from love and truth, we awaken as more conscious, connected, and compassionate humans. In this way, our experiences of grief and pain take us back to Source, back to the truth of our being.

This is a process of purification, a deepening alignment with what we really are, and it can continue throughout our lives. As the rigid layers of individual beliefs and personality dissolve and peel away, the qualities that are closest to the core of our being are revealed. Love and truth pull us deeper and deeper into what we are, into that which is real. Each death and dissolution opens us to a purer expression of our true nature. And each layer reveals another doorway to freedom from desires, fears, and suffering. Eventually, even our inner psychological or spiritual pursuits are seen through as just more endless seeking. The Project of Me no longer holds our attention or runs the show, freeing us to live our own unique expression of the love and truth that we are.

With nothing more to get and no need to resist, desire and fear no longer shape our perception and experience of the world, and our awareness is free to open and expand. Residing ever more deeply in the Heart, we come to live in unity consciousness. Gratitude and a sense of wonder emerge as we recognize the beauty of human qualities and experiences. Individual uniqueness, including our own personality, brings forth delight. We feel no hard separation or difference between "my" pain or joy and "yours." "You" and "me" are nothing more than mental constructs that we can move in and out of, knowing that behind and beneath and within "me" and "you" there is only One—that which truly IS.

CHAPTER 5

Taking Off the Armor

Take the armor off,
so the arrow of Truth can penetrate you.
—Adyashanti

I left the threat of physical violence behind, but at home the denial and repression of pain in the family hung over me like a heavy cloud. I felt a profound despair that I couldn't put my finger on. The immensity of the family suffering was more than I could bear and again the intolerable emotions and energies moving through me needed an escape valve. I couldn't allow myself to lose weight or I would end up in the state hospital again—I definitely didn't want that—but I was unable to handle the intensity of the emotions without an outlet. To my utter dismay, I developed bulimia.

I started binging and purging, stuffing down my emotions with food and then getting rid of them by sticking my finger down my throat. I still felt intense physical hunger all the time, which was both biological and a manifestation of the emotional and spiritual nourishment I craved. This hunger and desire for food seemed more evidence of my wayward soul as I had been taught that all desires except a desire to serve God were "craven idols." I didn't understand that the ability of my body and brain to register satiety had been dysregulated by years of starvation. I watched people eat and then finish, saying they were full. I never felt full. For many years I felt an intense connection to the starvation suffered in concentration camps and read every book I could find about the camps.

My family eventually figured out that I was purging and viewed my symptoms as another choice of rebellion and so I continued my role as the black sheep. Dad intentionally walked in on me once while I was purging. Ashamed and enraged, I yelled at him, "GET OUT!"

He stared at me coldly and asked angrily, "Why are you doing that?"

My shame was profound, and I assumed that my inability to overcome my symptoms was yet another confirmation that I was fundamentally flawed.

Wanting desperately to feel better, I got the phone book out of a kitchen cabinet and found Jay Broadwell's number. I worked up the courage to call him and began a journey of psychotherapy that was to last for years. Jay's kindness was a refuge from my family environment and I absorbed it like a sponge. Through inner child work, he taught me to have more compassion and kindness for myself and helped expand my ability to be with difficult emotions. He gave me cognitive behavioral tools that helped me identify and change habitual thoughts and behavioral patterns. With Jay's support, I learned to be vulnerable with him, with myself, and eventually, with others. I gradually increased my awareness of what influenced my thoughts and behaviors, and learned to listen to my own heart with patience and respect.

With Jay's guidance, I also began to explore the myriad ways that I had been affected by the fear-based Christian belief system I had been steeped in. I had always seen life through the conditioned lens of this rigid Christianity and experienced the world as split into people who were "saved" and those who were not. My first exposure to people who saw the world differently was during my hospitalization at Duke. Even there—where my heart could not deny the kindness of

Dr. Jones as he genuinely wanted to hear and understand my feelings and experiences—my mind still categorized the staff and patients as "unsaved" or "not Christian" and therefore evil and somehow aligned with Satan.

I hadn't known any other Christian paradigm even existed. I had been taught that anyone who didn't believe as we did was going to hell, plain and simple. I knew without a doubt that if I stepped outside of my family's belief system, I would secure my place in hell for eternity. Terror bound me to this fearsome image of God.

With Jay, for the first time I saw that Christianity came in different flavors. His Christianity was a kind, compassionate, forgiving tradition that was a balm to my heart. Because he didn't speak of people in terms of being saved or not saved, initially I assumed he too was not saved. But over time, our work together began to heal and open my heart, and my heart began to speak louder than my mind. As my heart softened and came forward, my beliefs also softened and receded.

During one session with Jay, I had an "aha" moment that served to break me out of the heavy belief system I had carried all of my life. I saw clearly that my past anorexia and my current bulimia were not only attempts to control and rid myself of my overwhelming Christian shame and terror, but my symptoms also crushed the truer aspects of myself. I had literally been trying to kill parts of myself, parts of my own heart, in reaction to this forbidding programming. I now had a stark life-or-death choice: I could continue with my childhood religious belief system—along with all the fear and shame that led to the anorexia and bulimia—or I could try to break free. I had been surrounded by constrictive Christianity all my life and didn't have any friends or other support outside of this framework. Gathering all my courage and strength, I chose to pull myself out of this deep indoctrination.

I was able to begin this process only because of the life-affirming experience of Dr. Jones' and Jay's kindness. Even so, I struggled to let go of the only reality I had ever known. The indoctrination had permeated deep into the fabric of my nervous system and for years I continued to be plagued with fear and guilt. Eventually, though, I was freed up enough to seek a different paradigm—one that resonated with the truth of my heart.

In spite of all my work and progress, the bulimia persisted. I intuitively knew that I needed to be aware of body sensations—the way the emotions manifested in my physical body—in order to overcome it. I began to journal not only about my emotions, but also about how I physically experienced the different energies of emotions as I was bingeing. It was really the last thing I wanted to do. After all, the purpose of bingeing was to escape emotions, at least temporarily. But I forced myself to journal, initially while bingeing, then before I started a binge. I slowly became aware of how my discomfort triggered these symptoms and I expanded my capacity to allow and experience difficult and intense emotions and energies. Over time, I was more and more able to be fully present with emotions in my body as they arose, and the symptoms of bulimia began to resolve.

As my capacity to experience discomfort increased, so did my capacity to experience joy, spontaneity, intuition, and connection. My spirit was waking up! In turning away from any single aspect of myself, I had cut off all aspects of myself. Closing off to pain and difficult emotions also closed off feelings of happiness, delight, and warmth.

Now allowing the parts of myself that I had resisted or repressed, my awakening spirit began to pull me to something deeper within. I didn't know what was drawing me; it lay beyond the mind, emotions, and body. But I sensed something more, and it was utterly compelling.

The tools and structure of psychotherapy could only take me so far. I became acutely aware of its limitations. It was as if I were moving the furniture around in my house by identifying thoughts, emotions, and behaviors and using tools to shift them, but I didn't know how to get out of the house. I began to experience intimations of the vastness I would later come to know as love and truth, and I wanted to go beyond the *me*.

• • •

I was now seventeen and I no longer had bulimia, but I was profoundly aware of my continuing dissatisfaction. My very being knew that there was more to life, but my mind despaired at its inability to get there. There was no need to suppress and get rid of emotions by bingeing and purging as the logjam of emotions had been unjammed and diffused. For the most part, I was now able to meet emotions consciously as they arose. I knew when I was hungry and what my body was hungry for. I continued to journal and to intentionally cultivate self-compassion, but something essential was missing and I still wondered what was wrong with me.

Once again I despaired, and my despair beckoned me inexorably deeper and deeper. Despair is impossible to ignore and impossible to escape; it rests on the razor's edge of surrender. Surrender emerges when there is nothing left to get, nowhere to get to, nothing to accomplish, nothing left to work on. Ultimately, my despair pulled me into surrender, into truth. After years of exploring emotions, thoughts, and body sensations, and using multiple techniques to manage emotions and thoughts, I realized that this work on myself was a bottomless pit. There had to be something beyond endlessly working on myself. From my work with Jay, I had a sense of a broader spirituality beyond the narrow religious world with which I was so familiar. Although I felt no connection to God, I called out to whatever higher power there might be and begged for help.

I found my way to a few spiritual bookstores. This was in the pre-Internet age, so books were only in print, and not many spiritual books were available in my world in the southeast. Over the course of my senior year at Shannon Forest Christian High School, three of those books fell into my hands. *I Am That* by Nisargadatta Maharaj literally fell off a bookshelf in a Unity bookstore in Greenville, South Carolina, right into my hands. I read the nondual teachings of this chain-smoking saint from India from cover to cover, not understanding the wisdom with my mind but sensing a depth of truth. Then a friend's mother gave me a book about another of India's great sages, Ramana Maharshi, which also resonated deeply with me. For the first time, I recognized that what I was seeking was REAL.

But it was in reading *Grist for the Mill* by Ram Dass that my mind and heart leapt with joy. Here was a living teacher whose words lit up my very being! I sensed the possibility of accessing the truth he shared within myself. My boyfriend Mike's mother, who was not aware that I had been reading Ram Dass's book, sent me a newspaper article announcing that Ram Dass would be in North Carolina for a workshop. I was pulled like a magnet and without a second thought drove five hours to get there.

At that first Ram Dass workshop I attended, I was flooded with relief and joy. His presence awakened within me a spark of that which I had been seeking. I stood in line to meet him during a break that day, wanting to share with him that I had grown up in Guatemala, knowing that the Seva foundation he cofounded had done work there. I wanted to connect with him and be important to him. I was aware that what my heart and spirit longed for was to be deeply *seen*; my personality, the *me,* was converting this deeper longing into a more superficial desire for recognition, but I couldn't help myself. When it was my turn to approach him, I opened my mouth to speak. Instead, I burst into tears.

Ram Dass and Mindy, soon after meeting

The floodgates of my heart opened and I began weeping. Ram Dass opened his arms wide and enveloped me in a warm, gentle hug. My heart had come forward, sensing the invitation and the space to open deeper than my mind had intended, trusting it would be fully heard, fully seen, just as it so longed to be. Eventually, the weeping subsided. I stepped aside, no words having been spoken, no words needed. My heart was full and empty all at once. I watched him as he engaged with each person, fully present, not just mentally but with his whole being, meeting each one right where they were at.

Meeting Ram Dass awakened in me an unstoppable seeking. I knew through and through that he "had" what I had been longing for all of my life. Nothing else mattered now but to find that which he had within myself. I didn't yet understand that the resonance of my spirit with his was itself *that*. The clarity of presence and love in him awakened these in me; in fact, there was no separation between *that* in him and *that* in me. I launched into a decades-long journey of spiritual seeking, my determination fueled by the awakening and longing of my heart and spirit.

After that initial workshop, I attended Ram Dass talks, workshops, and retreats whenever I could. Over the next several years I saw him in Prague, Raleigh, Atlanta (where I arranged to drive him from the airport to his hotel), San Francisco, Tampa, Detroit, and New York City. Early on, when I went to see Ram Dass at the Open Secret bookstore in Marin, I arrived several hours before the talk and walked into a dim room full of statues, flickering candles, and the scent of Nag Champa incense. Before my eyes had adjusted to the lighting, I was drawn to a sculpture of Ram Dass's guru, Neem Karoli Baba. I fell to my knees in front of it and wept for hours, connecting to the source of the love that had awakened in Ram Dass and had resonated so deeply in me.

My relief was profound. I felt I had found what I had been missing my whole life. I had come Home. I recognized Neem Karoli Baba, also known as Maharajji, as my guru. The immensity of his unconditional love reverberated through me and I absorbed it like a sponge. His pictures soon graced my meditation altar, the walls of my room, my wallet, and the rear-view mirror in my car. Maharajji's love and spirit were transmitted through Ram Dass, whose presence and stories of Maharajji captivated me. This was a love I had never experienced before—unspeakable, vast, holding all human experience and expanding beyond. Maharajji had planted himself in the center of my heart.

• • •

At eighteen I now had a guru and a living expression of my goal in Ram Dass. I had touched reality, but I was not able to live it. Day to day I was still living from inside the ego box— identified with my thoughts and emotions and trapped in mental projections still driven by my childhood conditioning. Love and spaciousness were often inaccessible.

I attended a retreat with Dr. Moss, a physician and visionary thinker in the field of personal transformation. As with all the retreats I was attending, everyone else was a few decades older than me. We sat in a circle, each of us sharing something about ourselves. When it was my turn to share, I went straight to the core of my pain—the separation I felt from the love and truth I had experienced with Ram Dass and Maharajji. I wept as I shared this with the group. It was too much for them, and for Dr. Moss. He shook his head, and responded to my suffering with, "You are too young for this." This triggered my familiar reactions; I felt shame, hopelessness, and despair. But I knew my age was irrelevant. This fire burned hot in me. My longing could not be turned off.

I started college at Furman University in Greenville, South Carolina. I was still geographically close to my family, but there was a great distance between us. Each time I spoke with them, I was thrown back into old familiar patterns and feelings. I realized I needed to cut off communication with my family for some time in order to support my healing process and to strengthen and integrate the spiritual insights that were arising. I moved to Dallas, Texas, and attended classes at Richland Community College. I also got a job as a mental health technician on an adolescent psychiatric unit and plunged into group therapy. Feeling a growing sense of inner strength, I resumed contact with my family. I was now much more able to reside in my own heart when I connected with them; old emotional patterns were no longer triggered when we interacted. Something was shifting in me: I began to see everything in daily life as a doorway, a potential portal to deeper wisdom, love, and truth. Even when I got stuck in identification with daily experiences, I began to realize that each experience could lead me straight to love. I saw that everything in my life was tailor-made to invite me to my higher self. Grief and sadness now opened me to tenderness, compassion, and love. Anger showed me pain, fear, vulnerability, and connection. I was beginning to realize that everything I was experiencing was born out of love, and could take me back to that love—the source of all.

I felt ready to devote more time and energy to my education and career. I applied to Wofford College in Spartanburg, South Carolina. I resonated with Joseph Campbell's teachings of "follow your bliss," and liked that Wofford had an Interim semester each year during which students could pursue independent studies of their own interests. Supported by my newfound inner strength, I was now able to appreciate my parents as human beings who were each doing the best they could. Even though I knew that my parents still viewed me primarily through the lens of being unsaved, their view of me no longer triggered shame. My mom and I began to share from the heart, and Dad and I spoke about practical issues and joked back and forth. I noticed that in relating to them, my attention now remained primarily on how and where we were connected, not on the separation created by their belief system.

At Wofford, I majored in psychology and completed pre-med science requirements, thinking I might want to continue my education by pursuing a PhD in psychology or an MD. I also ran for delegate-at-large on Student Council, and put up posters around the school with my motto of "Make it Work with Mindy," accompanied by a simple sketch of a school water fountain that had malfunctioned for years. Mischievous students crossed out the word "work" on most of my posters. I was mortified, but won nevertheless, and served on the Student Council until I graduated. I also started and organized a Big Brother Big Sister Program that connected college students with underprivileged children. We met with our little sibs once a week and engaged in a variety of activities with them, forging relationships that nourished all of us.

• • •

During the two Interim semesters I was at Wofford, I completed a sophomore internship with a neuropsychiatrist at Duke, Dr. Ed Coffey; then, during my junior year, I returned to Guatemala for independent study and visited Nahualá. It had been eight years since I had last been in Guatemala. After my plane landed in Guatemala City, I took the next bus to Nahualá, eager to see our old neighbors and friends.

Not much had changed in the village, although a small portion of the road into town from the main road was now paved. Once past this paved piece of road, though, I stepped back in time a few centuries. Adobe huts lined the dirt paths and cobblestone streets. Women washed clothes in the river and the town *pila*, and carried large *tinajas* filled with water on their heads. Men carried impossible loads of chopped wood on their backs, all held together by a rope extending from a strap wrapped around their forehead. Dogs and children ran in the streets and the smell of tortillas cooking on fire wafted from homes.

Although I told myself repeatedly that there was no way Henry would still be alive, I secretly hoped he would be. Dogs in Nahualá rarely lived beyond one or two years, typically succumbing to rabies, poisoning, or illness. I ran all the way to Juana and Baltazaar's home, walked into their familiar hut, and greeted Juana and their daughter Al'taleen in Quiché. "*Cheq ij, na'an!*" My eyes began to sting and water as soon as I stepped into the smoke-filled room. I squatted down instinctively, my body remembering there was less smoke lower down. Juana and Al'taleen had been making tortillas, but their hands froze when I stepped in, their faces stunned. I had grown up over the past eight years and I realized they didn't recognize me. "*In ri al'Mendy!*" With this they broke into giggles, speaking excitedly in Quiché; Al'taleen rushed out the door to spread the word of my arrival.

I sat with Juana, whose giggles turned to tears. She shared with me that Baltazaar had died the year before. They missed us. They missed Doña Patricia and Doctor Alas. She wept as she reminisced about the time they knocked on my parents' bedroom door in the middle of the night because her grandson had a high fever; she was sure they saved his life. She laughed about how she used to joke with Doctor Alas as he hung our wet clothes on the line between their house and ours.

As she shared her memories and gratitude, others began to arrive. Soon the room was full of people, others in the doorway and overflowing outside. Everyone was talking at once, laughing, crying, touching my face, touching my hair. Many shared with me how much my parents had meant to them. One man told me that his family had had no food for several days and my parents gave them the food they so desperately needed. Another lady wept as she shared how my mom had saved her son's life. He stood behind her shyly, now a teenager, and she pulled him forward by the hand to meet me. "This is the daughter of Doctora Patricia!" she exclaimed to him through her tears.

I had been a child when we had left, but now as a young adult I saw these beautiful people through a different lens; I recognized their gentleness, their innocence, their sweetness and purity. I was deeply touched by their intrepid spirit, and by their gratitude. Although I no longer held my parents' religious beliefs and had never shared their missionary zeal, I was being given a glimpse into the profound differ-ence they had made in this community. My tears were no longer just from the smoke.

I wept and laughed with the Indians around me, sensing a release of my own contraction around my parents' mission as my tightly-held judgment of their efforts to convert others to their beliefs dissolved. I saw that there were other forces involved, and that my parents had also brought healing and love to these people. I pulled some pens and stateside candy out of my backpack, knowing they had never seen or tasted anything like it, and handed a pen and a piece of candy to each of them to their great delight.

Henry loved shoes and sometimes took them
from the houses of the few Indians who had shoes.

As I moved through the crowd, I spotted a dirty, white dog slowly hobbling towards me. Impossible, my mind said. But there it was— the figure 8 on his back and his unmistakable eye patches. I ran to him and held him, my tears dripping on his dusty fur, creating muddy brown lines as they slipped down his back. Henry wagged his tail slowly and nudged his head into my body.

• • •

Although I excelled in my coursework at Wofford and had a modest social life, I was pulled to my spiritual journey by a force much greater than me and much greater than anything going on in my outer world. Ram Dass continued to be my primary spiritual teacher, but I did read other books and attended retreats offered by a number of other contemporary spiritual teachers. Unlike Ram Dass, they did not share their personal human experiences. They spoke of awareness, truth, and love, and talked about this world as being a dream—some dismissing human or personal experiences as unreal and therefore irrelevant.

While I resonated deeply with the energy they transmitted and the truth of their words, my day-to-day experience was much grittier than a blissful melange of awareness and love. Because they didn't speak about their day-to-day lives and how—or if—they managed to integrate and manifest their spiritual attainment, I thought their "teaching persona" was who they were. My mind projected onto them the wisdom and love I knew were real; I assumed they had gotten "it," but I had not. Later, my experience with spiritual teachers allowed me to understand how speaking the deepest truths while dismissing human realities as irrelevant was less than helpful. It made it very difficult for students to integrate deeper truths in the human realm. What ultimately led to my decision to share my personal experiences through this book was understanding how important it is to connect at a human level as a support for the spiritual journey.

When I realized that getting a doctorate in psychology would take almost as long as completing medical school and residency, I decided to go to medical school. Although my parents were supportive of any career path I chose and never pressured me to attend medical school, the world of medicine was familiar and comfortable to me. I had grown up walking into the clinic in Nahualá at any time, hearing my parents talk medicine, watching them care for patients, and at times participating in patient care myself. The world of medicine in many ways felt like home. Despite the Dean of Admissions' skepticism about my attendance at Wofford, I not only graduated but was also accepted to medical school.

I was pleased that my education and career seemed on track, but my spiritual journey was much more compelling than any other pursuit. I knew that once I started medical school, I would have little time to devote to my spiritual life. I decided to defer medical school for a year. I was drawn to go to Findhorn, Scotland, and to visit Auschwitz. It didn't feel like a decision I was making; I simply felt a pull that I couldn't deny. I hadn't yet figured out the practical aspects—I didn't have any money—but I sensed things would come together. This decision, without yet having a plan or resources, was the first of many such "decisions." When there was a pull to something on my spiritual journey, I simply knew that the calling itself would pave the way and the practical aspects would work out.

CHAPTER 6

The In-Between Time: Findhorn and Auschwitz

What you are looking for is what you already are,
not what you will become. What you already are
is the answer and the source of the question.

—Jean Klein

In spite of the very left-brain orientation of college, I was learning more and more to listen to my intuition, and felt pulled to experience being in a community that was living in this way. From the moment I read *The Findhorn Garden*, I knew I would someday visit Findhorn. This intentional community described itself as "a dynamic experiment where everyday life is guided by the inner voice of spirit, where we work in co-creation with the intelligence of nature and take inspired action towards our vision of a better world."

For years I also had felt a deep connection with concentration camp victims, and had devoured many books about them, including books by Elie Wiesel, Primo Levi, and Viktor Frankl. The experience of those who had been at concentration camps felt very familiar to me. I sensed that my pull to this aspect of human experience was a way for me to work out something within my own system. By the end of college, I knew that it was time to take the next step—to visit Auschwitz.

I had never mentioned my plans to travel to Europe but, out of the blue, Grandma Helen gave me a gift of $1200. Grandma had lived with us during my high school years. Although she never told me what prompted this gift, I sensed that she recognized how difficult my childhood had been and offered this as a gesture of compassion, love, and support. Her gift paid for my trip to Europe.

In late summer of 1991, I boarded a plane in Greenville, flew to London, and from there took a twenty-hour train ride to Scotland with my overstuffed black backpack. I was in a compartment with two friendly young Scottish men. For the life of me I couldn't understand their thick Scottish accent, in spite of asking them to repeat themselves over and over. Ultimately we all just laughed and smiled together. From Inverness, I took a cab to Findhorn. I rolled down the cab window, refreshed by the cool, damp air, and surprised by the vitality I felt in spite of having traveled for about thirty-six hours. Everywhere I looked, I saw lush green and felt my whole system absorb this rich nourishment.

I stayed at Findhorn for five weeks, initially taking part in Experience Week, and after that spending four weeks in the Living in Community Guest Programme. While there, I felt held by the gentle, loving, harmonious energy that permeated the community. The invitation of the community was to listen to and live from spirit and the intelligence of nature in daily life. The stay there "begins with clarifying your individual purpose and ends with a personal review to support you in integrating your experiences and to explore your next steps. Using the process of attunement you join the team of one of our service departments (gardens, kitchens, dining room, home care or maintenance) where the experience of Love in Action helps increase awareness, joy and freedom, creating an ever more meaningful experience of life."

I was made a member of the dining room team. We gathered at the beginning of each day, sat in a circle and practiced *attunement*—presented as "a meditative state, often using silence, aligning ourselves with goodwill and the desire to create the best outcome for all." After attuning, we each shared which specific task we felt pulled to that day. Invariably, we all felt pulled to different chores.

I learned to listen more and more deeply to my inner knowing, and to overcome shyness and fear in sharing my heart genuinely. I began to speak up more, and felt affirmed and strengthened each time I came forward. In groups, I realized that when one person opened their heart and shared in a vulnerable and intimate way, the rest of us were brought immediately into our hearts at that level and then shared from a similar place of intimacy. In this way, I experienced the power of vulnerability, and how this type of sharing brings others into their hearts. I experienced a flow, a harmony with this way of life, where we all were listening deeply to our own spirits, our own inner voice, letting go of limitations, opening to love and each other, and living in a gentle, conscious way.

I was moved by a fellow guest, Victoria from Spain, who was twenty years my senior. She had depth and a beautiful, quiet presence. One day, I tearfully shared with her that she had touched my heart deeply. Later that fall, I visited her in Valencia, Spain. She had a photo of Ramana Maharshi on her altar where she meditated each day. Although I had meditated in groups and occasionally on my own, I did not yet engage in a daily practice. I had experienced some deepening with meditation, but in my mind I was still uncertain about its benefits. I shared with Victoria that I was especially skeptical about the need to sit quietly through physical and emotional discomfort while meditating. I said to her, "I just don't understand why if you feel an itch, you don't just scratch it."

Victoria shared with me that being fully present with whatever arises, instead of impulsively discharging the energy through thought or action, allows for a deepening of capacity and expansion of awareness. She explained that growth comes from sitting with the physical, mental, and/or emotional discomforts in meditation and allowing them rather than "fixing" or alleviating the discomfort. What she said clicked. I remembered the intentional awareness of body sensations I had cultivated when I was struggling with bulimia, and how this had been the only tool that had taken me beyond those symptoms. This practice had enabled the expansion of my capacity to be with uncomfortable and intense energy/emotions without trying to discharge them. Without knowing it, I had been practicing meditation. I now recognized the power of meditation and my skeptical thoughts were laid to rest.

While at Findhorn, I met the spirit guide Emmanuel, an out-of-body presence channeled by Pat Rodegast. Pat was leading a day-long workshop. I was looking forward to participating as I had read and loved her books. I had been living with a burning question for months and I hadn't known who to ask. Now I felt to ask Emmanuel about the schism in my world, which seemed to be split between mind and spirit. I felt a deep inward pull to truth—to spirit—but I was mostly perceiving this pull through the lens of the mind. I was aware that the mind was not absolutely real, but I didn't know how to dis-identify with thought and connect with and rest in spirit.

During the workshop with Pat, I was terrified to speak up as there was such intense emotion behind my question. I kept trying to work up the courage, but didn't manage to speak until the very end of the workshop. As I began, the energy behind the question was so intense that I broke down in tears; it felt like my very life was on the line. Emmanuel was silent while I wept. Finally, I spoke. "Emmanuel, I know that thoughts and beliefs aren't real, but they are what the whole world is made of. I don't know how to get to what's real. Even you speak of beliefs such as past lives as if they are real. How do I get past the mind to the reality of truth and spirit?"

After a pause, Emmanuel said lovingly, "You are an angel so close to spreading her wings of freedom. It is true, beliefs and thoughts are not real. Know that beliefs are like clothing, you can put them on and take them off as it serves you. This is the art and dance of life."

With this light and joyful response, something in me unhooked. I could now see thoughts and beliefs as nothing more than aspects within a broader range of human experience. Although I longed to break free from the mind, I saw that unhooking identification with thought and its associated suffering was a process. But I got a wonderful taste of awareness as spirit, and of being free to adopt thoughts or beliefs and equally free to let them go.

• • •

After Findhorn, it was time to go to Auschwitz. I met others my age while I traveled on trains across Europe. We were all traveling with Eurail passes, and they eagerly described the various cities and tourist sites they had visited. I had no interest in tourism. I now felt only an intense, one-pointed pull to Auschwitz. Boarding the final train from Krakow to Auschwitz, I took a seat alone in a compartment. I was full of anticipation after years of connecting to the history of horror and anguish in the concentration camps.

An American girl around my age, with long brown curls draping her orange v-neck J.Crew t-shirt, joined me in the compartment just before the train left the station. During the ride we shared the basics of our lives. Ellen was an American college student, a sorority girl, and she looked the part. She had partied her way through Europe all summer and she told me about her fabulous trip. I was surprised she was on a train to Auschwitz as there was clearly nothing fun or superficial about a visit to a Nazi death camp. Curious, I asked her why she was visiting Auschwitz. Ellen's tone shifted immediately. She became serious and reserved, and quietly told me she had been traveling with friends and chose to part ways with them as she wanted to visit Auschwitz by herself. I sensed there was much more to be said.

At Findhorn I had realized that I could take others to a deeper place of truth and realness by being real and true with them. I shared with Ellen my nearly life-long pull to Auschwitz and my struggles with anorexia. I shared the connection I felt with the pain and suffering of the starving concentration camp victims. In turn, she told me that her last name was Topf. Looking down, she quietly said that the cremation ovens at Auschwitz and other camps bore her last name, as her grandfather had owned the factory that built the ovens. She looked out the train window, brushing away a tear. I felt the heaviness of her family legacy resting on her shoulders and weighing on her heart. We sat together quietly, our hearts raw, our pain held in the tenderness of our vulnerability.

Gate to Auschwitz. Photo by Frederick Wallace.

When we arrived at Auschwitz, we stood together in front of the entrance gate, looking up at the words *ARBEIT MACH FREIT* (Work Will Set You Free) etched in black against the cloudy sky. I was stunned by a profound silence that hung in the air. Although I was aware of the sounds of others talking in hushed voices, of a bird chirping, the heavy silence hit me hard and moved through my whole being. I pulled my rain jacket tight against the chill and looked down the muddy road ahead. I stared at the rows and rows of brick huts lining the road, the electric fences that went on forever, enclosing everything. Ellen and I looked at each other, then stepped through the gate where more than a million people had walked to their deaths. We walked together for a while, then parted ways, knowing that each of us had our own unique journey ahead.

The heavy silence of suffering, of death, was so intense that it swallowed my ability to feel or be aware of any other emotion. All felt eerily familiar as I walked through the camp filled with this pressing silence; I felt I *was* the silence. I wanted to absorb everything I could of Auschwitz into my very cells. I came to a hut and walked inside to a long corridor, lined with pictures on both sides—rows and rows of faces looking down at me. I stood in front of each face, absorbing the horror, the shock, the fear, the defiance in the prisoners' eyes, reading their names, ages, occupations, and nationalities, oblivious to others walking by.

Hours later I was only a third of the way down the hallway. I forced myself to walk on, ripping myself away, feeling as if each of the beings in the pictures was pulling me back, but knowing that if I didn't move on I would be in the corridor until closing time. I wanted to acknowledge—to bear witness in my heart and in my experience—the suffering of each person that had come here. In another building were huge piles of spectacles, wooden legs, human hair, and human teeth. I stood transfixed in front of a room with a giant heap of shoes, my feet glued to the floor, my heart aching. I again forced myself to move on, devastated by the impossibility of merging with every person who had been here. I stared at the room filled with suitcases, each with a name and date written on it, and staggered along rows of wooden bunk platforms. There was Hut 20, where doctors used prisoners to experiment with different ways of killing them more efficiently, and Hut 11, where guards tortured prisoners who rebelled. I stood where roll call was held every day and some nights, when prisoners were forced to stand motionless for hours, in thin clothing, in cold, rain, or snow.

I read the sign: "The one who does not remember history is bound to live through it again." I was struck by the truth of this, both on a personal level and on a collective level. I knew that for healing to take place, the remembering had to be in the heart as well as the mind. I stepped inside the crematorium and shivered in the cool air as my eyes adjusted to the dim light. My eyes locked onto the black iron door on one of the ovens. Emblazoned on the door was the logo TopF. The immensity of the tragedy bore down on me, suffocating me, and I plunged outside to get my breath.

I entered the courtyard between Blocks 10 and 11. Straight ahead stood a wall of large long concrete blocks pitted with holes. I stood frozen, unable to move. Horror crept up my spine, then into my throat. I wanted to scream, and feared that I would. Panicked, my system unable to bear the experience, I watched as something in me disengaged, as if short-circuited. Numb, I moved forward and stood in front of the Wall of Death, where thousands had been shot, aware only of my breath, my lungs rising and falling in my chest, my pulse thudding in my neck. I don't know how long I stood there before the clouds released a fine mist, then a cold drip. Soon, rivulets of water slid from my hair onto my face and mixed with tears I hadn't known were there. As the rain began to pelt down on my head and all around me, I wept aloud, dropped to my knees, and bowed, heaving with unspeakable pain. After some time, the rain stopped and so did my tears. I stood up and wiped my face with my sleeve. My jeans were cold and heavy with mud as I walked back out through the gates.

That day in Auschwitz something cracked open in my heart, alleviating the burden of horrific human suffering that I had carried with me for so long. My mind didn't understand, or need to understand, why I had carried this burden—perhaps I had been at Auschwitz in a past life, or perhaps I was somehow a conduit for holding and healing collective pain. The experience moved and changed me; I left Krakow feeling as if my heart was surrounded by light.

After Auschwitz, I headed to Prague to attend a much-needed spiritual conference with Ram Dass, Karl Pribram, Stan Grof, David Bohm, and other spiritual teachers and scientists. With the release at Auschwitz of a life-long burden and the nourishment of my spirit at Findhorn and at the conference in Prague, I felt ready to take on medical school.

PART II

Psyche

Love is the best medicine.
—Neem Karoli Baba

CHAPTER 7

Medical School, First Year

...after I had passed the final examination,
I found the consideration of any scientific
problems distasteful to me for an entire year.

—Albert Einstein

In the fall of 1992, I started medical school at the Medical University of South Carolina (MUSC) in Charleston. For the first two years all students took a mix of classes and labs. My first semester classes included Gross Anatomy, Biochemistry, Cell Biology, and Genetics. Through a school posting about available housing, I rented an apartment within walking distance of the school with two other medical students—Reg, who was in my class, and Shawn, a second-year medical student.

My parents drove to Charleston with me and helped me move in, lugging my belongings up the stairs to the apartment. They had never pressured me to achieve or make good grades and while they had been mildly positive about my academic achievements, their religious values were always more important. I was surprised that day to sense their happiness and pride in my chosen career path. Something shifted in our relationship, which expanded from purely parent/child to include the respect of professional peers. We began to enjoy exchanging and sharing our experiences in the medical world—a connection that continues to this day. The rigors of medical training and the challenges and joys of medical practice are unique and can best be understood by those who have experience of that world. Similarly, when physicians meet, within or outside of the context of medicine, there is an immediate, nonverbal sense of connection.

Reg and I knew that we were in for a very tough first year, and Shawn confirmed this. That first night, over a few beers, he told us stories about studying for days and staying up all night before tests, only to barely pass an exam. He told us about the horrors of gross anatomy class and lab, and the burdensome expectation that we learn to identify and name every branch of every blood vessel and nerve, all the muscles, bones, and organ parts, and every opening and passage in the body. He shared the seeming impossibility of biochemistry, requiring memorization of a two-foot thick syllabus, and the nightmare of physiology with a fast-talking professor who made it impossible to keep up with note-taking. Reg and I sat on the couch, beers in hands, feet propped up on the coffee table, our casual pretense belied by our saucer eyes glued on Shawn and our intense focus on every word he uttered.

The next day, Reg and I loaded our backpacks with our new textbooks, slung them over our shoulders, and walked the four blocks to Baruch Auditorium. Baruch, where many of our lectures were held during the first two years of medical school, was a large, old, and imposing brick building with four concrete columns in front. At 8:15 the sun was already hot and the air muggy. My forehead beaded up with sweat as we walked. Reg and I chatted and laughed nervously as we approached our new classmates on the steps outside the building.

I introduced myself to a few fellow students, then reached for the handle on the giant wooden door, which was warm from the sun. I pulled hard, but the heavy door didn't budge. I tried again, this time leaning back to throw my weight and the weight of my backpack into the effort. The door creaked open and a wall of cold, musty air rushed out. As my eyes adjusted to the dim light, I could see the main auditorium. Rows of chairs formed semicircles in front of the stage. Many of the seats were already filled with students and some students were studying textbooks in their laps. An uneven, watery brown line ran horizontally along the walls about nine feet up, encircling the auditorium. Later I was told this was the flood line from Hurricane Hugo, a category 4 hurricane that had devastated Charleston just three years earlier in 1989. I stepped into the auditorium and stood leaning against the wall, watching silently as more seats filled, and listening as the low din of voices gradually grow louder.

Off to the right of the auditorium were stairs to a mostly empty balcony. I climbed up, wanting to avoid absorbing more anxiety by sitting close to others; I already had enough myself. In the balcony's middle row sat a young woman. Her dark, permed hair was parted in the middle, bangs falling neatly just above her eyebrows. She wore gold hoop earrings, several gold bracelets, and a dainty gold necklace with a pendant that matched her red cotton blouse. Her white shorts were starched, crisp, and creased down the front, and her bright white Nike tennis shoes looked like they had come straight out of the box. She grinned at me, exposing a thin friendly gap between her front teeth. Her warmth was infectious. I smiled back and gestured a few chairs over from her. "Can I sit here?"

"Oh, please do! I think I'm just going to DIE with anxiety!" she said in a thick Southern accent.

I giggled. "Well, that makes at least two of us!" I sat down, heaved my backpack into the chair next to me, and slid my feet out of my Birkenstocks. The cool concrete floor on the soles of my feet was soothing, grounding, and calming to my nerves.

Christy and I became fast but unlikely friends. She had grown up in South Carolina, near Columbia. Her father was a hard-working peach farmer and her mother a full-time mom. Christy was a lot like her mom: she had a positive outlook on life and was outgoing, friendly, and always meticulous about her makeup and clothing. In contrast I was a bit of a hippie, having grown up running around the streets of Nahualá with my Indian friends. I was immediately drawn to the brightness of Christy's spirit and the generosity of her heart. We made a pact that we would help each other make it through medical school, and indeed we did. We studied together and shared class notes. We sobbed together before exams, exhausted and overwhelmed, and sobbed together after exams, convinced we had failed. We loved each other through thick and thin, and completely accepted each other as we were.

Between classes that first day, I walked downstairs and stood in line outside the bathroom, where I met Emily Ray, another soul sister who became a close friend. Emily was smart, world-savvy, and efficient. She grew up in Salt Lake City, where her mother worked in adult education and her father was a physician. Like the rest of us, she was Type A, task-oriented, and driven by stress. She also didn't have a fake bone in her body. She spoke her truth as she saw it, unconcerned if she offended someone, and never tiptoed around any issues. I loved her clarity and forthrightness, and implicitly trusted her. Emily recently said, "The friends you make in med school and residency are some of the best friends you ever have because of what you've been through together. No one outside of medicine can begin to understand what we go through in our training."

After classes that first day, Emily, Christy and I walked together on the narrow sidewalk along Ashley Avenue to the Basic Science Building. The humidity was now suffocating. Christy joked about the hair she had spent an hour curling and coifing that morning turning board-straight on her head after just a few seconds outside in the humidity. We entered the drab building, gulped in the cool air, rode the elevator up to the fourth floor, found the Gross Anatomy lab, punched in the entry code we had been given, and opened the door. All three of us stood silently in the doorway, staring into the room, stunned. The sharp pungent odor of formaldehyde assaulted and repulsed us. My eyes began to sting and water, and Christy began to cough. In front of us were thirty-two steel tables, lined up in rows, topped with long blue zippered bags, each outlining the vague shape of a human body. Under each table was a large white bucket.

Students were gathering behind us and we had to move forward. We filed into the room in silence and everyone stood in the spaces between the steel tables. The room was icy cold, and I was dressed in shorts and a sleeveless white blouse. I rubbed the goosebumps on my arms and found myself taking slow, shallow breaths, not wanting to inhale the sharp rank air. I squinted against the bright fluorescent lights.

Professor Harvey talked to us about the privilege of dissecting a human body. He spoke solemnly of the generosity of the donors who had given their bodies to us so that we could learn and help others, and advised us of the importance of respecting our cadavers, of honoring these gifts. He pulled a piece of paper from his white lab coat and began pointing to cadavers as he called out the names of the two or three students assigned to each corpse. We went to our tables to meet our lab partners for the semester, and then to unzip the body bags and meet our cadavers.

My lab partners were Kenny, a former college football player from Columbia, South Carolina, and Reg, my housemate. We stood around our table, each of us reluctant to reach for the zipper. We made small talk, noting that our body looked relatively small. Reg and I knew a small body was a good thing; Shawn had told us that a heavy-set cadaver brought with it the challenge of dissecting out endless sticky yellow globules of fat in order to make out the muscles, organs, blood vessels, and nerves. Finally, Kenny unzipped the body bag. Our cadaver was a small, frail, elderly lady. Her pale face was wrinkled, her eyes closed, and her lips shrunken into thin lines. A poof of short white hair sprouted from her scalp. We immediately felt a fondness for her, and wondered aloud about her life, her family, the cause of death. All of us named our cadavers that day (ours was Bertha), a gesture of gratitude and unspoken sadness about the passage of life, the recognition that each of these bodies had once been young and full of life, just as we were.

We quickly grew accustomed to the smell of formaldehyde. On lab days, it permeated our clothes, our hair, our nostrils. Although at first it turned our stomachs, soon many of us, not having had time to eat lunch, snuck food into the lab and ate as we dissected. Gross anatomy lab carried with it the classic pressure of medical school—we were always running behind and trying to catch up to the next section of the body we were to dissect.

Our minds were nearly always occupied with the tasks at hand, so there wasn't time to dwell on death. Nevertheless, we were all affected by the reality around us and the hard cold fact that, ultimately, each of us would be a corpse, just as lifeless and cold as these cadavers. Nearly all of the students in our class had grown up in the States, in a culture that tends to deny death; to pretend that we each don't have a death day just as we each have a birth day. Western strategies to defy aging through diet, fitness, surgery, and other means are manifestations of our desire to escape the certainty of decay and death.

I was surprised by all this, having grown up in Nahualá, where elders are honored and respected for their wisdom and life experience, and where death is seen as a natural part of life. But in spite of culturally-crafted denial, and in spite of how occupied our minds were with the tasks at hand, we were all faced with and affected by the inevitability of death throughout our training.

My new friend Emily was assigned to a cadaver two tables over from me. That first day she motioned me over to her table and pointed down at her cadaver. "Look, Mindy!" I looked down. Her female cadaver wore tattooed makeup—a stark contrast to the other cadavers, whose faces were a pale version of their natural skin color. Emily's cadaver was unnerving to all of us. She was one of the younger cadavers, perhaps in her thirties. Her eyebrows were dark black, thickened with solid black tattoos that matched her thick, long hair. Her eyelids were outlined in charcoal, and her full lips were a deep red. I looked at Emily. Her eyes were wide, beginning to twinkle. She raised the back of her hand to her mouth, trying not to burst into nervous laughter. Professor Harvey was still watching the room, and I was afraid of his reaction if she seemed disrespectful of her cadaver. "Emily, come over here and meet my lab partners, *now!*"

A few weeks later, several of us were in the lab after hours one night, working to complete a dissection of the face. I was working with Reg, and Emily was working nearby on her cadaver, whom she had named Lucy. We were each immersed in our dissection, gloves on, tools in hand, cutting through and peeling back skin, removing fat, finding the borders of muscles and carefully dissecting out fragile nerves and blood vessels. I held a scalpel and toothed forceps in my hands, which were beginning to cramp. As I dissected, I glanced frequently at my Netter's *Atlas of Human Anatomy* textbook, which lay propped open on a stool beside me, displaying detailed paintings of the muscles, nerves, and vessels of the face.

My head jerked up as I heard a loud knock on the door. Reg and I looked at each other quizzically. All the med students knew the code to get into the room. Who would be knocking on the door, let alone at this time of night? I turned back to my work, not wanting to sever the delicate superficial branches of the facial nerve that I was trying to identify and dissect out. I heard the door squeak open, then heard a sharp gasp coming from Emily's direction and the clatter of a steel dissection tool falling on the tile floor. I looked up to see Emily's pale face, staring wide-eyed at the door, her hand grabbing the side of the steel table for support.

I looked at the open door, and there stood Emily's cadaver—only it was alive, talking and animatedly gesturing with her hands and arms. The woman in the doorway was the spitting image of Lucy, identical down to the tattooed makeup. Involuntarily my head jerked back, my eyes locking on Emily's cadaver. It was still there, with outlined eyelids, thick black hair and deep red lips, but the skin from her face had been removed and the muscles, tiny nerves, and arteries were exposed. I heard the woman in the door explaining loudly that she knew her identical twin sister was here, and she had come to pay her respects. She hadn't yet spotted her sister's cadaver. Instinctively, I stepped into the woman's line of vision, blocking her view of her twin's mutilated corpse. Reg explained to her that no one was allowed in the lab without permission, but that she could call Professor Harvey to request permission (which she never received). Lucy's twin was apparently an employee of MUSC, as we occasionally spotted her around the campus that semester.

• • •

My friends and I—and most of our classmates—lived with a constant sense of anxiety and overwhelm, shell-shocked by the immensity and complexity of the material we had to understand and memorize. Having been at the top of our classes throughout high school and college, we were more identified with being the best than any of us cared to admit. Our first exam was a rude awakening.

The night before the test, Christy and I sat at the dinner table in her rented house, dwarfed by the giant biochemistry syllabi and textbooks before us. We were determined to power through the night, and sipped on giant mugs of lukewarm coffee as we quizzed each other on the molecular structures of carbohydrates, lipids, proteins, and nucleic acids. We drew and re-drew the molecular processes of the Krebs cycle, of glycolysis, of anaerobic metabolism, and gluconeogenesis, trying to cement each detail into our brains. We lost track of time, and several hours later our over-stuffed, exhausted brains began to resist any more absorption of material. We decided to run laps around the table, hoping the increase in circulating oxygen to our brains would give us a second wind.

Christy and Mindy during med school
having a brief celebration post-exam.

"What time is it, Christy?" I asked, short of breath, lifting my knees high and pumping my arms in the air as I jogged. Christy jogged into the kitchen to look at the clock. "OH MY GOD, MINDY! It's already THREE!" Panic gripped us both. We were only about halfway through the syllabus. Our plan to go through the syllabus two or three times quickly dissolved; we knew we'd be lucky to get through it once. Fueled now by fear and panic, we kicked up our pace. We didn't think about breakfast, or a shower, or even changing clothes as we sprinted through the material, every precious minute of memorization possibly the difference between passing or failing—possibly (we thought) the difference between making it or not making it through medical school. At 7:45 that morning, we rushed off to Baruch Auditorium and slid into our chairs as exams were being handed out.

Days later when word got out that the test results were up, Christy and I rushed to Baruch where the scores were posted outside of the auditorium. Apparently everyone else had gotten word at the same time—there was a large crowd gathered in front of a long piece of continuous computer paper taped to the door. The four or five students directly in front of the paper were taking a very long time to read it. The rest of us grumbled about the delay. When we finally reached the door that held our fate, the reason for the slow line was clear. The last four numbers of our ninety-six social security numbers were printed single space in a column on the left side of the unlined paper and our test scores were in a column on the far right side of the paper. I had to drag a finger across the page several times to match my social security number to my test score.

Christy and I both passed, only to begin cramming again the next day for a gross anatomy practical exam. That night, I thought I might explode from the pressure. We had been in the lab all afternoon and evening and were now back at Christy's house. At one point, I looked up at Christy. Her hair was in a high ponytail, her face tight, eyebrows furrowed as she leafed through the head and neck section of Netter's *Clinical Anatomy*. She felt my gaze on her, and looked up. Simultaneously, tears welled in our eyes. "Mindy, I don't think I'll make it through med school. I really think I made the wrong choice. I don't know what to do. I want to quit, but I've taken out so much in loans already, I don't feel like I can. And I don't know what else I would do. This is what I've always planned for." As we cried together, I shared with her that I felt like a fake, that it must have been a terrible mistake when they let me into med school since I clearly wasn't medical school material, and that I, too, wanted to quit but felt trapped.

• • •

And so it continued for weeks and months. The rigor of medical school was all consuming. There was room for nothing else, and by the end of that first semester I felt utterly depleted and parched, with no spiritual nourishment or nourishment on any other level. The pull I felt to a deeper Truth had not diminished in any way, and the limited and demanding world of medical school only served to highlight my longing. I didn't feel I could continue this for years. It seemed I had to make a choice between career and spirit, and hands down, spirit won.

Determined but scared, at the end of the semester I plucked up my courage and scheduled an appointment with Dr. Del Bene, the Associate Dean for Student Affairs. I told him that I had decided to quit medical school. From his response, I could tell he thought I was just another overwhelmed medical student. One of his jobs was to ensure there wasn't a high attrition rate as this would reflect poorly on MUSC. He told me it was normal to feel stressed, that things would get better during third year when I started to see patients. But third year seemed an eternity away and I didn't feel I could do this for one more day. I couldn't deny my spiritual longing any longer and didn't want to engage in a training process that seemed to negate that which was most important to me.

At first Dr. Del Bene tried to convince me to stick it out, but finally he realized I had made my decision. He asked if I would be willing to take a leave of absence instead of quitting, giving me the option of returning in a year. I agreed to this, although at the time I felt certain I would never resume my studies.

I was relieved to have the tremendous pressure and burden of medical school behind me and to be free again to listen to my deeper calling. Having been engulfed by the intensity of the medical training system—lost to my spiritual self in a haze of stress and fear—I now wanted more than anything to live from my heart. I wanted to recover and expand the softening that had taken place before med school began. I wanted to follow my intuition beyond the purely mental into a more awake and alive presence in the world.

CHAPTER 8

India

I can nourish myself on nothing but truth.
—St. Therese of Lisieux

All the threads of my spiritual longings, explorations, and discoveries led to India. I wanted nothing more than to travel there, but I was broke. I took a job as a mental health aide on an in-patient unit at MUSC's Institute of Psychiatry in order to save money. This was a locked hospital unit for patients in crisis, often committed involuntarily. Some patients were severely depressed and had attempted suicide; others, diagnosed with bipolar disorder, were hospitalized with symptoms of mania. Some with diagnoses of schizophrenia or schizoaffective disorder had had psychotic breaks, their paranoia or hallucinations leading them to be a danger to others or themselves. I found I connected easily with all of the patients and felt a sense of ease as I worked with them.

I started to relax again, and I began to consider the possibility of returning to medical school after the "leave of absence" I had thought was a permanent departure. I knew that if I could get through the training process, having the degree would allow me to work with others in a way that best served them, and that felt natural to me. I wrote to Ram Dass and shared with him my fear that continuing with med school would be a choice separating me from my very soul. I described the utter depletion I experienced from just one semester. I also told him that I thought medical school would allow me to help others in a way that other careers wouldn't permit.

Ram Dass replied with a letter full of compassion and love and advised me to complete medical school. He wrote, "Have no fear. Although your spiritual life may seem to go underground in that kind of intense environment, it is alive and well." He encouraged me to seek out spiritual support from others outside of medical school whenever possible. With this guidance from him, I prayed to Neem Karoli Baba, making a deal that I would return to medical school under one condition: I needed some sort of deep support for my spiritual journey during the rigors of medical training.

Several months later, I got word that Ram Dass had had a stroke and was in the hospital. Over the years I had come to know him not only from attending many of his conferences and retreats, but also through a variety of synchronicities where we ended up in the same place at the same time, usually at airports. Once I ran into him in the Atlanta airport and gave him a ride to his hotel. Another time, we ran into each other at the airport in Oregon before a retreat, and he and his secretaries gave me a ride to the retreat center. Later on, my friend Amita and I flew to Florida for a weekend retreat with him and on the plane I suggested that we visualize running into Ram Dass at the airport. After we got our luggage and boarded the van to our hotel, it seemed this was not to be. A minute later, though, the van driver got a call asking him to return to the airport to pick up another customer. We drove back up to the airport and, sure enough, there was Ram Dass standing on the curb with his suitcase, waiting for our van.

Ram Dass and I had exchanged letters a few times before I wrote him about my medical school dilemma. I shared my spiritual journey, my devotion to Neem Karoli Baba, the overwhelming pull to a deeper truth, and the challenges I faced in this unfolding process. It was Ram

Dass who had demonstrated for me, the very first time I met him, that what I was seeking really did exist. He was my living anchor, a spiritual grounding rod, and his very presence in the world served to open my heart. I was devastated with the news of his stroke.

I flew out to California to see him in the rehab center, where a picture of Neem Karoli Baba had been hung on a wall facing his bed. He was moving his body, reaching out towards me, but unable to speak coherently. Shaken by his fragility, I held his hand as I stood by his bed and looked into his eyes. I was met with the same spacious, all-enveloping love I had first come to know through him years ago. Although his body had changed, this love poured through him and filled the room. I was willing to stay and assist Ram Dass in the rehabilitation process, but he had excellent help. He had directed me to complete medical school, and it was time to find the spiritual support that would see me through the rigorous training process. It was time to go to India.

• • •

My pull to India was clear and specific: I was to go to Neem Karoli Baba's ashram in Kainchi and to visit Poonjaji in Lucknow. I had no desire to do or see anything else in India. When Ram Dass led me to Neem Karoli Baba, the love I experienced became my aspiration and my imperative—my whole being recognized Neem Karoli Baba's love as Home.

The gratitude born out of the experience of this love was profound. Sitting in meditation in front of his photo on my puja table, I would weep with joy and gratitude. My whole being longed to be a pure vessel of this love, first known through him, but also somehow not separate from my own being. I prayed fervently to Baba, asking for the grace to become such a vessel. I told him repeatedly and wholeheartedly, "Whatever it takes!" Although Neem Karoli Baba had "dropped the body" in 1973, his great love was still present and accessible. I was pulled to visit his ashram; being in the place where he had lived would help me know and realize this love more fully.

While Neem Karoli Baba—Maharajji—was the embodiment of love, Poonjaji was a living embodiment of truth. He was a direct disciple of Ramana Maharshi, one of the great sages of India, born in 1879. At the age of sixteen, Ramana had a "death" experience in which he became aware of a current or force that he recognized as the true "I" or "Self." Devotees were drawn to him and later an ashram grew up around him. Ramana Maharshi taught that the "Self" or real "I" is a non-personal, all-inclusive awareness, not an experience of individuality. He said the individual egoic self was a fabrication of the mind that obscures the true experience of the real Self. He maintained that this universal Self is always present, but the self-limiting tendencies of the mind must cease for one to be consciously aware of it.

A friend's mother had given me a book of Ramana's collected teachings while I was in college. I felt a deep connection with him and resonated with the truth of his words. Ramana had died in 1950, but Poonjaji had become a guru to many Western seekers. I felt a similar transmission of truth when I read Poonjaji's books, and wanted to be in the presence of a living realized being. Like Ramana, he taught the practice of "self-inquiry," which involved locating a person's sense of "I" and focusing on and investigating this directly.

Stepping out of the airport in Delhi, I was bombarded with . . . well, India. As I looked around for a taxi to take me to a hotel, several people came up to me at once, making offers, asking questions, begging for money. Hot, dark gray exhaust fumes billowed out from behind buses as they left the curb. The air reeked with an overpowering smell of diesel, gasoline, and decaying garbage. A cacophony of horns belted out, discordant in tune and in time. Unfamiliar with this amount of sensory input, my attention bounced around and my brain became foggier by the moment. Standing on the curb, surrounded by more and more people who wanted to "help" me, I closed my eyes, pulled myself back into my body, and gathered my energy and attention inward. As I did so, I realized I was smiling softly in spite of the sensory overload. Somehow, in the midst of this chaos, I felt quite at ease.

I opened my eyes and spotted a taxi a few yards ahead. "Excuse me," I said to the crowd that was gathered around me. They moved in closer, each person speaking louder, vying for my attention, blocking my way forward. I repeated myself, looked at each person close to me, and matched their volume with a loud "EXCUSE ME!" Instead of making way for me, they stood firm, more animated now, apparently excited that I was engaging. I laughed out loud, a freedom and joy rising up in me, a delight in the lack of traditional Western norms and etiquette.

After pushing my way through the crowd, I reached the cab and opened the cab door, slid my backpack off my shoulders, then shoved it in the back seat before I jumped in beside it. I slammed the cab door shut as I smiled and waved at the small crowd following me. I gave the cab driver the name of the hotel I had carefully chosen ahead of time from my *Lonely Planet* travel guide. He wobbled his head and said, "Oh, yes yes, no problem. I know that one." He told me his name was Vivek and said we would be at the hotel in twenty minutes.

Those twenty minutes were among the most harrowing I had ever experienced in my life. Vivek veered in and out of traffic, zooming ahead whenever a small space opened up, then slamming the brakes to come to a halt within inches of another car, bus, motorcycle, bicycle, or rickshaw. Every other car was doing the same. I grabbed onto the car door with one hand and the car seat with the other. There was no seatbelt. Vivek was completely unfazed and maneuvered adeptly (albeit in fits and starts) around a cow standing in the middle of the road, a washing machine that had apparently fallen off another vehicle, around potholes and people. There were no lanes; drivers were supposed to drive on the left side of the road, but often drove in the middle or on the right. The traffic lights were apparently optional and simply decorative in nature. Cars and buses honked constantly, often sounding joyful in nature, as if drivers were simply singing with their horns. I took a deep breath, tried to relax, and prayed for my safety. This certainly topped the chaotic traffic in Guatemala. Yet, as terrified as I was, I delighted in the chaos, in the lack of structure, in the inability of lines on the road or traffic lights or other structures to contain or control the vitality of the Indian spirit.

Finally, Vivek pulled in front of a building and said, "Here we are!" I looked at the name on the sign of the hotel. "Vivek," I said, "this is not my hotel." He turned and smiled at me. "Yes yes, this is it! It changed owners and now has a different name!" I looked at him skeptically, knowing that he would likely get a commission from this hotel owner for bringing me here. I weighed my options. I didn't want to get scammed, but also understood that scamming was a way of life here, and by this time I was ready to settle into the privacy of a hotel room for a long nap. The thought of dealing with the stress of getting back on the road made the decision easy. "Vivek, I know what you're up to. How much will this hotel cost me?" I was on a shoestring budget and had planned on staying at a cheap hotel overnight, before taking the morning train to Lucknow.

Vivek said, "This hotel is very very cheap but very very nice! Water runs very well and very nice roof terrace to sit on! Very nice people too! You will like this hotel. Very very nice." Unconvinced, but resigned to staying here, I paid and thanked Vivek, grabbed my backpack and stepped inside. It wasn't bad for a budget hotel, and at any rate I barely noticed my surroundings. I was led to my room by a friendly hotel owner, who asked if Vivek had brought me here. I pulled my thin sheet from my backpack, laid it on top of the bed, and slept for twelve hours straight. I awoke to the sound of loud music and laughter outside my window. The smell of Indian curry and exhaust fumes made their way into my consciousness as I awakened. I stretched my legs and opened my eyes to soft sunlight, muted by the grimy window. Fully refreshed from a good night's sleep, I was eager to get to Lucknow and to meet Poonjaji.

I set out to get a bite to eat with a young German woman I met in the lobby of the hotel. As we walked down the crowded street, men stared at us. I was uncomfortable but ignored the stares, until one man intentionally bumped into me and put his hand on my bottom. I instinctively slapped his arm away, yelling out, "You asshole! Get the hell away from me!"

As we walked on, Ingrid raised her left hand, which sported a wedding band, and said, "You need to get one of these. It helps a lot. If you don't have a ring here, you're fair game to all of the men in Delhi." I determined to do so as soon as I could. We stopped at a small cafe a few blocks away and filled up on *chana masala* and *pooris*.

After breakfast I took the train to Lucknow. Once there, I gave a rickshaw driver the address of an Indian home where I had made arrangements to rent a room. After dropping my backpack off, I took a rickshaw to a scheduled session with Poonjaji. These spiritual discourses or gatherings were called *satsangs*, a Sanskrit term meaning "being with the truth." I was full of anticipation as I stood in line surrounded by Westerners. One-pointed in my longing for Truth, I had little interest in socializing or making friends. Nevertheless, I was aware of a divide between those who had been there for some time and those who were new. The "oldies" didn't mix with or speak to the "newbies." Because I was new, I was instructed to come to the front of the line with the other newcomers.

Nearly everyone was eager to sit near Poonjaji in the front of the room, which set up a feeling of tension or competition among those waiting to be allowed inside. There was a rush inward as soon as the door opened. I found myself pushed forward by those behind me. I sat down quickly in the second row as all the spots around me rapidly filled up. I adjusted my position to have a clear view of the chair on the small stage at the front of the room. When everyone was seated, I glanced around. Many had their eyes closed, apparently meditating, while others looked eagerly at the stage.

Soon Poonjaji walked in. He was elderly (in his last year of life) and walked slowly, a devotee at his side, ready to assist. As he sat down, I fully expected to have some sort of extraordinary spiritual experience, some sort of opening, perhaps great joy or gratitude in recognizing a realized teacher. He sat in silence for some time. I waited in anticipation for my own opening, my own awakening . . . and waited, and waited. Everything felt very ordinary.

As Poonjaji began to speak, I studied him, thinking if I looked deeply enough, there would be *some* sort of experience. I saw only a human being. I did not feel the transmission of Truth or energy I had expected, or anything else extraordinary. Surely something was wrong! I tried to meditate, attuning to the energy in my body. I felt nothing special, no profound experience or insights; it was just a regular meditation. My experience was the same at each satsang I attended over the next week. Although his words rang true, I didn't feel a deeper resonance. Those around me spoke of their realizations and of their devotion to Poonjaji, and my mind sang the old song about there being something wrong with me. But I stayed attentive, and a deeper wisdom came forward, a simple knowing that Poonjaji was not my teacher, and that was not something I could change or influence. It was all in motion on a level beyond the individual "me."

One of Poonjaji's devotees, a young Italian man, invited me to go on a motorcycle ride with him. He wouldn't tell me where he wanted to take me, only that I would be glad I went. Although I felt a slight aversion to him, I overrode my intuition and climbed on the back of his motorcycle. My hair whipped out behind me as we drove out of town and down a long dirt road. I began to feel anxious about being alone with a man I barely knew, but had trusted solely because he was visiting Poonjaji.

We soon arrived at two trees that had grown together, twisting around each other in a clear embrace. I got off the motorcycle, putting some space between him and me. He came up behind me, put his arms around me, and pulled me to him. He told me the trees were sacred trees and described the local lore and spiritual meaning of the trees. I hardly heard his words. Daylight was fading and I was aware of his clear intention of having sex with me. I was furious with myself for having been so naive to have gotten myself in this position. I shivered in the cool air and felt him tighten his arms around me. Feeling vulnerable and afraid of angering him, I told him I was cold and asked if we could return to town. He hesitated, then got back on the motorcycle. I sensed his irritation and reluctantly climbed on the motorcycle behind him.

We drove into town, but instead of taking me back to my room, he drove to a plaza where he had pitched his tent. I asked if he would take me to my lodging, but he insisted that I come into his large tent for a cup of tea. I had no idea where we were, and no idea how to get back to the home where I was staying. I had not thought to bring the address of the home with me. I sensed the potential of his aggression, and felt a rising panic. I was afraid of him, afraid of angering him. In the tent, he tried to kiss me and reached to unbutton my blouse. I pulled back from him and moved his hand away. "No," I said quietly.

"Why the hell not?" he said angrily, loudly.

Sensing that he would escalate further if he felt I was rejecting him, I said, "This isn't about you. I just move much more slowly than this." He pushed me down on the ground and pinned me under his body. I pushed back with all of my might, rage now overtaking my panic. "STOP!" I yelled. "What do you think you are doing? You're going to force me? Are you fucking kidding me?"

He stood up, furious. "Why can't you just be free and in the moment?" He stormed out of the tent.

After catching my breath, I slipped out of the tent door and looked around, hoping he would be gone. I didn't see him, so I walked quickly towards a crowd of people. I had no idea how to get back to my rented room. I mingled in the crowd, not knowing what to do, tears stinging my eyes. Suddenly, out of nowhere, I heard "Mindy! Mindy! What are you doing here?" A young woman from Brazil, whom I had met standing in line at our first Poonjaji satsang, ran up to me. She was renting a room in a home near where I was staying and had come to the plaza to shop. Filled with relief, I gave her a tight hug. "I am so happy to see you, Francisca!" We took a rickshaw back to our rooms. She chatted all the way. Still overwhelmed with emotion, I was glad she was oblivious to my silence. I didn't tell her, or anyone else, about my experience. I knew that it was time to leave, and the next day boarded the train for Kathgodam, the nearest train station to Kainchi, where Neem Karoli Baba's temple was located in the Himalayan foothills.

Relieved to be leaving Lucknow, I settled in for the long train ride to Kathgodam. The slow clickety-clack of the train gradually sped up, almost drowning out the weak cries of a young infant coming from behind me. A faint scent of curry wafted over, then grew stronger as a nearby passenger gently pulled a piece of aluminum foil off a bowl.

I shifted my body towards the window and watched the streets and buildings of Lucknow disappear.

I was trying to get comfortable, but under my clothing was my traveler's pouch—containing my passport, travelers' checks, and cash—which was pinching the skin around my waist. I pulled my shirt out from my waist, unzipped the pouch, and stuffed my train ticket inside. As I pulled my hand out, a black-and-white photo of Maharajji fell out onto my lap. His head was tilted back, his bald head shining, a plaid blanket wrapped around his shoulders. I looked into his eyes, feeling love and relief that I was headed towards his ashram.

"Are you a devotee of Maharajji?" A man's kind, quiet voice broke through and brought my attention back to the train. Across from me sat a small, thin Indian man, dressed in dark gray pants and a white collared shirt. A gentle smile under his mustache greeted me.

"Yes," I smiled, my heart open, touched by this man's sweetness. "Are you?"

"Oh, yes, my whole family is. Are you going to the ashram?" He had grown up in Nainital and had been with Maharajji as a child many times before Maharajji's *mahasamadhi*—his departure from his body. He offered to help me get to the Hotel Evelyn in Nainital, where I would be staying. From Kathgodam, we took a bus to Nainital and he walked me to the Hotel Evelyn, where he was greeted as a dear friend by M.L. Sah, the hotel owner.

M.L. Sah was friendly and curious, asking questions about how I came to know of Maharajji and Ram Dass. After I had settled in, he met me on the terrace. The terrace was lined with potted flowering plants. In the midst of the flowers stood a faded but prominent sign: Please Do Not Pluck the Flowers. I giggled, imagining all the hippies that came through here in the past, plucking flowers to wear in their hair or to take to Maharajji. M.L. Sah set down a tray with two cups of hot chai on a table. We sat in two white plastic chairs, and he shared how during the fall of 1971 the hotel had housed Ram Dass and the group of Western devotees who were making daily visits to Maharajji's ashram at Kainchi, about ten miles away.

The next morning I took the bus from Nainital to Kainchi. As the bus rounded the last sharp turn, the bright red domes of the temples below suddenly appeared. A river flowed in front of the ashram. My heart leapt. When I arrived at the entrance to the ashram, I was pulled by an irresistible force straight to a large gray rock that sat in the shade of a tree. I sat on the ground in front of the stone and wept as waves of gratitude and love washed through my body. My hands came together in front of my heart in a spontaneous gesture of reverence, a *pranam*. I was truly Home in the heart—and world—of my guru.

The timeless love that Maharajji embodied had endured beyond space, beyond the death of his body, and was awake in my heart. I don't know how long I was glued to the ground. At some point I heard someone behind me say gently, "He would sit on this stone and devotees would sit around him." I stood up, my body as light as a feather; my whole being expanded outward, spacious, my heart full, my mind empty.

I moved through the ashram, bowing to the deities in each temple—Hanuman, Shiva, Durga, Laxmi Narayan, and at Maharajji's *mandir*, or temple to the Self. My personal will had disappeared, and I experienced myself flowing through time and space as not separate from my surroundings. The whole ashram was my body. Love was the substance of everything, and this love, freedom, and joy were more real than the world outside the ashram gate.

When I returned to the hotel that afternoon, M.L. Sah told me that his cousin, Krishna Kumar (K.K.) Sah, had invited me to visit. I knew of K.K. through Ram Dass's stories. K.K. had known Maharajji since he was a child, as Maharajji often visited his family's home. It was K.K. who insisted that Maharajji allow Krishna Das and others to come see him from the U.S. after Maharajji had initially refused their request.

I stood in front of the green door to K.K.'s home. As I raised my hand to knock, the door opened. A thin man in a plaid shirt and knitted cap, who could have been mistaken for a teenage boy, stood there smiling. There was a gentle, glowing presence about him. "Come in, come in, Melinda!" he said. I followed him up a narrow staircase. A palpable peace permeated his home. Two couches faced each other in front of a wall of windows. As we sat down, K.K. asked how I had come to know of Maharajji, and I shared with him my connection with Ram Dass. Soon his sister Bina came into the room with cups of chai and a plate of sweet biscuits.

I listened for hours as K.K. shared with me his experiences with Maharajji. I was unaware of time, absorbing and soaking up every word. I felt as if I had known K.K. all my life. His kindness, his gentleness, his giggle and delight were all a warm embrace welcoming me into his family and into the still vibrant family of devotees of Maharajji.

The unexpected connection with M.L. and K.K. Sah created a perfect context for the many weeks I spent in Nainital and Kainchi. Living in a culture that had emerged from and was defined by a profound spirituality was revelatory. Instead of a superficial "hello," people greeted one another with *namaste*—a loving acknowledgement of the divine reality and spiritual heart we all share. I was able to relax and live the boundless love that Maharajji had released within me.

Life was simple; nothing to learn and nothing to know other than the sweet enlivening presence that had drawn me to India and was now nourishing every dimension of my being. The depletion from my first year of medical school was far behind me, and a sense of grace and abundance supported my journey. I was not only full with the experience of my time in India, I sensed I would always have access to the limitless love that had become real for me by walking in Maharajji's footsteps. I had what I needed to hold my spiritual center while navigating the challenges of medical school. I headed back to the States with these great gifts.

CHAPTER 9

Vipassana Meditation Retreat

Be still, and know that I am God.
—Psalm 46:10; ESV

Upon my return to the U.S. I knew I would have to make time for meditation to maintain the awareness and presence that had been so abundantly available in India. I wanted to rest in stillness and feel the truth of love. I hadn't done much meditating and was pretty miserable every time I tried. My task-oriented mind, fueled by a medical school system that was created by a left-brain scientific mindset, just wouldn't quiet down, no matter how hard I tried to focus my attention while I sat. My mind raced off into the future, thinking about everything I needed to get done or imagining an upcoming event, or it turned back and rehashed the past. How could the "now" be so elusive? I kept bringing my focus back to my breath, but my attention followed the stream of thought before I even noticed that my mind had wandered off.

At Findhorn I had heard about rigorous Vipassana meditation retreats that were led by S.N. Goenka, an Indian who grew up in Myanmar (Burma) and was trained by the noted Buddhist teacher Sayagyi U Ba Khin. His organization had many meditation centers around the world. I decided I needed meditation boot camp and signed up for a ten-day Goenka retreat to be given at the California Vipassana Center in North Fork, CA, where all expenses for the retreat had been met by donations from those who had attended retreats in the past. I planned to give it all I had.

Once I had been accepted into the course, I booked my cross-country flight and waited for two months with great anticipation. When I stepped off the plane in Fresno, I was met with a wall of dry heat. As I drove onto the property, my rental car kicked up a cloud of dust behind me. Upon arrival I was dismayed to see that I would be sleeping in a large dormitory-style room with ten other women. I knew I wouldn't be sleeping much, as I was exquisitely sensitive to sound at night and awakened with the slightest noise.

We were informed of the rules we had to follow, which included:

- Noble Silence (no talking, no gesturing, no eye contact, no written notes, no sign language)
- no worship, prayer, or religious ceremony
- no physical contact
- separation of men and women (in different dormitories and sitting on opposite sides of the meditation hall)
- no smoking, drinking, or drugs
- no exercise
- modest dress
- no phone, internet, or outside communication
- remaining on the compound for the entire retreat
- no music, reading, or writing
- participation in all meditations

All attendees were also required to commit to the five precepts of Buddhism—abstaining from killing any being, stealing, all sexual activity, telling lies, and all intoxicants.

As I slid my suitcase under my hard bed, I met a few of my roommates. One girl who looked my age had heard that these retreats could cure people of addictions and had come to quit smoking. She sat atop her bunk, legs swinging, chatting nervously. In contrast, Amy, a veteran of seven previous ten-day retreats, was quiet, deliberate, and gentle. I sensed she could feel my heart and I found myself feeling jealous of what I thought of as her spiritual attainment. Ashamed of my jealousy, I feigned friendliness. Amy looked in my eyes and smiled as she said, "Even though on the surface it looks like we are all here trying to make progress on our spiritual journeys, underneath it all, we are all the same. There's nothing to attain." I was startled by her ability to read me, and touched by her kindness. Not until years later would I realize and experience the truth of her words.

Noble Silence began after dinner that night, as we did our first meditation. In the meditation hall, we were assigned spots on the floor where we were to place our meditation cushions, called zafus. My assigned place was towards the back, on the right side of the room with the other women. I sat down, crossed my legs, and soon heard Goenka's voice through an audio tape providing instructions on the meditation technique we were to follow. He spoke of the need for determination. I had plenty of that, yet already found myself frustrated with my wandering mind. Back in the dorm room, I got very little sleep with the chain saw snoring of two women rattling through the night air. I tossed and turned, put my pillow over my head, and plugged my ears with toilet paper—all to no avail. I began to worry about how sleep deprivation would affect my ability to meditate.

At 4 a.m. we were awakened by a gong signaling that a two-hour meditation would begin in half an hour. I stood in line at the sink for a chance to splash my face with water. Although my friends had doubted they could survive ten days of silence, I welcomed the silence and felt very comfortable with it. Some of the new students were ill at ease, at times smiling or gesturing to ease their awkwardness. I kept my gaze down and didn't look at anyone throughout the ten days, happy to avoid social interaction and grateful for the opportunity to dive inward.

I filed into the meditation hall and sat on my lavender zafu. My assigned position with the other new students in the back rows was presumably to prevent our agitation from distracting the students in front of us. I placed my feet on opposite thighs in the lotus position, spine straight. Eyes averted, I noted the long gray skirt taking its seat to my right; to my left, white socks, with the words "No Nonsense" stamped on the toes, wriggled and stretched before moving out of my field of vision. I closed my eyes and listened as the rustling of movement quieted into silence. I waited, eager to begin, eager to apply the force of my will.

The bell rang to signal the start of the meditation. Fueled by an intense determination, I brought my attention to the sensation of my breath on my skin, just above the upper lip and below the nostrils, as per Goenka's instructions. Soon, however, I realized my mind had wandered. I was thinking of a conversation about spiritual teachers I had with an elderly man on the plane. I quickly brought my attention back to my breath and intentionally sharpened my focus. Seconds later my mind again ran off, this time wishing that my neighbor would stop sniffling, then wondering what we would be eating for lunch, and which break might be the best to take a shower. With one shower for fifteen women, I would need to be strategic in order to avoid waiting in line. I heard a fly buzzing nearby and hoped it wouldn't land on me.

Suddenly I realized my mind had meandered for what seemed like a very long time. Deeply alarmed, I yanked my attention back to my breath. After multiple rounds like this, without any evidence of progress in quieting my mind, I was frustrated and agitated.

The room had gotten warm and I wished I hadn't left my jacket on. I had to stay still, so I couldn't remove it now. I felt the prickling of sweat on my forehead, and an itch just above my right eyebrow. I tried to ignore the itch and forced my attention back down to the space between my upper lip and my nose. The itch grew and grew in intensity, as did my impulse to reach up and scratch. I gave up on any attempt to follow my breath, intent now only on fighting off this overwhelming urge to scratch the itch. It became unbearable. Just when I thought I would explode, miraculously the itch began to dissipate. I exhaled with relief, noting that I had been holding my breath. Grateful for the reprieve, I resolved again to remain focused on my breath. I was successful for about three breaths, and then my monkey mind was off and running yet again, my agitation increasing each time I realized my mind had kidnapped my attention.

That first meditation was interminable. I was certain that the instructor had forgotten to ring the ending bell. I felt I couldn't sit for one more second or I would jump out of my skin, but I kept sitting. This wasn't working! I thought there was absolutely no way I would survive ten days. I came up with elaborate stories I could tell the instructor as to why I had to leave the retreat early. Finally, the ending gong rang.

And so it went for the first two days. Although I experienced some mild aches and pains during meditation, my wandering mind was much more of a challenge than any physical discomfort. I alternated between utter hopelessness that I couldn't make it through the retreat to forcing myself to think encouraging thoughts about staying. Not being able to come up with a reasonable excuse for leaving helped with the decision to stay, as did having a non-changeable, non-refundable return plane ticket. I told myself I could do anything for ten days; if I left early, I would never forgive myself. I forced myself to continue and gave it my all—a two thousand percent effort in focus and attention. I made every effort not to stray off into a single thought; when a thought did arise, I forcefully yanked my attention back to my breath.

By the third day, it wasn't so hard. I was aware of what seemed like a surrounding silence and presence, which felt like India. My mind was quieting down, and this profound familiar presence infused everything and followed me everywhere. It was not separate from me. I had put in tremendous effort and it now felt as if I had been meditating for lifetimes. Forgotten memories popped up, breaking through the intensity of my concentration. I remembered the terrifying silence I had experienced as a child that had awakened me from sleep in my bunk bed in Nahualá. Whenever memories or insights came, I immediately redirected my attention to the sensations in the body, determined to follow instructions to a T. I did not dwell on or dawdle with thoughts, psychological musings, or awe about whatever arose. I just pulled the attention immediately back to the breath.

The third afternoon I became aware of an intense burning sensation that felt almost like small balls of fire lined up down the center of my body. Initially I didn't give this much attention as I considered it a distraction from my focus on the in-breath and out-breath. However, my awareness of these balls of fire persisted throughout the retreat. There were seven—one just above my head, one in the center of my forehead, one in my throat, one in the center of my chest, one just below my diaphragm, another in my lower abdomen, and another in my pelvic area. The burning sensation was sometimes very intense and difficult to tolerate. After days of this, the word *chakra* popped into my mind. I had only heard of the chakras, the Sanskrit word for energy centers, once or twice in the past, and had not experienced them before. I hadn't given them much thought and had even questioned their existence, but now there was no question. They were real energy centers, and they were burning up.

After three days of practicing *anapana*, or breath awareness, we were given different instructions. Anapana was intended to sharpen our concentration, a preparation for the next step. We were now instructed on how to move our attention through a slow body scan, from the top of the head down to the tips of the toes. We were told to use *adhittana*, or strong determination, which I had already been applying. I dove into this new technique of body scanning in earnest.

The first thing I noticed was that some sensations would reveal long forgotten memories or emotions. Once, when I was scanning my back, a vivid image surfaced of me as a baby. I was clutching my mom, crying and screaming, as she handed me over to another woman at nursery school. At times emotions would surface without any associated memory or mental concept. Tremendous sadness or joy or anger would arise seemingly out of the blue, and then be released from the body where it had been held. The body alternated between tension and, after a release of the locked-up energy of emotion, a delicious and unfamiliar sense of looseness and freedom.

While Goenka's body scan instructions described different sensations we might be aware of—such as heat, cold, tingling, tightness—I soon discovered that when I placed attention intently on a sensation, whether the mind labeled it as muscle tightness or heat or cold, it would quickly dissolve into a tingling vibration. Soon all I experienced, no matter where I placed my attention, was this tingling vibration. I assumed I was doing something wrong, as I was no longer able to differentiate the sensations in my body. Every few days we were allowed to ask the meditation instructors questions about the meditation technique. I was called to the front of the room with the other new students. I raised my hand and nervously asked, "Goenka describes sensations of heat, cold, tickling, tension… I'm only feeling this tingling vibrating sensation. Everything else ends up turning into that immediately once attention is placed on it. What should I be doing differently?"

The teacher responded quietly, "Maybe that's what all sensations are made of." I was relieved that I apparently wasn't doing anything wrong, and only years later understood that this vibration was the energy out of which all matter is made.

I walked silently back to my zafu, tucked my long skirt under my legs, and sat back down to meditate. Suddenly I was startled by a loud toot coming from a few rows in front of me. A silent giggle erupted from me. I was unable to stop it. I clamped my eyes tightly closed, scolding myself harshly in an attempt to halt the laughter. The more I tried not to think about it—the more I tried to focus my attention on the body scan—the more my body shook with laughter. Tears slid down my face, and in my effort to stifle my giggles, I snorted loudly. Eyes closed, body shaking in laughter, I heard other snorts and giggles in the room. This was all so taboo! We were supposed to be in complete silence! I pinched myself hard and thought of as many tragic scenes as I could, like the death of my dog. All to no avail. Then suddenly I heard the teacher's voice, loudly and sternly saying, "Work seriously!" This set me off on another case of the giggles. My clothes were drenched in sweat from the effort of smothering my laughter. It was impossible. It was a joy to feel such spontaneous laughter. It had been a long time since I had really laughed.

The silence grew in intensity each day. It permeated every cell of my body and everything around me. My body and the world felt surreal as this silent presence filled the foreground and merged with my attention. The next day, as I scanned my body, I watched in slow motion as sensations moved into emotions, which then moved into thought. I was witnessing the very birth of emotions and thoughts, all from energy sensations in the body. In another meditation, I witnessed that everything in this world, everything in consciousness, everything in the universe, everything imaginable, is born of love. These clear and profound revelations—that all perception begins as energy in the body, and that all is birthed from love—shifted my entire experience of the world.

On the sixth day, applying renewed determination and one-pointed attention fueled by my burning chakras, I experienced a sudden opening—what felt like a cloud parting. I was given a glimpse of Truth—and it was so TRUE, so REAL that it seared my whole being. My nervous system couldn't have survived the intensity of more than a glimpse. Truth, not perceived through mind, just WAS, and it was more real than anything I had ever known or experienced, more real than anything in the world, more real than I was or anyone else. I felt my jaw drop open wide in stunned awe. My mind scrambled in: "Don't EVER, EVER forget this! Nothing else is real!"

The quest to fully know and live in—and as—this Truth was now fully established as the center of my life. After this glimpse—a "seeing" called *kensho* in the Zen tradition— there was no choice. It was as if Truth had chosen me and pulled me into Itself. Truth Itself, not ideas about truth, such as honesty or telling the truth. And so the compass of my life became Truth. Every cell in my body sought Truth and longed for it.

At the end of the retreat, when silence was broken, everyone began to laugh and chat, giddy with energy, joking about the hardships of the retreat. I couldn't speak. The silence was so loud, so pervasive, the awareness so profound, that I was unable to fit myself back into the constraints of my personality. The boundary between the others and me was much softer, looser.

I had always been aware of what others were feeling, but that sensitivity was now more subtle. I was acutely aware of energy, and this awareness was now in the foreground of my consciousness rather than the usual thoughts and emotions. I was often aware of someone's underlying energies or issues, and at times I was even aware of their thoughts. I could sense their openness, or where they were guarded or shut down. These experiential insights were spontaneous, realized in every cell of my body.

The realization that emotions and thoughts all arise from bodily energies went so deep and came from such depths of my being, that it transformed my life. I had seen the creation of thoughts and I also saw the reverse—that by simply placing attention on the sensations, an individual could unwind energetic contractions and physical knots that had been formed when these thoughts and feelings had been buried or rejected. Most importantly, I now saw that the contractions and holding of energies were actually what formed ego identity—they created the "me." This realization offered the possibility of loosening up identification with the "me" by attending to these sensations and releasing the underlying patterns. I had found a way to deeper revelations and truths beyond my individual consciousness.

Goenka's meditation style was traditional for the Indian sub-continent, focused on Buddhist teachings and technique without a Western framework or understanding of emotions or psychology. Psychological support was not provided during the retreat, nor was there any follow-up spiritual or psychological support. For some, old wounds were opened up during the retreat that did not release or resolve and there was no framework offered to understand what was happening. When the retreat ended, another student, Greg, drove me to the airport an hour away in Fresno. He was very emotional, alternately crying and yelling throughout the trip. He told me that prior to the retreat, he had been very stable emotionally and didn't tend to cry or get upset. I was alarmed at the intensity of his emotions and feared for our safety as we drove.

Greg shared that during the retreat, memories of childhood sexual abuse had surfaced. He had been completely unaware of the abuse before the retreat, having repressed the memories long ago. He was now having suicidal thoughts. As he drove, I kept my eye on the road and on the steering wheel while listening and offering support as I could. At the airport, he promised to call a friend as soon as he arrived home and to seek out counseling as he dealt with this open wound. From Greg's experience, I realized the power and potential danger of meditation in unlocking repressed memories and emotions. It was clear that an intense meditation immersion, like a ten-day vipassana retreat, was a risk if the meditator wasn't equipped psychologically for these types of revelations. I was soon to realize that intensive meditation could also precipitate an equally precarious psychic opening—all the more challenging amidst the immense demands of medical school.

The Goenka retreat had thrown me into a state of "premature" dissolution of separation. Even after the retreat ended, the structure of the world was continuously dissolving, with no separation between myself and others. As it had been earlier in my life, this dissolution—this awareness of the underlying fabric of existence—was terrifying. I had committed to a return to medical school and knew that navigating my life in that intense environment while in the midst of this spiritual earthquake would be challenging, to say the least. But the grace, grounding, and deep nourishment of my year-long leave of absence and Ram Dass's encouragement propelled me forward.

I was ready to return to medical school.

CHAPTER 10

Return to Med School, and Myself

When the mind, which is the cause of all cognitions and of
all actions, becomes quiescent, the world will disappear.
—Ramana Maharshi

It was the first day back, and I was on my way to Baruch Auditorium at MUSC. I was behind a student dressed in a long navy blue skirt; she was walking rhythmically, her legs poking out from under her skirt as she swished along. My consciousness shifted and suddenly I was flipping through hundreds of her past lives. I wasn't even sure I believed in past lives, but there it was. I continued to the lecture hall and sat in the balcony. Suddenly I was *in* some guy's body on the lower level, aware of his thoughts, his movements, his emotions. The dissolution experiences had evolved beyond awareness of formless existence and now I was accessing information and experience from outside of my physical body. I had hoped the medical school atmosphere would slow down these events, but they continued in full force.

My ability to identify separate objects and even the reference points that provided a framework in time and space would sometimes spontaneously disappear. Lying in bed at night, the sound of a truck triggered a dissolving of the world and "me." At times there were no boundaries between objects and myself: I couldn't tell where the dresser, my bed, or other objects started and ended. I watched from outside my body as it stood up on its own at the beach, without "me" doing it. I scheduled a massage, thinking it might help, but during the massage my sense of self dissolved into the background music and I had to ask that it be turned off. Time would also disappear. I would often have no idea what year, month, or day it was. This was especially poignant when I started working with psychiatric patients the next year. I'd have to ask them the date to test their orientation to time, while I didn't know it myself.

I lived in terror much of the time, as the dissolving of my mind petrified me and made everything very difficult. But it was that very terror that would bring me back into the sense of a "me." I knew I was undergoing a spiritual opening, so I continued my daily meditation practice despite the intensity and the demands of medical school. I meditated for an hour twice a day, every day, using my already very abbreviated sleep hours to meditate. Medical students hesitated to take time for a shower or even a bathroom break because of the overwhelming amount of work to be done, but I was compelled to never skip a meditation. A spiritual teacher told me to stop meditating, that it was too much for me at the time, that the dissolving of separation was premature for my system . . . but I couldn't stop. The inward pull was too strong. Enduring the rigors of medical school during this dissolution of "me" was extremely challenging, although the demands of medical school simultaneously served to ground me and keep me functioning in the world. Even so, I needed help.

Fortunately, my travels, retreats, and connections during my year off had created an essential network of spiritual support for my continuing journey. This was the late 1990s—before the internet, before the plethora of spiritual teachers that appeared in the 2000s, before a yoga studio ever existed in Charleston. You couldn't get the kind of help I needed from the Yellow Pages. I called Findhorn to see if there was anyone in South Carolina who had visited there, thinking that they would be spiritually-oriented and like-minded. They gave me the name of Ramita Bonadonna (who had no idea how Findhorn had gotten her name—she'd never been there or had any contact with them, and had just changed her phone number to the one Findhorn provided). Through a series of connections, Ramita introduced me to Amita Clark, a devotee of Osho, an Indian guru who had made quite an impact in the west.

Mindy lived at Amita's house during med school

Amita—gentle, utterly pure, full of unconditional love, and soft-spoken—quietly and gently welcomed me into her life. Amita was, and is, literally an angel on earth. We had an immediate connection. Her boyfriend had recently moved out and she offered to rent me a room. I lived with her for the next two years, until she married Duke, a bright Truth-seeker with an enormous heart, a twinkle in his eye, an infectious sense of delight and humor, and a crazy southern drawl. Amita and Duke became the core of my spiritual family and planted themselves in the center of my heart, where they both remain today.

I rented a small room and bathroom from her at Folly Beach, two blocks from the ocean, for $200 a month. The first thing I did was set up my meditation table with pictures of Ram Dass, Neem Karoli Baba, Ramana Maharshi, and Nisargadatta Maharaj. Amita and I meditated together and supported each other with a variety of tools we learned or made up on the fly. For some time, we intentionally laughed at challenging emotions as they came up as a means of shifting the energy and the identification with the emotion. Once, I felt terrible when I broke one of her dishes; she laughed, grabbed another plate, and tossed it to the floor. "There! Now we both broke a dish!" She and Duke worried about me—I would share my fear about failing every time I prepared for a test, then would end up getting an A. After a while Duke caught on that my fears of failure were unfounded and laughed each time I started to moan. His laughter inevitably rang through me and had me laughing at myself.

I shared with Amita my ongoing experience of the dissolution of the separate self, knowing she would get that this was a spiritual process and not label me as crazy. I knew that I was not psychotic. But the continuing challenge of navigating the world—and medical school—as an individual "me," even as the *me* was dissolving, created a tremendous stress and depression in my system. In my despair, I finally scheduled an appointment at the psychiatry residents' clinic at MUSC. I was randomly assigned to Michael Mithoefer, an ER physician who was shifting from practicing emergency medicine to a residency in psychiatry (and later would do research on the use of MDMA for PTSD). He had a depth of spirit and wisdom, had been on his own spiritual journey for decades, and had trained with Stan Grof in holotropic breathwork. Kind and compassionate, he understood that I was having a spiritual awakening.

After some time working with me, Dr. Mithoefer recognized that an antidepressant could help my overtaxed nervous system. Initially I refused medication, thinking it would somehow interfere with my spiritual process. As I told Dr. Mithoefer, "I'm not interested in doping myself up." I feared that medication would hide the one doorway that would bring me to freedom, or that medication was somehow an admission that something was wrong with me. I held a belief that if I dove in deep enough, the depression would resolve. But the symptoms of depression persisted and I finally realized that there might be a biochemical component. After many months of delay, I agreed to take a low dose of fluoxetine, a medication also known as Prozac. After three weeks, I began to notice a big difference, and after a few more weeks my symptoms of depression had resolved. I was able to move through my life much more fluidly. Instead of feeling "doped up," I felt much more like myself in a way I had not experienced in a long time.

For the first time that I could remember, the despair was gone. After so may years of "being with," "diving into," and trying all kinds of therapies, tools, and spiritual practices to get rid of the despair, now it had dissipated. I was able to experience joy, spontaneity, and compassion fully, in a way that had not been possible. My heart was moved by others' experiences. I could feel the full range of human emotions—sadness, grief, joy, love. Now able to feel more compassion for others and myself, I opened to all suffering, which softened and then dissolved my die-hard, effort-full approach to spirituality. I thought many times: *If I had only known...*

My newfound balance also allowed me more equanimity around the difficulties of my career path. Towards the end of the second year of medical school, we had to take Step 1 of the United States Medical Licensing Examination. The USMLE is a series of three tests taken at different times during training. Step 1 is a one-day exam, consisting of seven 60-minute blocks, that covers all of the Basic Sciences from the first two years of medical school. The sheer volume of material to review, recall, and re-memorize is staggering. One estimate of the average time needed to prepare for the exam is at least five to six hundred hours of study, or ten hours daily over a six-to-eight week period. That time is a blur for me. But with my spiritual, psychological, and biochemical supports in place, I persevered and passed. It was time to start working with patients in my third year of training.

A Note on Psychiatric Medication and Spirituality

It's not uncommon for spiritual teachers to claim that taking psychiatric medication is an avoidance of something that needs to be experienced. The belief or ideology is that if you can be present with everything that arises, all suffering will dissolve; if you are suffering in any way, this means you are not being fully present with an experience. The flip side of this viewpoint is that if taking psychiatric medication alleviates suffering, this hijacks your process and therefore prevents your spiritual growth.

This may be true for some who need support or encouragement in facing issues and emotions. But many have fully opened to their experiences yet continue to suffer with debilitating emotional, mental, and behavioral patterns. They assume that somehow they aren't doing it right or aren't going deep enough. In some cases it may be that the hard work of facing issues pops people out of their suffering and identification, but to assume things unfold the same way for everyone is to deny the vast range of human experience.

Some former seekers who have become spiritual teachers, like Byron Katie and Eckhart Tolle, have sudden profound spiritual experiences that radically alter them. This is rare, however, and a grace that cannot be expected. Many spiritual seekers have had the experience of going on a meditation retreat, having a profound spiritual experience, and returning to daily life only to resume the familiar dysfunctional patterns that cause the suffering. Spiritual teachers rarely have training in mental health issues and may lack perspective beyond their own experience. Their ideological beliefs about psychiatric medication can exacerbate their students' suffering and prevent them from getting the help they need. This mindset can delay or prevent a seeker from finding the biochemical balance that might allow them to open more deeply.

For someone like me, with a history of repeated trauma and a genetic makeup leaning towards depression and despair, a biochemical imbalance in the body is often reflected in symptoms, painful emotions, and negative thought patterns. Would we deny a diabetic insulin because he or she needs to "be with" the experience of hyper-glycemia? Biochemical imbalances that create emotional suffering are not different from imbalances that cause physical suffering. Deeply ingrained patterns may not be possible to unwind with therapy, will-power, meditation, or with spiritual insight. Being fully present with all that is arising is a tremendous spiritual practice. But in many cases, medication can help shift a person out of a cycle of suffering and thereby allow for a deeper opening and spiritual awakening—a deeper and fuller human experience of love, kindness, and compassion.

A technical note about psychiatric medication

Before prescribing antidepressants, I always sense into the patient's willingness to be with their pain as a tool for their own growth. If he or she has been avoiding being with their pain, I will begin by supporting them as they open more to the contractions that keep them from experiencing their own heart. Often, there is a mixture of avoidance along with ingrained patterns that need to be treated with medication. I don't usually prescribe certain medications, such as benzodiazepines like Valium, Ativan, Klonopin, and Xanax, except rarely for a very brief period of time to help someone through the aftermath of a trauma, or to keep someone out of the hospital. Benzodiazepines have a long-term likelihood of harmful side effects, including addiction and dementia.

Further, it is important to know that therapy and spiritual awak-enings have no effect on psychosis. Only antipsychotic medication will work to rebalance the brain chemistry that causes symptoms of psychosis, such as paranoia or auditory and visual hallucinations. Someone with paranoid schizophrenia cannot be talked out of their paranoia or their delusions. For someone with milder mood swings, spiritual practices and psychotherapeutic tools can be helpful, but for bipolar disorder type I, medication is generally needed to prevent a patient from engaging in potentially catastrophic behaviors during a manic or depressive episode.

CHAPTER 11

Medical School, Third Year

I went inside my heart to see how it was.
Something there makes me hear the whole world weeping.
—Rumi

The first morning of third year, my alarm went off at 4 a.m. I had slept lightly, activated by both excitement and anxiety. I sat to meditate but was hardly able to sit still. I showered and slipped into a pair of tan dress pants and a light blue blouse, intentionally choosing muted colors. We all knew to expect plenty of humiliation this year. Residents and attending physicians notoriously "pimped" medical students, drilling them with questions about disease processes, interpretations of lab and radiology results, diagnoses and treatment options. *Pimping* was such a common word used to describe that aspect of medical school that I never questioned the origin of the word. I looked it up recently and found that it stands for "Put In My Place." Typically, pimping occurs during rounds, in front of the entire treatment team. The intention behind this rite of passage, on the surface, is to further learning, but the questions are typically accompanied by subtle or not-so-subtle authoritarian dominance and intimidation.

On that first day, I dressed with the intention of not standing out, terrified that I would be questioned and my chronic lack of confidence in my medical knowledge would be exposed. I had been wearing shorts and jeans for years, and felt awkward wearing nicer clothes. Christy had advised me to wear low-heeled shoes as I would be walking back and forth from rounds to patient rooms, back and forth to the nurses' station, and to different parts of the hospital for conferences and Grand Rounds.

I had prepared my white lab coat the night before, filling its pockets with the *Tarascon Pocket Pharmacopoeia*, blank note cards for patient notes, pens, laminated cards with detailed instructions on physical exams and review of systems, and my stethoscope. The thick, heavy *Washington Manual for Medical Therapeutics* was crammed into my right pocket, nearly bursting the stitches. I stood in front of the full-length mirror as I slipped each arm into the white coat. I tried to ignore how lopsided I felt, the weight of the manual pulling on my right shoulder. I was determined to have it at my fingertips for looking up anything I might not know. Although I didn't have time to reference it once during that rotation, I carried it in my pocket all day, every day, as a sort of security blanket. I paid the price at the end of each day with a painful crick on the right side of my neck.

I arrived at the VA Hospital on the Medicine floor at 6 a.m. and gathered at the nurses' station with the three other medical students assigned to my team. I tugged at my lopsided lab coat collar as we talked and joked, our chatter and laughter infused with our anxiety. One student asked a nurse where we might find our resident. She looked pointedly at us, silently pursed her lips, and turned away. We soon realized that as medical students, we were at the very bottom of the hierarchy. Just as abuse is perpetuated through generations within a family, from perpetrator to victim to perpetrator, the medical system had in place its own system of abuse, passed down by generations of attending physicians, residents, nurses, and medical students. We very soon understood our place.

Our resident soon appeared, Styrofoam coffee cup in hand, his rumpled scrubs and untidy hair belying his energetic voice. He had been up all night, on call, admitting patients from the ER and managing issues with patients on the floor. "Hey guys, my name is Mark. I'm your resident this month." He peered over his coffee cup at each of us as he took a sip. "We're going to have a lot of fun. And get ready to be thrashed. I'm going to work you HARD, and you're going to learn a lot."

Well, at least he was straightforward. He explained that we were to arrive at 5:30 a.m. each day, six days a week. "You will be assigned four to six patients each. Start each day by reviewing your patients' vital signs, labs, and imaging results; review their charts; check in with the nurse assigned to your patient; if applicable, get an update from the med student who was on call that night." After these tasks, we were to see our patients, assess their symptoms and responses to treatment, complete a physical exam, and then write a progress note for each patient that included all of the information we had gathered.

At 8 a.m. we would be "rounding" with the team—*attending physicians* (the doctors in charge, at the top of the hierarchy, who had long since completed their training), *residents* (physicians who had completed medical school, obtained their MD degree, and were now completing their training in their chosen field of medicine), and *medical students*. Our resident went on: "During rounds, you will present your patients to the team. Make sure your presentations are thorough but concise. We don't have time or care to hear about your patients' dislike of their nurse, or their stress on the home front. Or yours for that matter. Read up on everything there is to know about your patients' disease processes and medications. I guarantee that you will be asked questions during your presentations."

My throat aborted my attempt to swallow; it was too dry with anxiety and anticipation. I looked at the other medical students, who were looking to each other and peering back at me, silent and wide-eyed. An image of the four of us in army fatigues in a war zone, bullets flying overhead, flashed through my mind. We were already comrades in combat, comrades in survival.

After team rounds, we were to attend patient rounds. The entire team visited each patient in their hospital room, with the resident leading the interaction with the patient. The attending at times joined in the conversation, highlighting any valuable teaching points for residents and students and answering any questions. After patient rounds, the resident would "run the list"—a review of the "to-do" list for each patient that day—then give us our assignments, such as helping with medical procedures, completing history and physical exams on newly-admitted patients, following up on tests, obtaining medical records from outside institutions, etc.

At noon, we attended an Internal Medicine conference, during which residents presented interesting or difficult cases to the entire department. This was also lunch time. Pharmaceutical companies typically provided lunch for the team. During our first lunch, we students instinctively understood the unspoken rule: wait until all attendings and residents go through the lunch line first; then you're free to get lunch . . . if there is any food left. In the afternoon, we completed tasks and checked in on our patients again.

Mark, our resident, said normally we could leave between 6-8 p.m., once all of our tasks were completed, unless we were on call that night. We were on a Q3 call schedule—every third night we remained at the hospital all night to assist residents with admissions from the ER, and then we'd continue to work through the next day until 6-8 p.m. that night. "We expect you to be on time, alert, and prepared, always," Mark said. "If you nod off or fall asleep during rounds—well, let's just say that it has happened before, and it didn't go well. At all." He slid his hand across his neck in the classic gesture of throat-cutting.

"Oh, and make sure you are reading and studying every night. You'll need to, not only because you'll get pimped during rounds, but also to pass the exam at the end of the rotation." Internal Medicine's exam was notoriously difficult because of the sheer volume of material. "Any questions?" Mark looked at us expectantly.

If we had any, we were too scared to ask. "Okay, grab your patients' charts, learn about them, and then do H&Ps on each of them." He handed each of us a list of four patients. We had been taught how to do History and Physicals during our second year of medical school, but I froze at the prospect of doing an H&P on a live patient. I instinctively reached into my lab coat pocket for my laminated H&P instruction card, relieved to find its sharp edge with my fingers. If I had a brain freeze while doing an H&P, I could rely on its detailed instructions on taking a thorough history—including chief compliant, history of present illness, allergies and medications, medical history, and social and family history—and its detailed instructions on completing a thorough physical exam. For each patient, I would also need to provide an assessment, or differential diagnoses, based on the history and physical exam, and a plan that addressed each of the patient's problems.

I was relieved that I would get to meet my patients alone at first, without the pressure or stress of anyone else observing or critiquing me. Although I lacked confidence in my medical knowledge and my clinical skills were still in their infancy, I instinctively knew that I could communicate well with my patients, as long as my own stress didn't override my natural ability to connect. I also knew that my brain would be most receptive to learning if I was relaxed and not in fear mode. Unfortunately, the medical school system did not seem to understand this simple biological fact.

At the VA, my first patient was a 49-year-old, divorced, Caucasian Vietnam veteran named Edward Syracuse. He had a history of hypertension, hyperlipidemia, Agent Orange exposure, COPD (chronic obstructive pulmonary disease), and PTSD (post traumatic stress disorder), and had been admitted two days earlier status post MI (myocardial infarction or heart attack). Prior to admission, he had been noncompliant with all medications. As per his chart, he had refused all medications since admission. Nurses' notes indicated that he had been belligerent, often yelling at them.

I found myself curious about this patient, wondering what lay beneath his anger. I tapped gently on his door, pushing it open a few inches. "Mr. Syracuse, my name is Melinda Edwards. I'm a student doctor. Can I come in and talk with you for a few minutes?"

"Another med student? What the hell do you want? I am so sick of y'all, coming in here and asking me all of your same questions, over and over. I don't give a damn about your questions. I just want to feel better, and y'all are making me sicker!"

Well, he hadn't told me to go away. I took that as permission to enter the room. "I am so sorry, Mr. Syracuse. I know it really stinks seeing so many different people and answering so many questions. I've been assigned to look out for you and to help you in whatever way I can, and I really do want to help, not make you feel worse—"

Mr. Syracuse interrupted me. "Get over yourself. You ain't even fifteen years old yet. What the hell are they doing assigning me a teen-ager? This goddamn VA don't give a shit about us vets. They ruin our lives and then throw us to the wolves. I tell you what, if the head of the VA were ever to walk into my room, he'd best run for his life. I ain't messin' around. I am so SICK of y'all. You're just another one come waltzing in here, makin' me your guinea pig, and not giving a SHIT about me, or any of the other veterans here!"

Unfazed by his angry verbal assault, I sensed into him and understood that all of the anger, all of the attacking, was a valiant effort to avoid his own deep pain. I stood silent, at the end of his bed, taking it all in, unflinching, open, nodding from time to time, seeing in his heart the pain, sensitivity, and tenderness that were masked by his anger. He continued his ranting for some time. At one point, I sensed a small opening, a turning point. "HELL, you're young enough to be my granddaughter. How the hell you think you're gonna help me?"

I smiled and laughed out loud. "Now Mr. Syracuse, I am NOT young enough to be your granddaughter, but I appreciate the compliment!" His lips pressed together almost imperceptibly, and I understood that he was withholding a smile. "Mr. Syracuse, I know you are less than thrilled that I've been assigned to you. But here's the thing. You are my first patient, ever. I am so excited to *finally* meet you, my first patient. Do you know that I've been waiting for

TWO YEARS to meet you? I know you may not like me, but could you at least try working with me? Maybe I can't really help, but maybe I can. And what else have you got to do in this hell hole except talk with me?" I smiled at him, squeezed his big toe and shook it gently.

Somehow disarmed, Mr. Syracuse pulled himself together, now with a twinkle in his eye. "Well, you sure got some nerve, Dr. Teenager. Alright, I'll talk with you, but that don't mean I'm gonna like you."

"It's a deal," I said, extending my hand across the bed. He hesitated, then shook my hand.

I somehow sensed that being a bit bossy with Mr. Syracuse would work best with him, that he appreciated and enjoyed having someone stand up to him in a lighthearted way, that he really wanted to connect, and that his attempts to intimidate others were just a defense that he was unable to control. He feared any semblance of intimacy and pushed everyone away with his anger, but he wanted to be heard and understood. If he allowed anyone in, his old wounds would open, as pain does in the face of intimacy. I somehow understood all of this in a flash.

"Alright, Mr. S. We've got a deal now. I've got tons of questions for you, and now that we have a deal, you'll have to answer every single one of them! And by the way, if you go back on our deal and don't help me out, I will get into HUGE trouble with my boss, I may fail the rotation, never be able to be a doctor, and I will hold YOU personally responsible!" I smiled at him and sat down in the chair next to his bed.

"You got some balls, Dr. Teenager. I don't go back on my word. That's something I just don't do." He looked me in the eye, unblinking, his masseter muscle contracting as he set his jaw firmly in place.

I met his gaze, meeting and understanding the warrior qualities that were woven into the fabric of his soul—his integrity, his trueness, his fierce loyalty. I held his gaze. "Thank you, Mr. Syracuse. I got it."

For the next thirty minutes, he answered all of my questions, and then cooperated with a physical exam. At the end of our meeting, I thanked him, then cupped my hand to my mouth, and whispered, "I see your huge heart underneath all that angry fluff. You can't fool me."

He smiled sheepishly, in spite of himself, his cover blown. "I don't know who you think you are, Dr. Smarty Pants. Go on, get outta here. I've had enough of this cow manure for one day!" I walked towards the door, waving as he spoke, then closed the door behind me, popping my head back in once to say, "Oh, and I'll be back tomorrow! You don't have to throw up that smoke screen, and if you do, I'll see through it anyways." I closed the door before he could say anything else. My heart was full after that first meeting with Mr. Syracuse. I went on to meet my other patients, jotting down notes after meeting each of them.

That first day, our attending told us he would give us a break: we would not need to present our patients until the next day. The residents would present all of their patients today and we were to learn from their presentations. For team rounds, we stood in a loose circle in the hallway, surrounded by patient rooms. I stood in awe as Mark presented all ten of his patients. He glanced at each patient notecard once, then launched into a detailed description of the patient, the diagnoses, the lab and imaging results from the previous twenty-four hours, and the patient's progress over the past twenty-four hours. How could he spout off all of those labs—such as electrolytes, blood glucose levels, blood cell counts—just from having looked at them that morning before rounds? How did he remember all those details about the patient? I couldn't even keep my patients' diagnoses straight. I felt deflated, thinking yet again that there was no way I would ever make it.

Those first few days, Mr. Syracuse met me initially with yelling and ranting. He couldn't help it, it was just a habit. But each day, it was less loud, less long, less intense. I bickered with him, "Enough of this hogwash! We've got work to do! Hey now, we talked about this yesterday! I told you I wouldn't have any more of this nonsense!" After several days, he was no longer yelling at me, and we began our meetings with our easy banter. I knew that I had earned his trust, that his heart had cracked open to where I could touch on some sensitive subjects and plant some deeper seeds.

One day, I said, "Mr. S, what's this about you STILL refusing your medication?"

"I AIN'T taking it, so don't even go there. All those goddamn side effects. I read up on all of it. Y'all are trying to kill me!"

I sat down and looked at him seriously. "Mr. S, you know me now. I'm not trying to kill you. Your blood pressure is through the roof and if you don't take your blood pressure medicine, you will end up having another heart attack or a stroke, or both. I don't want that for you. Yes, there are potential side effects from the medicine. If you want, we can take a look at different medication options." He argued with me, a stubbornness born of fear and mistrust disabling any capacity for a rational informative conversation. For a few days, we had similar conversations. I couldn't seem to find a crack in the rigid wall he had erected. I stood my ground, though, and told him that he needed to let his stubbornness soften, that his stubbornness could end up killing him.

One morning, when I checked the MAR (Medication Administration Record, the record of medications administered to a patient), I saw that he had taken his medication.

"Mr. S, I can't stop smiling. I am so happy you took your medication."

"I don't even want to talk about it," he said gruffly, unaccustomed to giving in, to not clinging to his stubbornness.

"We won't, then. I am just so happy today." After I asked him my usual questions about his symptoms, I looked into his eyes, and my voice softened as I said, "You know, Mr. S, it can be uncomfortable and sometimes painful when our walls start to come down, and our hearts start to open. But that's what life is all about." I saw his eyes begin to water. "We don't have to talk about it, because I know you know what I'm talking about," I said as I reached for his hand. He fought back the tears, his lip trembling. "Your heart is beautiful, and precious. Thank you for letting me in." We sat in silence for a few minutes, both of us basking in the gentle love that was present in the room.

Over the years, each veteran I worked with was unique, but I recognized in each of these warriors the qualities of integrity, service, loyalty to death, and honor. Many of them also carried the same defense pattern as Mr. S—anger and lashing out at the world that served as a cover-up for an aching heart. When the heart is seen, even through the smoke screen of anger, the heart knows it is seen, whether or not it is spoken. And the heart responds. With my veteran patients, once they let you in, you are in. For life. Their loyalty is fierce, and they manifest their love and gratitude by wanting to defend and protect you.

• • •

My connection with my patients was the very best part of medical school, but felt very removed from the rest of the training process and did nothing to allay the stress and anxiety of patient presentations during rounds. Typically, one of us med students would get the brunt of pimping on any given day, and we never knew who it would be. My turn came on the fourth day of our Internal Medicine rotation.

Our attending had paged Mark to let him know he would be arriving early. Mark called us to join him in our now-familiar circle in the hallway as the attending approached. "Mindy, you can get us started today." As I pulled my patient notecards out of my pocket, my stethoscope caught on my sleeve, slid out of my pocket, and tumbled down onto the tile floor. Flushed with self-consciousness, I leaned over to pick it up and stuff it back in my pocket. I looked at the top notecard and started out with one of Mr. S's neighbors on the ward. "Mr. Murphy is a 75-year-old widowed World War II veteran with a history of Parkinson's disease, Parkinson's dementia, hypertension, and glaucoma, who was admitted two days ago with acute renal failure (ARF). He—"

"What are the symptoms of ARF?" the attending barked at me.

"Well, prior to admission, Mr. Murphy had decreased urine output, peripheral edema, weakness, shortness of breath, and confusion." My thoughts scrambled to get back to my presentation, but the attending jumped in again.

"What are the causes of ARF?"

I had read up on ARF the night before, but my thoughts froze in fear. Take a deep breath, try to relax, I told myself. I saw bits and pieces of the chapter appear in my mind, flashes of thoughts that I grabbed before they could disappear. "Causes of ARF are categorized as prerenal, renal, and postrenal. Prerenal causes can include volume depletion from decreased fluid intake or diarrhea. Renal ARF involves actual damage to the kidneys, like acute tubular necrosis, acute tubular nephritis, and damage from nephrotoxins like medications. Postrenal ARF involves obstruction to the tubules or more distally, for example with an enlarged prostate."

Although I felt some relief, knowing that I had at least partially answered the question, I knew this would not end well. I had seen the other students on the team answer questions well, only to be drilled further into humiliation. "In Mr. Murphy's case, the etiology of his ARF is likely prerenal and renal. He was dehydrated when he came in, hadn't had much to drink for a few days, and it looks like his ACE inhibitor benazepril may also have contributed."

"Which diagnostic tests should you order when you suspect ARF?"

"BUN, Creatinine . . ." My brain again scrambled, freezing under pressure. I thought back to my patient, his admission lab work. My mind was blank. As the seconds ticked by, I felt my face turn red, my brain stop in its tracks, refusing to cooperate. I felt the dampness of sweat on my forehead, a drop of sweat trickle down my back. I glanced furtively around the circle, hoping for some help. The other medical students were looking down at the floor, averting their eyes, experiencing my shame and discomfort vicariously, not wanting to bear witness and not wanting to add to my discomfort. The attending was staring at me, his arms crossed as he waited, the silence accentuating my shame. The attending and the resident, Mark, slid their eyes sideways at each other, smirking.

The attending pounced. "Congratulations, Dr. Edwards, you have just killed your patient. Why the hell would you just order BUN and creatinine? Why wouldn't you order a CMP to look for electrolyte imbalances and metabolic acidosis? What about a CBC to screen for infection and anemia? What about urinary sodium, protein, urinary sediment? And what about an ultrasound or CT scan of the bladder and kidneys to rule out obstruction? After your patient kicks over from respiratory failure or the sepsis that you missed, you'll get to face his wife in court and explain why you decided to kill him."

"Got it," I said weakly, looking down at my shoes.

"Tonight read up on diagnosis and treatment of ARF and give us a five-minute presentation tomorrow. Okay, you can proceed with presenting your now dead patient, Dr. Edwards," the attending said mockingly.

I fumbled through the rest of my patient presentations, embarrassed and humiliated, wishing only for the day to be over. The scene ran through my mind like a nightmare that night, reviving the humiliation with each play. What little confidence I had gained had been shattered and I feared that my lack of knowledge would harm or even kill my patients. The attending knew exactly which buttons to push to undermine a student, but surely there was a better approach to teaching.

• • •

When we started our rotations we were full of memorized facts, but we lacked preparation for the practical application of the basics. During my first night on call, our senior resident Mark asked me to write standard *prn* (*pre re nata*, meaning "as needed") medication orders for a patient that was being admitted from the ER to the hospital, which Mark would co-sign later. I panicked, having no idea how to write medication orders.

Sheepishly, I asked Mark how to write the orders. "Oh, just write for Tylenol and Phenergan prn," he said. I gulped. I didn't even know the appropriate doses for Tylenol or Phenergan. Too embarrassed to ask, I strode casually to the chart rack in the nurses station, pulled out another patient's chart, and looked at his admission orders. I snuck a look around. Whew. Everyone was busy with what they were doing. No one seemed to notice. I walked back to Mark, picked up the new patient's chart, and wrote the medication orders.

We were on call every third night which meant being at the hospital for a thirty-six hour stretch—all day, all night, and the next day. Nights were often just as busy as days. We were in the ER most of the night, seeing patients that were being admitted from the ER to the Internal Medicine ward. We took histories, completed physical exams, and wrote admission notes, including differential diagnoses and plans for treatment, then presented the patients to the resident on call. We worked through the night, drinking coffee or Mountain Dews when we could, and then rolled right into rounds the next morning, cotton-mouthed and rumpled.

One day, Mark assigned a patient to me that had been admitted the previous night. Mr. Brooks was a 69-year-old widowed Caucasian veteran with a history of diabetes, schizophrenia, and PTSD, who had been admitted with complaints of abdominal pain and decreased appetite. We had admission lab results, which were normal. His diabetes had been well-controlled with metformin, and he had not experienced auditory hallucination, visual hallucinations, or paranoia since he had begun clozapine a year earlier. He described ongoing symptoms of PTSD, including frequent nightmares and flashbacks from his combat exposure during Vietnam, as well as hypervigilance and hyperstartle. He complained of side effects from the clozapine, including sialorrhea (drooling) and constipation. Mr. Brooks was clearly in discomfort. He told me he had not eaten in two days and had not had a bowel movement in eight days.

On exam, his abdomen was distended and I didn't hear any bowel sounds with my stethoscope. When I presented my findings to Mark, bowel obstruction was at the top of my differential diagnosis. The radiologist examining his x-rays confirmed bowel obstruction as the diagnosis. Bowel obstruction, if severe, can cause bowel perforation. Mark said, "Glove up, girl. You're about to do your first manual disimpaction."

Usually, we students were excited to do procedures, although this was not one I was looking forward to. But I was finding that my clinical, objective self kicked into gear reliably with all things biological/medical, and this was no exception. Mark guided me through the process of manually disimpacting Mr. Brooks' rectum and then giving him an enema. I was so intent on the process that I barely noticed the smell or the mess. Mr. Brooks' relief when it was all over was profound.

Several weeks into our rotation, I noticed the other students and I were remembering our patients' lab values, able to recite them after having glanced at them that morning. I realized my brain had somehow adjusted and was becoming more adept at retaining this new language, this new system. Although I never got used to getting pimped, as I gained more knowledge and learned to present patients more concisely, my anxiety during patient presentations lessened.

CHAPTER 12

Finding My Way

You are awareness, disguised as a person.
—Eckhart Tolle

One day I met a physician named Dr. Cohen, who had completed his residency and was in the midst of a fellowship. Near the end of my long work day, I stood in my short white lab coat with a stethoscope draped around my neck in the busy hospital nurses' station, my lab coat pockets bulging with my pharmacopoeia, medical notes, and patient notecards, searching for my patients' charts on the large rack behind the desk. I was looking forward to sitting down to update the charts on the patients I had seen that day, knowing that after this last task I could go home and rest, at least until I woke up early the next day to start all over again.

It was after 11 p.m. and my exhausted mind was distracted by the bustle of the nurses' change of shift. I scooted forward as a nurse gathered her sweater and lunchbox from the desk behind me. Laughter erupted from the nurses' report room as they filed out. A persistent, loud repetitive beep, the sound of a patient's unanswered call button, seemed to sound in time with the beginning throbs of a headache in my temples. I hadn't had time to eat or drink since early that morning and felt a sudden and familiar thirst rushing through me, all the more powerful at having been ignored all day. I pushed the thirst away, not wanting to take the time to seek out a glass of water, determined to get my charting done so I could finally go home. I heard a patient retching and the sound of a nurse's footsteps rushing towards his room across the hall.

Pulling my attention back to searching the charts in front of me, I became aware of someone in a long white coat standing beside me. The length of his coat distinguished him as a resident or fellow, further along in his training than I was, having already completed medical school. His hand reached for a patient's chart just as mine did. I quickly dropped my hand, knowing that residents, fellows, attending physicians, nurses—pretty much everyone—outranked medical students and had priority over everything, including access to charts. We looked at each other and smiled. I sensed the kindness in his smile, in his face and demeanor—a rare thing in this realm of very busy, task-oriented health care workers. I looked at the name sewn into his white lab coat. "Help yourself, Dr. Cohen, I have plenty of other charts I need to work on."

He asked me to give him a thumbnail on the patient, as he was doing a cardiology consult and had not yet read the chart or seen the patient. Instead of my usual anxiety when doing a patient presentation, I found myself relaxed in his kindness, sensing he had no inclination to probe me with questions until he reached the limits of my knowledge in an attempt to humiliate me, as so many attendings, fellows, and residents did. We medical students understood this daily ritual of anxiety, fear, and humiliation as a rite of passage—but our understanding did not make the experience, or the anticipation of it each day, any easier. We lived in a state of overwhelm, without time to care for our bodies, let alone our emotions or spirits. We knew the humiliation would end after our fourth year of medical school, when we became interns.

Surprised, I felt none of this with Dr. Cohen. Instead, I found myself absorbing his gentle nature. I felt my shoulders relax and loosen, a sense of nourishment seeping into my long-depleted spirit. As we sat down in the nurses' station, I pulled my stethoscope from around my neck and stuffed it into my lab coat pocket. I told him about our patient, reciting in the traditional SOAP format: the patient's **S**ubjective symptoms and medical history; **O**bjective findings, including vital signs, physical exam, and labs; **A**ssessment with problem list and differential diagnoses; and our team's **P**lan for treatment. I was exhausted but my computer brain kicked in, pulling out the details needed for a concise patient presentation.

No longer rushing to get home, I found myself wanting to stay, to enjoy this relaxed professional connection. As I spoke, I felt my heart soften and my eyes begin to water, a physical manifestation of the softening taking place. In the middle of my presentation, vivid images began to interrupt my brain's near auto-pilot. The drip-drip-drip of an intravenous bag of fluid; the sensation of cool, nourishing fluid flooding my veins; standing with my chest up against the cold metal plate, hands cupped behind my head, holding my breath for another X-ray; and finally Dr. Cohen in his office in Quetzaltenango, smiling down at me, reassuring me with his kindness and gentleness.

I watched myself from a distance as I completed my patient presentation. With a sense of the surreal, I asked this Dr. Cohen, "Any chance you know a Dr. Cohen from Guatemala?"

He looked at me quizzically. "Yes. That would be my dad."

I laughed out loud, with a sense of internal puzzle pieces coming together. There was no doubt they were father and son. They shared the same energetic make-up, both true healers not only by profession but also in spirit. I shared with the younger Dr. Cohen my childhood experiences as his father's patient. "You remind me of him," I said as I looked into his eyes. I couldn't bring myself to put into words the undercurrent of kindness I felt coming from him, not only because this kind of talk and intimacy was taboo in the medical world, but also because I feared I would weep in gratitude. "Please, please tell your dad thank you for all that he did for me, for diagnosing me early on before I even had typical symptoms of TB, and for his kindness all those years."

He promised to do so. We sat for a minute in silence, this surreal meeting of these other aspects of our lives breaking open the rigid realm of medicine that we inhabited. Our paths did not cross again. But somehow, this cracking open of the wall of rigidity and fear that is woven into the very fabric of the world of medical training created a permanent fracture. This fissure provided an opening through which a deeper nourishment could trickle in.

• • •

My next rotation was Obstetrics and Gynecology. Each rotation was a completely new field of medicine and we had to start over gathering the knowledge necessary to care for our patients. Rotations were often in different hospitals, or different parts of large hospitals—and my deficient navigation skills made it tough to find my way around the labyrinth of hallways, nurses' stations, patient rooms, clinics, and lecture halls. Each hospital and clinic also had different charting systems. Some were just beginning to implement EMR (electronic medical records) and had clunky systems that were quite difficult to use. With each rotation, we also had new attending doctors and residents. Getting to know their personalities and expectations took some time. Typically though, as we familiarized ourselves with our environment, and as our experience and knowledge grew, so did our confidence.

We all looked forward to the OB/Gyn rotation, in large part because of the experience of delivering a baby, but we simultaneously dreaded it. At MUSC, the OB residents and attendings were notorious for their harshness and abuse. I had heard stories about students not allowed to get food for eighteen hours, of being ignored and then attacked as they attempted to do their work. Some who had planned to become obstetricians changed their career paths because they couldn't tolerate the environment. I braced myself, determined to learn as much as I could, to deliver as many babies as I could, to do as many procedures as I could, and to keep as low a profile as possible in order to avoid the abuse.

Meeting the residents that first day during rounds, the tension, anger, and unhappiness were palpable. Dr. Simpson was the resident in charge and she didn't bother to greet me or the other medical students. She spoke with an air of condescension and arrogance to the haggard-looking interns, who in turn treated us medical students similarly once rounds were over. I shoved aside the heaviness as best as I could each day, keeping my head down, numbing out when I was being criticized or yelled at, waiting until I got home late at night to nurse my humiliation and anger.

In spite of this, the joy of new life when I scrubbed in on C-sections, or delivered babies, could not be dampened. During my first delivery, in my excitement I failed to clamp the umbilical cord completely and was sprayed by blood as I cut it. The miracle of birth brought me to tears and overrode the thrashing I got from the resident. Her harsh words and criticism bounced off the bubble of joy this new baby brought into the world.

• • •

In the wider medical community, surgeons are much more likely than obstetricians to lack patient communication skills and compassion. They are notorious for their egos and for loving surgery, but otherwise for not being too interested in their patients, who are under anesthesia most of the time they are in contact with them. I wasn't looking forward to my surgery rotation as I knew that I wouldn't be choosing surgery as a career. I liked connecting with my patients, and I wasn't drawn to the rigorous lifestyle of a surgeon, so I was completely surprised to find myself enjoying surgery. The rotation was fast-paced and exciting, and I loved being in the OR and participating in surgeries to whatever extent I was allowed.

During this rotation I typically got up at 4 a.m., slipped into my scrubs, gulped down a cup of coffee, stuck a granola bar in my pocket, and got to the hospital for pre-rounding on my patients by 4:30 a.m. By 7 or 7:30 a.m., we were scrubbing in for our first surgery of the day. A nurse instructed us about pre-surgery protocol our first day of the rotation. She first warned us to make sure we didn't drink much in the morning, and to use the restroom before surgery, as surgeries sometimes went on for hours. Next, she taught us how to scrub, gown, and glove. After diligently scrubbing our hands and forearms with a scrub brush three times, we were instructed on how to don the sterile gown and gloves. We were then told to not touch anything that wasn't blue or sterile, to keep our hands above our hips, and to not pick up anything if it fell.

During surgeries, my job typically included retracting a flap of skin and tissue for the surgeon or suctioning blood and fluids. I was happy to be participating in my first surgery and was asked to retract a flap, which I did by manually pulling back on the metal retractor with my arm. After fifteen minutes the surgeon asked me to retract further. I pulled harder, my arm beginning to cramp, not sure I could keep it up but knowing I had to. I felt my forehead bead up with sweat from the exertion and feared that my sweat would drip into the sterile surgical field, so I leaned back as I pulled on the retractor, my face mask absorbing the sweat. I used all the will and determination I had developed doing vipassana meditation to hold my position. After ninety minutes, the surgeon was finally done, and I was greatly relieved when told I could remove the retractor. I flexed my cramped hand and arm, careful to keep both arms above my waist, resisting the urge to wipe the sweat dripping down my temples. The reward for my stamina was being allowed to suture the incision at the end of the surgery. I had practiced suturing with bananas and had learned not to put too much tension into the stitches, to grab the skin gently with my forceps, place my elbows at my side to steady my hands, and to slowly work my way down the incision. It was exciting to do this in real life!

After mornings in surgery, during the afternoons we attended clinics for post-op patients and for patients that might need surgery, then returned to the hospital to see our post-op patients who hadn't yet been discharged. We drew blood and ABG's (arterial blood gases), changed wound dressings, and assisted patients with breathing exercises and mobility.

At the end of outpatient surgery clinic one day, Dr. Scott, my attending, instructed me to come by his office. My first thought was that I was in trouble for screwing up somehow that afternoon. Dr. Scott was a typical surgeon, a workaholic with a substantial ego. I don't know if the field of surgery attracts individuals with a particular personality type, or if doing surgery, cutting into bodies and saving lives, creates their notorious God-complex—most likely a bit of both. When a surgeon walks into a room, he fills up the space, whether or not he is in scrubs. Dr. Scott carried himself with the ultra-confidence tending towards arrogance that was characteristic of many surgeons.

When I arrived at his office, he was seated at his large desk facing the door. I stood in front of his desk. "Hi Dr. Scott. What did I do? Am I in trouble?" I smiled, pretending to half-joke, camouflaging the fear I felt.

"Hello, Dr. Edwards," Dr. Scott said somewhat sarcastically as he put his feet up on his crowded desk and leaned back in his chair. As a medical student, you have not yet earned your M.D. degree. You are not yet a doctor. When an attending calls you "Doctor," you are either being put in your place or the attending is accentuating the power differential between you. Dr. Scott was clearly asserting his power with me. "Do you need to be in trouble?" he joked.

"No sir, not at all, in fact I was thinking it was more likely you wanted to let me know how well I'm doing on this rotation, how you've been admiring my suturing skills." It was risky for me to joke in this way, but I found myself pretending to match some of his arrogance, trying to manage my own discomfort.

"Oh, is that so?" I was relieved to see him laugh, but still not sure where this was going. "As a matter of fact, you have done well on this rotation, Dr. Edwards." He began talking about a patient who had to have a splenectomy that morning after their spleen had ruptured in a motor vehicle accident. I had scrubbed in on the surgery and performed my usual role of holding the retractor and occasionally suctioning fluid. Dr. Scott seemed to be going off on a tangent and I still didn't know why I was here. Eventually, he stopped talking for a moment and looked at me intently. "I was thinking we might get together sometime after work."

Oooohhhhh. I wanted to kick myself. I could be so naive. I looked down at the dirty carpet in front of my feet, felt my face flush, and scrambled to come up with a way to navigate the awkwardness. I was keenly aware that whatever I said could make or break my grade for the rotation, and I was even more aware of the resounding "NO" I felt inside of me. No way in hell would I get involved with him—socially, sexually, or otherwise.

I took a breath and looked up at him. "Thanks for the invitation, Dr. Scott. Maybe some time," I lied, keeping the tone light and resolving to never be alone with him in a room again. I realized my vague response could accurately be perceived as rejection so I abruptly shifted the conversation. "I do have a question for you." My mind scrolled through a few patients I had seen that afternoon, trying to find a reasonable question I could ask him. I launched into a description of a patient I had seen in the surgery clinic. Later, another medical student shared with me that she had been sexually involved with Dr. Scott. The power differential between medical students and attending is one more med school hazard—this one with a potential to promote or derail career plans, depending on students' interactions with attendings.

By the middle of third year, as much as we wanted to feel enthusiastic, we were losing steam—the constant stress, long work hours, sleep deprivation, and overall lack of nourishment on any level were taking their toll. My classmates all struggled in their own ways. A few classmates seemed to be relatively unaffected by the stress. Gordon was one of those few. He was the only other student in my medical school class who came from Wofford College. Gordon had blond hair, gentle eyes, and was physically solid as a rock from his regular workouts in the gym. He was kind and soft-spoken, always methodical, meticulous, and intentional. I knew that he had type I diabetes, but never heard him mention it. Actually, I never heard him complain about anything, even when the rest of us were moaning and groaning about the rigors of medical school. I was shocked to my core when I heard he had committed suicide by a self-inflicted gunshot wound. At his funeral, those of us who were his classmates sat in stunned silence, our hearts broken by this tragic loss. We had all been touched by his kindness, had all assumed he would be one of the best physicians of our class. None of us had recognized signs of his depression. Later that year, a resident friend who was two years ahead of me found her husband, who was also a resident, hanging in the garage. She was barely recognizable in her grief—pale, thin, devastated and shell-shocked.

Typically one or two medical students in each class commit suicide—somehow an accepted casualty of a system tasked with training healers. With Gordon's death, that statistic became a devastating reality. My grief brought to the foreground the sense of helplessness I felt—I was helpless to bring Gordon back so I could reach out to him more, and I was helpless to change a system I was powerless to change. It was a system we were all struggling to survive.

A Note on the Mental Health of Medical Students and Residents

Medical students are three times likelier to die of suicide than their counterparts in the general population, and suicide is the leading cause of death among male residents and the second leading cause of death among female residents. In one recent study, about ten percent of fourth-year medical students and residents reported having suicidal thoughts within the previous two weeks. Only one-third of medical students who are suffering from depression seek help, mainly because they're afraid of what it might do to their careers. The system is beginning to change, starting to recognize that the stress inherent in medical training is not conducive to learning or patient care, and certainly not to student/resident self-care.

When I work as an attending with medical students these days, I give voice to how medical training is driven by fear and stress and share my own experience. I ask how they might learn best—by observing my interactions with patients, by interviewing patients themselves, or a mix of both. I ask them to let me know each day what they feel will give them the best learning experience, not only in terms of medical knowledge, but also in connecting and communicating with patients. If they are exhausted or need to schedule an appointment, they are free to leave early. In this way they take charge of their learning experience and take care of themselves.

Most students are tense and formal at our initial meeting, having learned to try to please and impress the attending. When I share with them my perspective on learning, I watch as they visibly relax. Their shoulders drop a bit, their hands relax their grip on the book or paperwork they hold, their tight faces soften. They smile or laugh, relieved to be understood, to be respected. I talk with them about the importance of not perpetuating the culture of abuse within the system and how each of us can shift the dynamics of the system with mutual respect and kindness. This energetic undercurrent is perceived by our patients and supports the healing process, regardless of the field of medicine we are in.

After I had completed my training, the Accreditation Council for Graduate Medical Education (ACGME) in 2003 limited the number of work-hours to eighty hours weekly, overnight call frequency to no more than one in three, thirty-hour maximum straight shifts, and at least ten hours off between shifts. While these limits are voluntary for residency programs, adherence has been mandated for accreditation. From my recent research, it seems that medical training is no longer quite as harsh or abusive. At least the need for adequate sleep is now acknowledged (after a patient in New York died from being given the wrong medication by a sleep-deprived resident). I'm hopeful that this trend will continue and caring for oneself on every level will be recognized as a necessary foundation for learning and caring for others.

CHAPTER 13

Choosing Psychiatry

The mind creates the abyss, the heart crosses it.
—Nisargadatta Maharaj

When doing clinical rotations, attendings and residents inevitably asked medical students which field of medicine they were planning on pursuing. Although some students started their training intending to be surgeons or internists, most didn't know. We hoped to get more clarity as we rotated through the different specialties. I had loved my work as a mental health technician during my year's leave of absence from medical school, and was leaning towards psychiatry. I felt at home in psychiatry; I knew how to talk with patients, and they responded and opened up to me. I also felt comfortable setting firm limits with them when necessary. I loved seeing patients respond to therapy and medication—to see mood, anxiety, or psychotic symptoms resolve or improve, to see patients with substance use issues get the support they needed to turn their lives around. And I loved that there seemed to be more room in psychiatry to address the whole patient—mind, body, and spirit—than in any other field of medicine.

Even though I was leaning towards psychiatry, I wanted to stay open to the possibility of making a different choice. I saved my psychiatry rotation until the end of my third year so I could consider other options before I dove into the field. I learned quickly that psychiatry had its own unique place in the larger world of medicine—it was viewed by many physicians as illegitimate or pseudo medicine. When I mentioned to residents or attendings that I might go into psychiatry, I was often mocked. "What? Don't you want to be a real doctor?"

Psychiatry had been viewed as "soft" medicine since the days of Sigmund Freud and the birth of psychoanalysis. Compared to other fields of medicine, there were limited psychiatric medications available when I was in medical school, although more and more were being approved for use. Psychiatry was fighting hard to prove itself in the world of hard science, trying to legitimize itself with double-blind, placebo-controlled studies—the gold standard of medical research. Personally, I loved that psychiatry didn't reduce patients exclusively to their biology; it included not only hard science but also the softer, holistic aspects of healing, including psychotherapy.

As I approached my psychiatry rotation I felt the pressure mount to make a definitive choice about my field of specialty. It was almost time to apply to residency programs, the next phase of medical training. I had loved the family medicine and pediatrics rotations, and was considering each of them.

My first day of my psychiatry rotation I walked into the nurses' station at the Institute of Psychiatry, grateful for the familiarity of the hospital. I knew some of the nursing staff, the charting system, and the building from my time there as a technician. I sat down with other medical students at the conference table to wait for the attending and resident to join us. I heard them arrive at the nurses' station, joking and bantering with each other. Their laughter and ease were a surprising balm. They joined us in the conference room and the attending, Dr. Carson, asked us our names, what specialty we thought we might go into, and a little more about ourselves. He and the resident listened carefully to each of us. We were surprised by their interest and the respect they showed us. I found myself feeling more and more at home, happy to be part of a team that seemed to hold the space for more than the left-brain practicalities of medicine.

As we rounded on patients with the team that day, Dr. Carson and the resident treated each patient with the same attention and respect. Later, when I met with the patients that were assigned to me, I felt as if this was what I was born to do. I didn't have to think about it anymore. I was going into psychiatry. As I completed my third year in the psychiatry rotation, I began to settle a bit and to envision my future career.

• • •

Fourth year of medical school brought with it a very noticeable change. We had made it through the rigors and abuse of third year and had now earned the right to a little respect (or at least less abuse). Attendings and residents turned their attention to third-year students, pimping them relentlessly, but usually left us alone. We were given more responsibility with our patients, and our patient assessments were often accepted as facts.

Most of us took the USMLE Step 2 exam early in our fourth year—two days of rigorous testing on physiologic conditions, diseases, and physician tasks that we were to have learned and studied during our third-year clinical rotations. With this behind us, we could shift our attention to the future. Not long after taking the USMLE, we applied to residency programs. We had been well aware throughout medical school that our grades during the first two years of basic science courses, our grades during our clinical rotations, and our USMLE test scores would in large part determine which residency programs would grant us an interview, but we were also acutely aware that good letters of recommendation could open doors. We teased each other about brown-nosing whenever any of us went the extra mile to please an attending, knowing full well that each of us was guilty, each hoping to leverage our standing in the eyes of our attending in whatever way we could.

I strategically used my intuition and innate ability to connect to my advantage with attendings, especially those from whom I wanted to get a letter of recommendation. During my third year of medical school, I had boldly asked to meet with the dean of the School of Medicine, who was a psychiatrist. I told him that I had decided to go into psychiatry—even before I had made that final decision—and asked if he would be my advisor. I did want guidance, and I also knew that his position as dean of the medical school would carry weight in a letter of recommendation. To my delight, Dr. McCurdy not only agreed to be my advisor, he seemed pleased to connect with a medical student in this way—to have some real contact with a student outside of his administrative duties.

We met regularly for a year, discussing psychiatry, residency programs, and my personal and professional intentions and goals. Although in a very traditional role at a very traditional medical school, he was sympathetic to my hopes that the field of medicine would become more holistic, and that the medical training process would become more humane and more in alignment with the healing role for which we were being trained. Although I didn't share with him the extent of my own spiritual experiences, we spoke at length about the tendency of western cultures to pathologize experiences that are considered spiritual awakenings in other cultures. We spoke about how cultures that honor spiritual openings will also support individuals in integrating those experiences. We were both interested in the important capacity to differentiate a spiritual opening from a psychotic break, and to recognize how they might also overlap. We shared the book *Saints and Madmen* by Russell Shorto.

At one point, Dr. McCurdy set me up on a lunch date with his son Robbie, who was visiting from San Francisco. His son was not in the medical field, and was irritated when I was late for our lunch date because of an unexpected patient emergency. These were the days before cell phones and I was unable to let him know that I was delayed. His irritation highlighted how difficult it was to have or maintain a relationship or friendship with anyone outside the world of medicine while in the midst of training. Most of our connections with others dropped away, not only because there simply wasn't time to foster or nourish those relationships (even a two-minute phone call was a luxury we rarely had), but also because it was almost impossible for anyone outside our world to relate to the immensity of the demands placed on us. Our lives were completely consumed by medicine. Many weren't able to understand, or weren't willing to stick with us when we had nothing to give to the relationship. They fell by the wayside.

After gathering my letters of recommendation from Dr. McCurdy and several attendings, I wrote my personal statement and filled out applications for residency programs around the country. Hoping to complete my residency in California, I applied to several programs there. We all waited to hear where we would be invited for interviews. The interview process, in the midst of fourth-year rotations, was a whirlwind, involving travel to interview at different residency programs around the country. Once we had completed all our interviews, we anxiously awaited Match Day, when we would find out which residency program we had "matched" into.

Match Day finally arrived the third week of March. All ninety-six of us gathered in an auditorium, given permission to abandon our rotations for a few hours to take part in this ritual. Most of us had not seen each other since our first two years of basic science classes. The room filled with an electric excitement as we gathered together again—excitement at seeing each other and the anticipation of finding out where each of us would be for the next four years of our lives. The insecurity of the first three years had been replaced with a hard-earned growing confidence in our abilities as soon-to-be physicians, and a rock-solid strength that came from having survived hell. For most of us, finding out whether we had matched or been rejected at one of our top choices would serve to affirm or diminish this new-found confidence in ourselves.

I sat at the back, in the last row of the auditorium where I had sat during the first two years of medical school classes. Others also gravitated to their old seats. The auditorium buzzed with chatter as we all caught up with each other, but when Dr. del Bene walked onto the stage in his starched white lab coat and thick black glasses, the room went totally silent. He placed a cardboard box full of envelopes on a table. "Well, now," he said, smiling as he crossed his arms, "look at all of you! You've grown up. Congratulations on making it through. As you know, today is an important day, the culmination of all of your hard work up until now. Getting into medical school is hard enough, but getting through it and matching with a residency program is even tougher. I am proud to tell you that each of you matched into a residency program."

We were all stunned to hear these compliments and words of congratulations from the assistant dean. Up until then, he had been tough on all of us. His shift in attitude was a sure sign that we had indeed made it through those first harsh years of medical school. Dr. del Bene took each envelope out of the box, one at a time, and called out a name. The student walked up to the front of the room, took the envelope, and shook his hand. Some students opened the envelope immediately, too excited or nervous to wait a second longer. A few hollered out with joy, having matched with their residency of choice. One or two did a victory dance on stage. Others waited to open their envelope until they got back to the privacy of their seat. Some of us, including me, kept our envelope sealed until we were all dismissed.

I made a beeline for the privacy of a bathroom stall as soon as we were dismissed. I pushed the door closed and slid the cold metal latch through the notch. I leaned my back against the door, took a deep breath, and held the envelope up, watching it shake in my trembling hands. One more deep breath, accompanied by a whispered prayer as I exhaled: "Not my will, but thine"—my feeble attempt at surrendering attachment to the outcome. I giggled at my half-hearted attempt at spiritual piety and surrendered to being attached. I ripped open the envelope. *Stanford.* My first choice. "WOO HOOOOOOO!" I whupped, and twirled around in the stall as I held the paper, my future, high in the air. As no one else was in the bathroom, I soon found myself singing "Dancing Queen" by ABBA and doing the disco finger dance à la John Travolta in front of the stalls. After a few rounds, I straightened up, ran all the way back to the apartment, and called my friend Christy. She, of course, screamed as loudly as I did at my news, sharing my joy and excitement.

• • •

It was a well-known fact that after Match Day, medical students could finally breathe and let their hair down a bit. We now had a pretty-much guaranteed spot in a residency program, unless we did something terrible. We no longer had to work so hard to impress attendings. Nevertheless, we still had several elective rotations left. Fourth year rotations were chosen either because of an interest in the specialty, or because they were relatively easy.

During third year, I had arranged to do an elective rotation in Complementary and Alternative Medicine with Andrew Weil, a physician in Tucson. My great interest made the rotation easy. Dr. Weil approached medicine from a wellness and preventative perspective—a holistic approach that made much more sense to me than limiting medicine to the treatment of symptoms. Now in fourth year I opted to do an HIV/AIDS Psychiatry Consult-Liaison rotation at the University of California San Francisco (UCSF). I knew that Ram Dass and many other spiritual teachers lived in the San Francisco Bay Area and I knew of several meditation retreat centers nearby. I wanted to have this type of support for my spiritual journey during my psychiatric residency training, and I thought that a rotation at UCSF during medical school could help with matching at a residency program in California. I also set up elective rotations at MUSC in ENT surgery, rheumatology, and cardiology.

You didn't always get your first choice of an elective rotation, and otolaryngology—ENT surgery—was not my first choice. I had heard that it was not as rigorous as other surgery rotations and resigned myself to just getting through the rotation. I was to meet the residents in their office at the VA clinic on the first day. I arrived early, allowing myself time to find the clinic. As I walked through the labyrinth of hallways at the VA, I hoped to come across a person or a sign that could direct me.

Peering down a long, dark empty hallway, I turned back around and bumped into a young man rounding the corner. I backed up as we both apologized. He was about my height, with dark brown hair and matching eyes framed by high cheekbones and a strong jaw, and wearing a long white lab coat. We looked at each other for a split second, an unmistakable spark of chemistry in the air. I glanced at the name sewn into his lab coat and saw the word "Otolaryngology" under his name. Whoa. "You're in ENT, Dr. Davis? I'm the fourth year med student rotating through this month. I'm looking for the residents' office," I said. I fought to maintain my composure as I looked in his eyes.

Dr. Davis cleared his throat. "That's exactly where I'm headed. I'm your resident. Please, just call me Joel. What's your name?" he spoke with a quiet confidence and precision, each word carefully chosen.

As soon as I got home that evening, I called Christy. When she answered the phone, I screamed. "CHRISTY! I'm in LOVE!" I told her about Joel, and she teased me about seducing him, about wanting to be my maid of honor at our wedding, about the beautiful babies we would have, and on and on.

Joel was a third year ENT resident. ENT was one of the most competitive residencies to match into and typically drew brilliant, highly-skilled residents. Joel was no exception. I loved his intelligence, his quiet confidence, and his kindness. He was drawn to my spontaneity and humor, and to my spirituality. Although our attraction to each other was palpable, we didn't speak of it or go on a date that month, knowing that a resident dating a medical student was taboo. Withholding our attraction only served to intensify it. I wasn't surprised the last day of the rotation when Joel took me aside and asked me for my phone number. He didn't explain why he was asking for it, and I didn't need an explanation.

In love and elated, I floated through the rest of fourth year. Joel was even-keeled and a bit formal. He loved my unconventionality and I loved his stability. Eventually we moved in together. Joel had one more year left of residency at MUSC, and I was scheduled to head across the country to Stanford in a few months. After completing his residency, he was hoping to do a fellowship in facial plastic surgery and reconstruction in the Bay Area. Neither of us wanted to be apart for the next year. Never afraid to think outside the box or ask for what I wanted, I explained our situation to the psychiatry residency training director at MUSC, Al Santos, and he said I could do my first year of residency at MUSC in order to stay in Charleston with Joel that year. With that cleared, I called the residency training director at Stanford, Barr Taylor, and asked if I could skip first year of residency there and join in as a second year resident. To my surprise, he agreed. The Stanford residency program would be one resident short that first year—a sacrifice that he and the other residents would be making. I was astonished and grateful for the flexibility that would allow me to be with Joel for the next year.

Graduation!

Before I knew it, medical school was over. We had all been so busy that graduation day seemed to come upon us suddenly. As I walked down the aisle in my cap and gown, I thought I might burst with the joy, the bliss, the elation of being DONE, of being FREE . . . at least for the next two weeks until residency started. I was now officially a doctor!

Reveling in that achievement was short-lived. I knew what lay ahead.

From Intern to Resident

Our separation from each other is an optical illusion.
—Albert Einstein

I didn't sleep at all the two nights before my first day of residency. I was lost in an all too familiar feeling—once again I was terrified. As a medical student, I always had an intern or resident overseeing what I did with patients. The interns and residents had spent time teaching me, telling me what to do, correcting my mistakes. They had co-signed my patient notes and patient orders. Now, as an intern myself, I bore the title of MD—and with the title came full responsibility for diagnosing and treating patients; for another human being's life and health. Residency also came with a teaching role with medical students. My chronic insecurity had me dreading this prospect.

I settled into being an intern, the very busy first year of residency. All my rotations were now in psychiatry. I loved it, and knew without a doubt I had chosen the right career. My days were full and often I didn't have much time with each patient. I learned that the quality of time was more important than the quantity of time I spent with them. Deep listening came naturally to me. I saw that my patients were connecting with me, and I often sensed what needed to come forward in them for healing. I knew what called for gentle, open, receptive listening, what called for a mirroring back, and what called for a firm confrontation. I sensed into the wounding behind superficial habit patterns and symptoms. In retrospect, I know that the journey into the depths of my own psyche had helped to dissolve boundaries that would otherwise have prevented my deep seeing of each patient. Some of my insecurity about my medical knowledge began to dissipate as I gained experience and confidence in treating different psychiatric and medical conditions, including psychosis, mania, depression, anxiety, substance abuse, and personality disorders.

Psychiatry was known to be a bit more humane than many other residency programs. Nevertheless, my schedule was rigorous, and exhaustion was a constant companion. As with medical school, I knew the system was flawed, and now it felt exploitative. As medical students, we paid tuition for our training, but as residents we were earning a salary, of sorts. When the hours we worked were accounted for, we were paid far below minimum wage, making it difficult to make ends meet. We were exhausted, and many of us were strapped financially. I spoke with friends about the possibility of forming some kind of residents' advocacy group, or a residents' union. But at the end of my long days and nights on call, I didn't have enough energy left to do anything more.

One of my last rotations during my internship was a one-month rotation at the MUSC outpatient psychiatry clinic. My attending physician, Cindy Hope, struck me as compassionate, real, and open. The power differential between attending and resident just wasn't there with her. She was my mentor, yet my input was genuinely valued and respected. I felt seen by her. Cindy was curious about my experiences with meditation and spiritual teachers. I shared openly with her. I began to experience the possibility of science and spirit coming together, and of more consciously allowing my spiritual experiences to inform my work as a psychiatrist. Cindy and I became close friends and attended many retreats together over the years, and later shared a connection with a spiritual teacher. Sharing a similar spiritual journey with a dear friend who is also grounded in the world of psychiatry has been a true gift.

• • •

The summer of my intern year, Joel and I rented a house at Folly Beach, where we lived with my chocolate lab, Buddha. The honeymoon stage of our relationship had begun to wear off and we were beginning to recognize our challenges. Joel was emotionally distant. My childhood fear of being left behind by Jesus and my entire family, along with the trauma and grief of being left at boarding school, now expressed itself as fear of being left by Joel (and later by future partners).

This fear of being left manifested as jealousy. It would burst forward out of the blue, unexpected and uncontrollable. If I saw Joel interacting with an attractive resident or medical student, or found out he had spoken with his ex-girlfriend, a urology resident at MUSC, or came across a card he had kept from another ex-girlfriend, I got triggered. A surge of terror and burning in my heart transmuted instantly to jealousy. Even though I was fully aware that it came from my past, that it had nothing to do with Joel's actions, time and time again I found myself arguing with him, at times yelling. When my reaction subsided, I always felt remorse and a deep sadness at having allowed it to overtake me.

Understanding that my fear of abandonment triggered my jealousy at first did nothing to temper or get rid of the emotion. I used a variety of tools, including utilizing therapy and spiritual practices, to work with this old wound. Over time, I was able to tolerate the fiery energy of jealousy in my body for longer and longer periods, to recognize it, and intentionally choose not to act it out. When I was able to be fully present with the fire, without my mind getting involved by labeling it as jealousy or going into thought about its origins, I came to experience it as an intense but neutral energy, no different at its core than any other energy.

As I had seen in meditation, all emotions are pure energy. When we recognize that thoughts about these emotions are unreal and empty—including the labels or names we give to the energies and the stories we tell ourselves about their source—our attention canstay with the energy instead of getting wrapped up in the mind's thoughts. We can see that energy is the source of all emotions, all experience. But the habitual patterns of our mind and nervous system are very powerful and can make it very difficult to halt the thought patterns, to stop acting out and discharging the energy (in my case through bouts of jealousy). Clear intention, determination, and repeated efforts are often needed to hold the energy of habitual patterns without discharging. This holding of the energy and momentum, instead of releasing it, in turn expands our capacity to be present with all energy. For me, this was a process, and my bouts of jealousy kept us both on our toes that year.

Between these disturbances, though, Joel and I continued to share a sweet affection, a delight in being with each other, and humor. I played practical jokes on him—several times I surreptitiously turned on his fancy car seat warmer during the summer, pinching myself to contain my giggles as I watched him lower the temperature of the car air conditioning and wipe his damp forehead before he realized why he was so hot.

One warm and humid summer Sunday, we both had the day off. Neither of us had been on call the night before and we were delighted to have a full day together with no plans or obligations. We sat side by side on the back porch, sipping coffee from our over-sized mugs. Buddha was ecstatic to have both of us outside with him. He dropped his slimy muddy tennis ball over and over again at our feet, wagging his tail wildly. At one point, he raced back to us with the muddy ball and dropped it right in my lap. "Buddha! That is so gross!" I jumped up, wiped off my shorts, and threw the ball into a large bush. Buddha couldn't find it, so Joel and I jumped off the bench to search for the ball, our search quickly evolving into a playful game of tag. I chased Joel across the yard and caught up with him just as a couple was walking by. Cornered by the fence, he tried to fake me out by dodging to one side and darting the other way. By now Buddha was in front of him, blocking his escape. I laughed with glee, grabbed Joel's elastic-waisted shorts, and tugged down hard—revealing to the passers-by the bright red and purple hearts on his boxers. Joel was by nature quite modest, and I loved pushing his buttons. He chased me down and tackled me. We laughed our hearts out together, then made out in the grass, Buddha hovering beside us, ball in mouth, tail wagging happily.

• • •

Towards the end of my internship, I took the USMLE Step 3—another long and rigorous exam—and was ready to head to Stanford for the final three years of residency. To our relief, Joel matched with a fellowship in Facial Plastics and Reconstruction in the San Francisco Bay Area. When my internship and his residency were over, we had exactly one week to move to California before the start of our next level of training.

My friend Pam, whom I had met at a meditation course, decided to move with us. Pam was a tall goddess with long thick blonde hair down to her hips and green almond eyes. She was athletic and vibrant and had a hearty, spontaneous laugh. Pam was intense; she was creative and powerful in her life and open and loving with the people in it. She filled every room she entered and pulled everyone into her orbit. But Joel and Pam didn't like each other. Her intensity rubbed him the wrong way, and she didn't feel he was a good match for me. She saw his emotional distancing and a rigidity underlying his kindness, and she knew that he did not share my spiritual interests. Nevertheless, we still made plans to drive out west together. Pam started packing up the U-Haul while Joel and I finished up our last few days of training at MUSC. We took off, taking turns driving the U-Haul (with Joel's car in tow), Pam's car and my car. Four days later, after a night in Tennessee with my uncle and aunt and a few nights in budget hotels, our entourage arrived in San Francisco.

These were the days before internet, so the first thing we did was buy a newspaper to check out the For Rent section. Joel and I had decided to live in Hayward, which on a map looked to be halfway between Palo Alto, where I would be at Stanford, and San Francisco, where he would be at UCSF. Pam planned on helping us settle in while Joel and I jumped into the next stages of our training. She would live with us for a few weeks until she found her own place. We were all physically exhausted from the trip, and emotionally exhausted from the palpable tension between Joel and Pam. After a single day in our new home I started my residency at Stanford.

• • •

That first day I was out of the house at 5:00 a.m., giving myself plenty of time to find the outpatient psychiatry building by 7:00 a.m., where I would meet the residency training director, Barr Taylor. I fumbled in the dark for my keys, unlocked my car, placed my heavy satchel on the passenger seat and my mug of coffee in the console cup holder. I shivered, unused to a chill in the air in June. I popped open the glove compartment and pulled out my newly-purchased, laminated, Rand McNally Easy Finder San Francisco Bay Area map. GPS wasn't yet even in the realm of imagination. I had pored over the map the night before, and written out the directions for the trip across the bay to Palo Alto. I started the car, full of anticipation. My first rotation was to be at the VA Hospital, on the same inpatient unit where Ken Kesey had worked as a nurse's aide and written *One Flew Over the Cuckoo's Nest*.

My anticipation quickly turned to dread fifteen minutes later when I saw the traffic waiting to get on the Dumbarton Bridge that would carry me across the bay. Joel and I had been living in Charleston, where traffic never had to be taken into consideration. When we had looked at where to live, we had chosen an area that was equidistant from where each of us would be working. We didn't know that I would be driving in heavy traffic for my commute while he sailed along in the opposite direction. I crept across the bridge, gripping the steering wheel, terrified that I would be late for my first day at Stanford.

I arrived at the parking lot in front of the outpatient psychiatry building at 6:58 a.m. I pulled my heavy satchel over my shoulder and slipped a few power bars from the bag into my lab pocket. As a teenager I had been diagnosed with hypoglycemia, so I always carried a few granola bars or power bars in my pocket, partially opening up the package of each bar before I put them in my pocket for easier access. When I felt hungry, weak, shaky or sweaty, I would break off a piece of the bar in my pocket and pop it into my mouth when attendings and residents weren't looking. If I couldn't orchestrate that, I would pretend to take a bathroom break and eat the bar in a bathroom stall as quickly as I could. I never even considered asking for an accommodation or permission for a quick snack break. Ironically, I knew that a medical diagnosis of hypoglycemia wouldn't get me any slack. The need for a snack would be seen as a weakness, and I certainly wasn't going to push the issue.

I met briefly with Dr. Taylor, the residency training director. He was genuine and kind, and welcomed me to the program. In turn, I thanked him for allowing me to defer my training at Stanford until my second year. He then discussed my rotation schedule for the next year, gave me a key to the psychiatric ward at the VA, and sent me off for my first rotation.

The air was crisp that first morning at the Palo Alto VA; the sun beginning to rise and peek through the buildings. The parking lot was busy. A loud humming noise came from a machine on the rooftop of the main hospital, adding to the sense of a bustling hospital waking up and starting its day. I walked down the sidewalk and into the main hospital, looking for someone who might give me directions to the psychiatric ward. To my surprise, the hospital felt clean and fresh and modern, and had clearly been renovated recently. A candy striper in the lobby directed me back outside, pointing across the parking lot at another building. I cut across the lawn towards the psychiatric unit. The grass tickled my feet through my sandals, the tips of my toes wet from the dew. In front of the door of the psychiatric ward I stomped my feet to shake off a few blades of grass.

I was hopeful that the renovation had extended to the psychiatric unit, as psychiatric wards were typically drab and depressing. From my own experience, I knew that a patient's environment can contribute to their healing or impede it. Maybe California was more progressive than South Carolina and understood this. I peered through the small window in the door to make sure no patients were standing nearby plotting their escape. After unlocking the heavy door, I pulled it open and stepped inside. The door slammed behind me. I stood for a moment to allow my eyes to adjust to the darkness. The ward was dim and drab, with a low ceiling, and filled with the heavy energy of decades of suffering. I walked down the hallway towards the nurses' station and noticed the missing pieces of grout between the brown floor tiles, the dirty, tan paint on the walls. Clearly the Department of Psychiatry had been left behind in the renovations.

A cart filled with breakfast trays stood in front of the nurses' station, the smell of scrambled eggs and biscuits mixing with a faint smell of urine that wafted from one of the rooms lining the hallway. A patient stared at me, unblinking, from the doorway of his room, still as a statue. Three patients stood in line in front of a half door at the far end of the nurses' station, waiting for their morning medication. They watched me as I walked down the hall. One of them, a tall, muscular man with long, stringy gray hair, pointedly looked me up and down and said loudly, "I wouldn't mind having some of THAT for breakfast," then chuckled loudly. I felt my face flush. I knew from my past work, both as a mental health technician and as a medical student, the importance of establishing boundaries and respect with patients from the beginning. I didn't yet know anything about these patients—including whether or not they had a history of violence. I had to set limits, but also had to be careful not to trigger or escalate this patient.

I approached the patients, maintained my distance, and said, "Good morning. My name is Dr. Edwards. I'll be making rounds with the team later today and will get to know each of you then." I smiled, then looked at each of them. "I'll do my very best to give each of you the best care possible. I do expect to be treated with respect, and that includes not making inappropriate comments." I felt my heart thumping in my chest, not knowing how this would go on my first day of the rotation.

The tall patient laughed loudly, uncomfortable with this boundary being set. He looked at the other two patients, hoping to get them to laugh with him. They continued to look towards me and returned my smile, one with a toothless grin. "What are your names?" I asked them.

"I'm Jack, and this is Don."

"It's good to meet you, Jack and Don." I smiled again as I turned to the tall patient, my heart thumping, and asked, "What is your name?" I was giving him an open opportunity to connect in a respectful way. I saw something shift in him as he watched me—a decision to settle back, to go down a different path. "I'm Darrell. Sorry about that, Dr. Edwards. We don't get many attractive women in here and I got carried away." He grinned at me, attempting to make amends.

I let his last comment slide, and said, "It's good to meet you, Darrell. I look forward to working with you. And I'm glad we all see eye to eye about the need for mutual respect. I'll see you all in a bit." I turned and walked to the door of the nurses' station, a big sigh of relief escaping my lungs. I was ready to meet my attending and the rest of the team.

It turned out I had two attendings this rotation. Dr. Baker had just completed his residency two years before. He was young, opinionated, and talked . . . a lot. Usually, Dr. Baker was in a good mood, almost euphoric, but occasionally he was irritable, complaining at length about the VA, or about politics, or anything else that struck him as unfair or out of alignment with his opinions. Stacy, the other resident on the unit, joined me in wondering if he had bipolar disorder. He certainly seemed hypomanic; he was always full of energy and his speech was pressured.

The medical hierarchy was firmly in place at Stanford, just as it was at MUSC and at every other teaching institution in the country.

As residents, we had to sit and listen to him. We couldn't interrupt or excuse ourselves to get on with our duties of seeing patients, charting, and writing orders. We sat for hours, tensely waiting for Dr. Baker to wind down or realize he was expected elsewhere. We were painfully aware that the time we spent listening to him was time tacked on to the end of our already very long days, when we would be trying to finish up our work.

One morning, I woke to my loud alarm at 5 a.m. Against my better judgment, I pressed snooze, trying to squeeze in a few more minutes of sleep, knowing I would be pressed for time after I got up. When the alarm went off again, I forced myself to roll out from under the blankets into the chilly air. I was on call that night, and pulled on a pair of blue scrubs, the on-call attire of psychiatry residents. I turned on the coffee maker before splashing my face with water, putting on deodorant, and brushing my teeth, then went through my routine of checking my lab coat and satchel to make sure I had everything I needed for the next thirty-six hours. I reached into the pantry for a few power bars, and found an empty box. Dang it. I grabbed an apple from the fridge and stuffed a few pieces of sliced bread into a sandwich bag, putting the apple in my lab pocket in case of emergency and the bread in my satchel. I poured hot coffee into my travel mug and rushed out the door.

A few hours later, I sat at the conference table during team rounds. Dr. Baker was in a bad mood today, irritable and ranting about the salary the VA gave to psychiatry attendings. He had found out that neurologists at the VA were given a higher salary and was furious. Our other attending, Dr. Keller, was quiet and passive. He often charted while Dr. Baker spoke, or slipped out of the room to see patients or attend meetings. Dr. Baker carried on for some time that day, keeping me, Stacy, and the two medical students from our work. I began to feel hungry and weak. I told myself to hang on, but he kept talking and soon I found myself wiping sweat from my forehead. I felt dizzy and confused, and feared I would pass out.

This was the worst possible time, and I knew it—but I didn't have a choice. I waited for Dr. Baker to take a breath between sentences, and interjected weakly, "Dr. Baker, I am so sorry to interrupt. My blood sugar is dropping, and I have to have a snack." I knew how this sounded. I had never mentioned my hypoglycemia before, knowing it wouldn't go over well even in the best of circumstances. I pulled the dark red apple out of my pocket, my hands shaking, even as he turned on me.

"Oh, really? Hypoglycemia?" he said sarcastically. I wiped my forehead again, realizing I had to choose between his wrath and the possibility of passing out. I forged ahead bravely, biting into the apple, unable to respond, trying to stay focused on biting, chewing, and swallowing, biting, chewing, and swallowing. Dr. Baker unleashed his anger on me, ranting about lazy residents. I felt the onslaught as if from a distance, using my willpower to focus on the mechanics of eating the apple. I was vaguely aware of Stacy shifting in her seat, her anger at this tirade and her inability to speak up because of the power differential adding to the tension in the room. At some point, Dr. Bakers' attention shifted to my apple. "Why would you be eating an apple? Look at all the dye on it. You know it has all kinds of chemicals, don't you? Why the hell would you be putting that into your body?"

I heard Dr. Keller clear his throat, clearly uncomfortable with what was happening, but not comfortable chastising his colleague in front of residents and medical students. He finally interrupted with a loud "Dr. Baker!" Each of us, including Dr. Baker, turned and looked at him, stunned. We had only known Dr. Keller as quiet, gentle, kind and passive, clearly overshadowed by the immensity of Dr. Baker's energy. "This is not appropriate," he said quietly, looking directly at Dr. Baker.

After a stunned moment of silence, Dr. Baker gathered himself back together, stood up abruptly and said, "Appropriate, my ass! I'll show you what's appropriate!" He stormed out of the conference room and slammed the door behind him. We sat in shocked silence. After an eternity, I spoke up, wiping a tear and sweat from my face with the palm of my hand. "I'm so sorry, guys. I'm not making it up. I had to eat." Dr. Keller cleared his throat, reached into his blazer pocket, pulled out a packet of crumbled saltine crackers, and laid it on the table in front of me. "Here you go, eat this," he said gently.

Exhausted the following morning after being on call all night, I walked to the conference room for team rounds, expecting to face Dr. Baker's wrath. To my great relief, Dr. Baker was back to his baseline mild euphoria. It was as if yesterday had never happened. I sensed that Dr. Baker wouldn't hold it against me or go to my residency training director with some sort of complaint. I resolved to always eat before I arrived at the hospital, either at home or in the car, and to never run out of power bars again.

CHAPTER 15

Residency Continues

The wound is the place where the Light enters you.
—Rumi

A few months later, I began a rotation at the Stanford hospital. The psychiatric ward was a locked unit, as were nearly all inpatient psychiatric units. It had a sterile look and feel to it, but not the drab heavy energy of the VA. Bright fluorescent lights lit the hallway and day room, and the scent of rubbing alcohol hung in the air. The psychiatric unit had the fast-paced, buzzing energy of a cutting-edge research institution with brilliant researchers. The attendings at Stanford were all driven, efficient, and accomplished. Some were eccentric. As a resident, it was impossible not to be caught up in the exciting forward-moving energy of the place. This translated into motivation to be well-versed and up to date with all aspects of psychiatry. It also meant a further activation of the desire to achieve, and for some residents, a heightened sense of competition with other residents.

I started out with eight patients on the inpatient unit. One of my patients was a forty-eight-year-old single Caucasian female with a

long history of anorexia nervosa. Miss Lawson was a walking skel-
eton. She weighed seventy pounds and looked as if she were seventy
years old. Her cheeks were sunken, dark circles sucked in around her
eyes, and her thin brown hair was dull, lifeless, straw-like, and broken
off in places. Her leggings hung on her like limp windsocks, and her
thin hands poked out from under the oversized light pink sweatshirt
she wore each day. Her dry, pale skin hugged and outlined the bones
of her hands, displaying the details of the phalanges, metacarpal and
carpal bones.

Miss Lawson had been hospitalized with anorexia seventeen times
since she was sixteen years old; three times due to cardiac arrest
resulting from the anorexia. She had been on many different psychiatric medications and had engaged in psychotherapy over the years.
She had been admitted to psychiatry this time after an ICU stay, having suffered another cardiac arrest that required intubation. When
she stabilized, she had been transferred to the internal medicine floor
and fed via nasogastric tube until she was physically stable enough to
be transferred to psychiatry. At this point, her IV and NG tube had
been removed.

Miss Lawson was lucky to be alive, but her prognosis was not
good. Her pattern was to gain enough weight to be discharged
from the hospital, only to begin starving herself again once she was
discharged. She was hospitalized on a 5250 hold—a fourteen-day
involuntary psychiatric hospitalization—because her anorexia was
life-threatening. Already, the nurse weighing her in the morning had
found two water bottles shoved in her socks—one of many attempts
to inflate her weight. She sat in the hallway when she was not engaged
in group therapy, as she would exercise vigorously if allowed to stay
alone in her room, attempting to burn off calories. Even as she sat in
the hallway, she swung her legs back and forth, back and forth under
her chair. She ate her meals sitting beside the nurses' station so that
nursing staff could monitor her intake.

From her history and the nurses' reports, I knew that hospitaliza-
tions where she was forced to gain weight and all the therapy in the
world would not be enough to save Miss Lawson's life. Miss Lawson

was psychologically very savvy. She understood the past family dynamics and emotions that led her to develop anorexia, her tight control of her food intake and weight. But there was a disconnect between her cognitive understanding and her will or desire to be free of her eating disorder. I knew that we had to find a part of her that wanted to be healthy, that wanted to be well, even as we unraveled and treated the aspects of her that were driven to starve herself—the aspects that were driving her towards death.

I had often viewed my own choices as either aligned with life, health, and an alive spirit, or aligned with harm and self-destruction. Every person has aspects and tendencies that are healthy and other aspects that are unhealthy. In speaking with my patients, sometimes I frame their choices in this way to encourage them to align their will and their decisions with the part of themselves that truly wants life and health, while standing up to the aspects that are not healthy. Miss Lawson was the first patient with whom I had this conversation. For her, this was a life-or-death matter; all her aspects were aligned with starvation. Her will was fueling the path towards death of spirit and body; her mind and emotions were aligned with supporting her anorexic self. We had to find a part—however small or hidden—that wanted to be healthy and free. If we couldn't help her awaken and nourish even a small part of her that wanted to live, she would die.

When I spoke with Miss Lawson, I searched for a spark, anything that we could work with, a healthy part of her that I could support and encourage. I couldn't find it anywhere. It was as if her spirit had flat-lined. Although she was willing to engage in conversation, she spoke in a flat voice, saying all the right things but without the ring of truth behind her words. Each day I tried to reach her, tried to engage her, knowing that her life was at stake, but without success. I told her that she would die if she did not make an effort, hoping that fear of death could save her life. Freedom from her suffering was possible—not easy, but possible. But there was nothing in her that was motivated to work towards health, to be free of the psychological entrapments that were weighing her down. I felt as if her spirit was already partly gone. Hard as I tried, I couldn't reach her.

I thought about my own history of anorexia, how it now felt almost like a past life, and wondered why I had somehow had such a strong motivation to move through the eating disorder, to work so hard to be free of the underlying psychological and emotional oppression that fueled the symptoms.

Miss Lawson gained enough weight to be discharged from the hospital. After saying goodbye to her, I unlocked the unit door and held it for her as she walked through. I watched her through the small vertical window in the door as she walked down the hall, rolling her suitcase behind her, and then disappeared into the elevator. I stepped into the bathroom and cried. I knew I was discharging her to her eventual death, and that no amount of my willpower could keep her alive.

Another patient was a forty-two-year-old, Chinese-American male with no prior psychiatric history. He had developed new-onset psychosis, including paranoia and auditory hallucinations and had been admitted from the ER to psychiatry with a likely diagnosis of schizophrenia. In my assessment, though, his history didn't match up with the typical course of schizophrenia. It was late in life for a new diagnosis of schizophrenia—typically men are diagnosed in their late teens or early twenties. Mr. Liu had never had the negative symptoms so characteristic of schizophrenia—the blunted affect, poverty of speech and thought, apathy, anhedonia (the inability to feel pleasure), lack of motivation, and reduced social drive. Mr. Liu was animated and engaged, almost in spite of his psychotic symptoms.

He also had had a gradual loss of appetite over the past year. I was concerned that a medical issue could be causing his symptoms and decided to do a work-up for delirium, a sudden change in mental status that is caused by an underlying medical issue. I ordered labs and a CT scan of his head and looked over the lab results carefully when they came back that afternoon. His CBC didn't show any evidence of a hidden infection or anemia. His blood glucose, electrolytes, and liver, kidney, and thyroid function were all within normal limits. He didn't have a urinary tract infection, his drug and alcohol screens of his urine and blood came back negative, and his thiamine and B-12 levels were normal.

The CT scan results came back the next morning, indicating a large left frontal mass. My heart sank. I ordered a neuro-oncology consult and walked slowly to my patient's room, thinking carefully about how to share this news with him. He was seated in a chair in his room, staring out of the thick glass window. The only light in the room came from the window, glinting off his glasses and creating a silhouette of his body slouched in his chair.

"Mr. Liu, could I talk with you for a few minutes?" He nodded his head, straightened up, and turned towards me. I pulled up the other chair in the room and sat down. "All of your lab results came back normal, but the CT scan of your head didn't. I'm really sorry to say that it looks like you have a tumor in the left front part of your brain." I put the fingers of my left hand over my left forehead, indicating to him the location of the tumor. "I'm pretty sure that's what is causing your loss of appetite and the voices you've been hearing." He stared at me, clearly having difficulty absorbing this information. "I wish I had more I could tell you right now. Neuro-oncology will see you this afternoon, and you'll likely be transferred to another floor in the hospital after that."

He blinked a few times, then swallowed. "Am I going to die?" he asked.

"Mr. Liu, I can promise you that there will be treatment options for you. Once they find out what kind of tumor it is, the oncologist and neurosurgeon can let you know what treatment or treatments will be the best for you. It might include chemotherapy, radiation, surgery, or some combination of those three options, depending on the specific type of tumor." We sat in silence for a while. After some time, I said quietly, "Mr. Liu, I know this is really hard news. How can I best support you right now?" I leaned forward, and saw his eyes water behind his glasses. "What can I do?" I asked.

"Maybe just stay here for a little while," he whispered, choking back tears.

I scooted my chair up to him and held my hand out, palm up. He reached over and put his hand in mine. Tears fell silently down his face as we sat silently together. I wasn't supposed to touch my patients unless I was doing a physical exam. I knew if a nurse or another staff member walked in, I would get in trouble. I also knew I was going to be late to team rounds—a huge taboo. In all of my years of training, I had never seen a med student or a resident late to team rounds. I didn't care. I couldn't override the natural and very literal urge to reach out to another human in pain, and if being late in order to be with a patient got me kicked out of residency, I was in the wrong profession.

As it turned out, I was about ten minutes late to rounds. The room went silent when I walked in. The other resident and the med students stared at me, wide-eyed and bodies still as stones. "I'm so sorry I'm late," I said. The truth was, I didn't feel sorry at all, or afraid. I knew I had done the right thing, and didn't care if there were consequences for me. "I had to break some hard news to a patient."

"Dr. Edwards, you can talk with your patient any other time. Being late to rounds is not only not okay, it is disrespectful and rude to the rest of the team. Don't let this happen again."

"I'm very sorry," I lied, sitting down at the conference table and looking as humble as I could. I didn't even consider explaining the situation, knowing that I had committed a cardinal sin of medical training, and that there was no situation that could absolve me from the attending's perspective. I was surprised to find no fear, shame, or guilt rising up in me. To the contrary, I felt a sense of freedom—a simple knowing that overrode all the structures of medical training I had been indoctrinated with, all the heaviness of the hierarchy, the rules of the system, the fear built into the training process. The confidence and trust in my own knowing as a physician felt established in me at that moment, and it continued to grow from then on.

Later that afternoon a resident from neurology visited Mr. Liu. After her consultation, Mr. Liu was transferred to the Neurology floor. The resident invited me to attend their rounds the next morning, when she would present the patient to the neuro-oncology team. The next day, I arrived on the psychiatry floor early and saw my patients so I'd have time to attend neuro-oncology team rounds before our psychiatry team rounds. I arrived a few minutes early for neuro-oncology rounds and chatted with the resident while we waited for the rest of the team to arrive. As team members began to arrive, the resident introduced me to each person. One attending literally took my breath away. Not only did he look like he just walked off a men's fashion photo shoot, he was also a shining light; his whole being filled the room. As the resident introduced me to him, I looked into his eyes and was met with a depth of presence I had not yet encountered in the world of medicine. I sensed that he was seeing me, deeply.

Everyone sat down in the crowded room. I pulled up a chair near the door, just behind the team's circle of chairs. I was a guest, not part of the team, and knew my place. I also was happy to be able to relax, knowing I wouldn't be called on during their rounds. When Mr. Liu's case was presented, I was merely acknowledged with a nod. The treatment plan proposed for him seemed sound, and his prognosis hopeful. As the residents presented different patients to the team, I found myself more and more relaxed, barely listening to their words with my mind, instead dropping into a meditative state of sensing the energy in the room.

I began to notice soft light around each person. Most were surrounded by yellow light, but a few also had reddish or blue-ish patches. The handsome attending, who had been introduced to me as Dr. Sternberg, was surrounded by a billow of yellow light with lavender splotches. I realized that I was seeing auras—energy fields extending from each body. I noticed that when I focused on and thought about what was being said, the auras disappeared. I played with the phenomenon a bit, alternately relaxing and expanding into this altered state of perceiving energy, then intentionally shifting and contracting my attention to focus on the patient presentation.

As the team began to wrap up their rounds, I sat up straighter, took a deep breath and moved into everyday, task-oriented, person-ality-centered mode. I knew I needed to re-engage my left brain and get back in gear for the day. After rounds, I stood up and thanked the attendings for allowing me to come to their rounds that day. Dr. Sternberg was the last to leave. He looked me in the eyes again. Again, I felt as if he was seeing through me. "Would you like to meet for lunch in the cafeteria today?" he asked. I was taken aback. Being asked by an attending to have lunch, let alone an attending from another team, was unusual to say the least. I also knew that I was running well behind with seeing my patients and completing orders and tasks on the psychiatry floor. But you don't say No to an attending, and I certainly didn't want to say No to Dr. Sternberg. I let all the practicalities drop away, and heard myself say, "Sure, what time?"

I rushed through my morning, my mind repeatedly pulled back to Dr. Sternberg. I was curious, nervous, and excited all at once, and felt myself buzzing with energy. Clearly I had not imagined what we recognized in each other. Until then, my spiritual life and my training had been worlds apart, split off from each other. If a fellow medical student or resident asked what I had done over a weekend, I always shared openly about satsangs or meditation retreats I had attended. I was often teased about my spiritual inclinations, but I didn't mind. I sensed the teasing came from affection, or sometimes from discomfort in the other person. Some were curious, a few perhaps pulled to embark someday on their own spiritual exploration. My openness about my spiritual path allowed my colleagues to share with me their personal struggles, sensing I could receive what they shared, openly and without judgment, and always knowing that what was said would stay between us.

When asked about my spiritual journey by fellow medical trainees, I usually described some aspects of my journey in a left-brain, practical sort of way, sensing that their questions stemmed from a mental curiosity, not the deeper and undeniable pull to Truth that was my constant companion. I had met many people at satsangs and on retreats that shared this pull inward, this deeper connection, but never in the medical arena. The split between my spiritual life and the medical world seemed to mirror the split between spirit and mind. The depth of presence I sensed in Dr. Sternberg was my first experience within the world of medicine of this deeper knowing in another. The whole encounter felt surreal, occurring at another level.

I stood inside the open cafeteria doors, scanning the large, noisy room as residents, medical students, and nurses walked by me, some heading in to the cafeteria, others just finishing lunch and heading back to their floors. The smell of cooked chicken and burgers hit me hard, as it always did, bringing with it a brief wave of nausea. Most of the tables were full. Residents sat crowded together around small tables, each small group of residents easily identified by the color of their scrubs. Surgery residents wore green scrubs, a few still with their matching surgical caps in place on their heads. OB/GYN residents wore white scrubs, internal medicine blue. Many were draped in their long lab coats, stethoscopes poking out of pockets or hanging around their necks. Medical students also sat together in bunches, their short white lab coats pointedly marking their place at the bottom of the hierarchy. At other tables, a few nurses clumped together in mostly pastel scrubs. All the groups of residents and medical students were engaged in animated conversation, their energetic voices echoing together in the large room as an excited, unintelligible hum. An energy of purpose, importance, confidence, and enthusiasm filled the room, each person embodying their role as a physician or physician-to-be at a leading medical institution. Everyone was in a hurry; moving, speaking, and eating quickly.

I scanned the room again for Dr. Sternberg, thinking I had missed him with all the movement in the room. Then I heard a friendly voice behind me. "Hi, Mindy. Sorry I'm a little late." I turned around and returned Dr. Sternberg's smile. I was surprised by his apology. Attendings never apologized for being late and the rest of us never considered them late; the rest of us simply revolved our world around them.

"No problem, Dr. Sternberg," I said. "I just got here a few minutes ago." I felt my heart rate increase, overwhelmed by his striking physical presence.

Dr. Sternberg glanced around the crowded cafeteria. "It's a little crazy in here. Do you want me to get you something to eat while you grab a table?" I asked him to get me a salad, and waited for a table to open up while he stood in line to get our food. Soon we were sitting across from each other at a small round table. As he put the food on the table, I noticed a wedding band on his finger. Okay. In my book this meant he was completely off limits, even for light flirting. I felt myself shut down the attraction and excitement I had been feeling, and hoped he wasn't going to hit on me. We turned our Styrofoam salad containers sideways on the tiny table so they would fit, and turned our legs diagonally, so our knees wouldn't touch.

"So what's this about, Dr. Sternberg?" I said boldly, hoping that a direct approach would ward off any less than professional intentions on his part. I had been naive enough in the past to learn that even simple friendliness was often misinterpreted by men as sexual interest. Dr. Sternberg carried with him not only the confidence of being an attending physician at Stanford Medical Center, he also carried the confidence of a life-long striking physical presence whose good looks stunned everyone. And he wasn't just good-looking. His whole being was enormous. He knew that all eyes would be on him whenever he walked into a room.

He laughed at my question. "Don't worry, I'm not going to hit on you," he said, meeting me again with his eyes. I was taken aback. How had he known I was afraid that was where this lunch was headed? "I noticed you were reading energy and seeing auras during rounds today." His eyes twinkled, knowing I would be shocked—not only that he knew this, but to hear this kind of talk in this realm of traditional medicine.

My jaw fell open. "What the heck?" I said, at a loss for words.

"Well, weren't you seeing auras?" he asked, challenging me with his confidence.

"Okay. How did you know?" I lowered my voice and looked around us to see if anyone was listening. "I can't believe we are having this conversation, right here in the Stanford Hospital cafeteria." I wanted to pinch myself to see if I was dreaming.

Dr. Sternberg told me that a few months earlier he had started doing yoga at home with his wife for about thirty minutes each morning. They were doing yoga as a form of physical exercise, not as a spiritual practice. Dr. Sternberg had never engaged in any spiritual practices, other than traditional Catholic rituals with his family as a child. After about a week of yoga, he said, "Something just opened up. I can tune into people at will and know what's going on with them.

I also have what feels like unlimited energy. Honestly, I don't know what's going on, but it's pretty cool. When I tuned into you, I sensed that you could tune into people, too. I thought you might know what was happening with me, especially when I sensed you were seeing auras. Do you know what is happening?"

My left-brain medical mind kicked in. This was just bizarre. Psychic or intuitive abilities are typically innate from birth, or develop over a long period of time with intensive spiritual practices. Could he be manic? I went through my check list, screening for mania or hypomania. I cleared my throat. "Well, you're right, I've been pretty intuitive most of my life, and more so since I started meditating about ten years ago. Were you intuitive or psychic before you started doing yoga? Are your thoughts racing? Are you able to sleep at night?" I pelted him with questions. He didn't exhibit any symptoms of mania or hypomania. His speech was not pressured, he was not having racing thoughts, he was sleeping good at night, and he wasn't engaged in any spending sprees or other risky behaviors such as sexual promiscuity.

Although he was clearly excited about his new-found psychic abilities, he was not grandiose or euphoric, and although he spoke of having a lot of energy, it was not manic or hypomanic energy. "I'm not manic, Mindy. I'm psychic, all of a sudden. It's like a whole other realm has opened up to me that I didn't know existed before. I love it, but I just don't know how or why it's happening to me."

"I don't have answers for you, but I agree that you've had some sort of sudden psychic opening. Probably you had a lot of latent psychic ability under the surface all your life, just waiting to be cracked open. For you, all it took was a little yoga to open it up." I looked at him curiously. He was clearly enthralled with his new-found abilities, like a kid in a candy shop, playing and experimenting with them. I had known many people with abilities outside the normal curve of human abilities, but I had met all of them through my "other" spiritual life outside of medicine. Everyone I had met who had abilities of this nature shared either my inward pull to Truth or my intense longing to be a vessel of Love in this world. Their *siddhis* (powers and abilities) were secondary to their spiritual journey, and although they might identify with them from time to time, their own pull inward was the primary driving force of their lives, as it was for me. I hadn't heard Dr. Sternberg mention anything about a spiritual journey or a pull inward, and wondered if he was aware of that in him.

I shared with him about my spiritual journey, my life-long pull to Truth, the force that continued to pull me inward. As I spoke, I searched his face, his energy field, for a spark of recognition, of understanding or resonance. It wasn't there. He lit up when we spoke about psychic abilities, but only listened politely when I spoke of my spiritual journey. This was the first time I had met someone who was dazzled by playing in the realm of spiritual phenomenon, but was not on an intentional spiritual journey.

I was utterly surprised, not understanding how or why this inward pull was so forceful, so powerful, so unstoppable in me. For me, being on a direct road to Truth was all that mattered. I had no interest in taking an exit ramp to a playground. Even so, I was happy to have someone in the world of medicine that I could speak with about psychic phenomenon without being labeled as crazy, and I was happy to support Dr. Sternberg with a loose understanding of what he was experiencing. I held open the door for the possibility that his psychic opening would precipitate a deeper spiritual opening, but during the course of our connection, this didn't happen.

• • •

As residents, we saw our patients in the hospital in the mornings and early afternoons and patients in the Stanford outpatient clinic later in the day. Some patients at the clinic were Stanford college students or staff members, and others were residents of the Palo Alto community. One of my patients, Daniela, was a sophomore at Stanford who had a skin-picking compulsion, a type of obsessive-compulsive disorder. She had been on a multitude of medications over the past several years, including SSRIs (selective serotonin reuptake inhibitors) and TCAs (tricyclic antidepressants)—the standard treatments for compulsive disorders. Nothing had helped. She picked nearly constantly at real or imagined blemishes or bumps, and had open lesions all over her arms, legs, and face.

Obsessive Compulsive Disorders (OCD) are notoriously difficult to treat. Daniela and I were working to identify situations and stressors that exacerbated the picking so we could find alternate ways to release her stress and anxiety. She was also implementing behavioral techniques, like wearing gloves when she was at home and gently snapping a rubber band that she kept on her wrist each time she noticed she was picking or noticed the urge to pick. Because she had been on all of the standard medications used to treat OCD, I spoke with my attending about alternate treatments. He suggested trying risperidone, a new medication that had been FDA approved for the treatment of schizophrenia. Although she didn't have schizophrenia, and there wasn't any research available on using this new class of medications to treat OCD, she was beginning to suffer from symptoms of depression related to shame and the self-imposed social isolation due to the disfigurement her picking caused. She was willing to try anything that might help. Risperidone did not miraculously rid Daniela of her symptoms, but after several weeks, she noticed the urge to pick was less intense, and with therapy and the behavioral techniques she implemented, she was able to curb the picking enough to allow many of her lesions to heal.

One afternoon, she walked into my office smiling. This was the first time I had seen her smile. "My goodness. What's going on?" I asked her, my heart warmed by her joy.

"I went on a date last weekend," she said shyly, unable to restrain her smile.

"Daniela, this is such a big deal. You have worked so hard to get to a place where you have the confidence and willingness to put yourself out there and to connect with others. And a date! Tell me about him. Tell me how it was for you." Daniela shared with me the details of the date, including the awkward moments, the spontaneous, fun moments . . . and the kiss at the end of the date.

• • •

Living in the Bay Area was not cheap, and when we weren't on call many of us took moonlighting jobs in the evenings and on weekends to boost our income. I had a job at an outpatient clinic in Gilroy, about an hour south of Palo Alto, where I worked late afternoons and some weekends. It was a busy community clinic that served local underprivileged individuals. We were short-staffed, as are many community clinics. Before I even started working, my schedule was booked solid for two months. Many patients arrived in crisis, and occasionally required emergency psychiatric hospitalization.

I saw one patient every thirty minutes—barely enough time to assess and treat a stable patient, let alone these very complex patients who were often in crisis. I found myself running later and later as my shifts wore on, feeling the stress of patients piling up in the waiting room, even as I tried to move quickly through the details of patient care, not wanting to miss something important. Here I learned to be ultra-efficient and honed my ability to be fully present with a patient—giving them my full attention and allowing them to feel as fully heard as possible, even as I pointedly steered the conversation to the information I needed for a thorough assessment.

Patients were frequently angry or frustrated because of the wait to see me. It was impossible for them to know how busy I was, impossible for them to know that I had been working my tail off, not twiddling my thumbs or taking a lunch break. I listened to their frustration and simply apologized for being so late. I found that a humble and gentle approach helped to diffuse their anger and frustration. Next, I had to elicit details about very specific psychiatric symptoms associated with their illness, and ask about or test for specific side effects associated with their medications. Patients often launched into descriptions about events or home life that weren't relevant to their treatment. There just wasn't time. Often they didn't realize the difference between a medication management appointment and an appointment with their therapist or case manager, and wanted to discuss very involved psychotherapy or psychosocial issues with me. At the Gilroy clinic, I learned that when I listened deeply and was fully present with my patients, they didn't mind if

I gently interrupted from time to time in order to ask about the medical information I needed.

Staff often asked me to "work in" a crisis into my schedule. I always felt my chest tighten when I was asked, knowing that a crisis meant a patient that would take significant time to assess. My schedule was already bursting at the seams. But I always agreed, concerned that the patient literally might not survive if I didn't see him or her. Some patients were in crisis because they were suicidal or threatening to harm someone else, others were manic or psychotic, and some were having side effects from their medication. One afternoon, I was asked to find time for a new elderly patient who was living in a residential care facility. Staff said they didn't know if she was a true crisis; the facility staff had said that the patient was confused. I was already overbooked and running an hour late. I sighed, set aside my stress, and agreed to see the patient; I knew that otherwise she might not be been seen for weeks.

Mrs. Perez was wheeled into my office in a wheelchair. She was accompanied by a young staff member from her residential care facility who had just come on duty and had little information. The patient occasionally mumbled unintelligibly. When I asked her questions, she tried to respond, but I was unable to understand her. I asked the staff member what her baseline was: was she normally able to engage in conversation and be understood? Was she able to ambulate on her own normally? The staff member said that the patient had not been able to walk since she had suffered a stroke several years ago, but until a few days ago she could talk, carry on a conversation, and was normally oriented to person, place, situation, and time. Okay, at least now I knew we were dealing with altered mental status, possibly delirium.

As I waited on staff to bring me her chart, I did a physical exam. Her eyelids drooped at half-mast, and she dozed off even in the middle of my exam. When I asked her to squeeze as tight as she could, her hand only loosely wrapped around my finger. Her muscles were weak. When she raised her arms, she had a noticeable tremor. She was hyperreflexic and exhibited myoclonus (jerky muscle movements).

During the exam, I noticed the smell of urine, and asked the staff member if she was normally incontinent. She wasn't. "Has she had any new medical issues, or new physical complaints, or been started on any new medications lately?" I asked.

"She mentioned the other day that her arthritis was acting up, but nothing else," the staff person responded.

The secretary opened the door to my office and handed me the patient's chart. I looked through her medical history and medications, searching for clues. She had a history of a stroke, as the staff person had mentioned, and high blood pressure, which was well controlled with a beta blocker. She had a diagnosis of bipolar disorder, and had been stable on lithium for over fifteen years. I ran through a mental check list of possible causes of delirium as I wrote orders for stat labs—infection (urinary tract, respiratory, or other), medication interactions or side effects, hypo- or hyperglycemia, stroke, cardiac issues. I ordered a panel of delirium labs and added on a lithium level, uneasy about her condition, and still unsure of what was going on. I asked the patient to return to the waiting room after she had labs drawn.

I continued seeing patients as I waited for Mrs. Perez' labs to come back, my concern about her condition weighing on me even as I saw other patients in crisis. Two hours later, the secretary knocked on my door and handed me a fax from the lab. I scanned them quickly. She was lithium toxic and her kidneys were already affected. I took a sharp breath in, walked to the front desk and asked the secretary to call EMS. I hoped that her kidneys were not permanently damaged, and that she would not end up on dialysis. As we waited on the ambulance, I wheeled the patient back into my office from the waiting room, and explained to her and the staff member that her lithium level was too high, that it was affecting her kidneys and her ability to think, and that I was sending her to the emergency room so that she could get the medical treatment she needed.

Why had she been stable on her current lithium dose for fifteen years and all of a sudden was lithium toxic? What had caused her lithium level to rise? Suddenly, I remembered a comment the staff person had made earlier. I turned to her. "You said she has been complaining of arthritis pain. Has staff been giving her anything to treat the pain?"

"Just some ibuprofen," she replied, "nothing prescription strength."

"How often has she been getting the ibuprofen, and what dose?"

"I don't know the dose, but she got it a few times the last shift I worked."

There was the explanation. Staff members at her facility had been unaware that NSAIDS like ibuprofen tend to raise lithium levels, and should not be taken with lithium.

Mrs. Perez did end up in kidney failure and needed life-long dialysis. Even though there was no way I could have prevented this complication, I felt sick about it and never forgot her. Lithium is a very good medication used to treat bipolar disorder, but since then I am wary of prescribing it and go out of my way to make sure my patients who take lithium, and all of their caregivers, know not to take NSAIDS with lithium.

• • •

My long commute back and forth from Stanford made my already long days much longer, adding to my stress and exhaustion. When I asked Joel if we could move closer to the Dumbarton Bridge so that my commute wouldn't be as long, he refused. At one point, after Pam had moved out of the house, I was on call at the hospital. I had washed my lab coat the night before and had forgotten to fill my pockets back up with their crucial contents: my stethoscope, reflex hammer, pharmacopeia, and patient note cards. Pam was visiting someone in Palo Alto that day and agreed to stop by our house, get what I needed, and bring it all to me. The next day, she called and told me that she had seen a porn magazine in the house that Joel had apparently been looking at. I felt the sudden burn of terror and jealousy—familiar by now, but still hard to be with. By this time, the mounting pain and resentment in the relationship, along with our exhaustion and limited time together because of our schedules, left little room for shared joy or spontaneous affection. We hung on for several more months, trying to work things out, but were unable to overcome the heaviness that hung between us. We parted ways.

The break-up with Joel opened up all my past grief and feelings of abandonment. I continued to move through the motions of residency—seeing my patients at the clinic, admitting patients to the hospital, meeting with attendings and other residents, and teaching what I could to medical students assigned to my team. On the surface I was doing everything I needed to do, but for months I was devastated.

After the break-up with Joel, Pam and I rented a house in Palo Alto. My commute was now only fifteen minutes—a huge relief for me. I was hoping I would be able to get more sleep, but my nervous system was so high-wired at this point that it took me a few hours to fall asleep at night, and I awakened at the slightest noise. Pam tended to stay up late and get up late, and I heard every sound she made, quiet though she tried to be.

Whenever I could, I attended satsangs with different spiritual teachers in the Bay Area. Pam resonated with Gangaji's satsangs, and we often attended those together. We shared our spiritual insights, and supported each other as we each encountered aspects of ourselves that were in the process of transformation.

After some time, Pam fell into a depression. She had shared with me previously that she'd had a troubled childhood and suffered from bouts of depression, but I was unprepared for the depth of her hopelessness. She didn't see a reason to live and expressed suicidal thoughts several times. I tried my best to be there for her in the midst of my exhaustion, but Pam stayed in her room much of the time. She was not interested in therapy or antidepressant medication. Over time, Pam's depression shifted into anger, which she often directed at me. She was sharply critical, and I felt the unmistakable thrust of her anger. I was deeply hurt and didn't understand where the anger was coming from. Years later, I was stunned when a mutual friend told me that Pam had been jealous of me. As powerful and brilliant as she was, she was insecure about never having completed college and my academic achievement triggered her insecurity.

Pam eventually pulled out of the depression, but over the years she continued to suffer recurrences and said several times she wouldn't make it to fifty years of age. Years later, for reasons unknown to me, she abruptly stopped responding to my phone calls and cut off all communication. I reached out once again after my daughter was born, but Pam didn't return my calls. Several months later, I learned from a friend that she had been found dead, intentionally overdosed on pain medication.

Pam's suicide broke my heart open. In my own life, I was struggling with the discrepancy between my spiritual insights and the aspects of myself that had not yet "caught up" with my spiritual development. I had been so aware of Pam's depth, but hadn't known how to reconcile this other part of her that seemed so out of alignment with the brilliance of her spirit. Her suicide left me with an undeniable truth: this dance of being human is itself the integration of psyche and spirit—the transformation of all aspects of ourselves, all aspects of humanity, with nothing left behind. Her suicide broke my heart open to the tenderness and fragility of life… and to the understanding that we are all doing the very best we can.

CHAPTER 16

The Undeniable Pull

Our yearning for Truth actually comes from Truth.
—Adyashanti

During my three years of residency at Stanford, the pull inward, the pull to Truth, intensified even more. In San Francisco, I gravitated to teachers of non-dual spirituality, resonating deeply with the profound truths they spoke of. I attended Eckhart Tolle's first talk at a church in Palo Alto, and a few years later attended his retreats at the Omega Institute and in Costa Rica, where an earthquake in the middle of the night shook the tent I was in with Cindy. I attended Adyashanti satsangs and meditation retreats, and Gangaji satsangs. I saw Ram Dass at Open Secret bookstore in Marin many times, and visited him in his home in San Anselmo. I also went to as many ten-day silent Vipassana retreats at Spirit Rock Meditation Center as I could.

I loved Spirit Rock. After attending several Goenka meditation retreats at the Goenka retreat center, I realized that the intensity of their structure was feeding my pattern of being hard on myself. This pattern began taking front seat instead of insights, unwinding, or spiritual progress. My intense effort was co-opting my longing for

Truth. I decided to attend meditation retreats that were less rigorous, with teachers that also acknowledged and addressed the psychological aspects of being human. I had read and loved Jack Kornfield's books, and attended retreats at Spirit Rock with Jack, Tara Brach, James Baraz, Sylvia Boorstein, and other meditation teachers. While retreats at Spirit rock were intense, retreatants were held in an environment that was imbued with kindness and love.

During medical school, I had contacted Roger Walsh, a psychiatrist who had written books about meditation and spirituality. We exchanged letters and spoke by phone several times. Once he also attended a retreat I was on at Spirit Rock. We were all in silence, but one day I noticed a bulging envelope with my name on it pinned to the bulletin board. In it was a kind, supportive note from Roger and a Ferrero Rocher chocolate, a truly divine treat during an otherwise austere experience. I was deeply touched by his note, and felt warm tears sliding down my face as I read it. As I turned my attention to the chocolate, my mouth watered in anticipation. I slowly unwrapped the gold foil, mindful of all the sensations in my body. I sniffed the chocolate, inhaling the fragrance that filled my whole body. As I savored each bite, I entered a state of bliss. I tasted chocolate as I had never tasted it before; its sweetness filled my mouth so intensely it was as if nothing else existed. When I swallowed the last bit of chocolate, I wept. I was so grateful to Kindness Itself for having come through Roger in such a pure and beautiful way, and grateful for the gift of having a body so I could experience love, energy, and sensation—the true grace of being human.

My resonance with the truth that all of the teachers spoke of magnified the intense longing for Truth that burned throughout my being. During residency, this intense longing for Truth expanded into a deep, constant longing and prayer that I would become a pure vessel of love, that love flow through me freely, unimpeded, and that I exist to serve love, only love.

At that time, many of the non-dual teachers didn't share any personal experiences other than their awakening. Some had come to the deep realization that "none of this is real," including their own personal challenges—and hadn't yet embraced the paradox that *everything* is real. There was a tendency to deny the human experience and only speak about deeper spiritual insights. In this way, human aspects that were calling for attention were often bypassed. This split often was evident in the organizations they headed; their blind spots ultimately got played out in the communities devoted to them. I saw this first hand years later when I lived in a spiritual community.

I had also had the realization that this world is not real, that everything is consciousness and is a projection of the mind. The absolute Truth—the unchanging source before, within, and beyond manifestation in time and space—was all I cared about, and I had experienced this as Presence. But on the human level, there was still suffering. My spiritual realizations had not fully permeated my daily life. I didn't know how to bridge this gap, how to make the deep insights a part of my moment-to-moment experience, and many spiritual teachers I turned to were bypassing the process of integration of insights and realizations into the fabric of the individual human life. I continued seeking and searching for a way to integrate the Truth that had come to me into my daily life.

During my last year of residency, I asked my residency training director if I could delay completion of residency in order to attend a two-month silent meditation retreat at Spirit Rock. During breaks in my training, I had attended several ten-day retreats at Spirit Rock, but it was unheard of to take time off from residency. I knew I was to go, and wasn't surprised that Dr. Taylor was supportive and gave me the green light.

During meditation retreats, I always felt the sense of homecoming, and this two-month retreat was no exception. Without daily distractions and with the quieting of my mind, the palpable presence that *is* permeated my awareness. Meditation retreats were always intense energetically. The patterns I'd developed through my life to avoid discomfort had created walls and contractions around my heart. During the two-month retreat at Spirit Rock, more and more subtle contractions in my system opened and released. This release dissolved perceived boundaries, and my identification with my thoughts, emotions, and body began to loosen. My awareness expanded and ideas of "other" dropped away. I realized that all boundaries are born of the mind—and that when the mind drops away, there is no separation.

But there was the keen sense that I was still pretending to be a "me," pretending to be limited to this body, pretending that the thought "I" was real. For much of my life I had felt that I was playing the role of "me," or that this or that mattered to me, when I was actually experiencing the emptiness and unreality of the world. I assumed everyone felt they were pretending, that everyone had this deeper sense that the individual "me" and the world were not real. When I searched inside to find anything that I could identify as the true "me," I didn't find it. During this sixty-day retreat, I finally realized that the feeling of pretending to be someone arose out of a deeper awareness that, in truth, there is no "me" to be found.

At the end of the two-month retreat, retreatants had a day of re-entry. Silence was broken after breakfast. We began easing into the awkwardness of talking after sixty days of silence and intense inward focus. On shorter retreats, re-entry had always been a challenge for me. This re-entry, though, felt different. There didn't seem to be a split between the state of pure presence and the "me." I could carry on a conversation as if there was a "you" and a "me," even as the awareness of non-separation remained in the foreground. Outside the dining area, I joined a group of three others who were talking. I remained mostly quiet, aware of a young man in the group who I felt I knew intimately, although I had not met him previously. Ty had light blue eyes, clear and steady. He wore his blond hair and his beard in pony tails. I learned from the conversation that he worked at Spirit Rock and that his spiritual teacher was Gangaji. He lit up when he spoke of her. I shared with him that I had been to many of her retreats, although I had mixed feelings about her because of what seemed to be spiritual bypassing in her teachings and in her community.

Ty and I ate supper together that evening. We took our food outside and sat down on the cool grass. Our talk was interspersed with long periods of comfortable silence as we ate. He was from Arizona, but was living a nomadic life, unaffected by the traditional structures of society. He was spontaneous, and real to the core, true to his own intuition and living in the moment. In many ways, he was the opposite of Joel. While Joel was responsible and measured and thoughtful, Ty was a free spirit, unencumbered by responsibility or commitment. He was a breath of fresh air for me.

We fell in love. While my world was full of people who were ultra-responsible and intellectual, Ty would burst into song, dance around the room, or tickle me spontaneously, and take joy and delight in things others wouldn't even notice. We spent hours reading each other poetry—our own or Hafiz—weeping with gratitude or joy as we read. Our spiritual paths and realizations were similar, and we attended many retreats together.

Over time, the very qualities that brought us together began to pose challenges in our relationship. Initially, my responsibility in the world served to ground his free spirit. His free spirit gave me breathing room and fresh air from the weight of my responsibilities as a resident. I was functioning in a very left-brain, task-oriented world; his was the opposite. We balanced each other out. Eventually, though, my jealousy, although more tempered than in the past, started coming up. For someone who treasured freedom and warded off any constraints, my jealousy only served to bring forward Ty's insistence on freedom. He moved in with me and chose not to work. I was working long hours and making less than minimum wage as a psychiatry resident, and over time felt drained by his lack of financial contribution. As in all relationships, we served as mirrors for each other, exposing and highlighting the other's challenges and tendencies.

Ty's free spirit was occasionally punctuated by a sense of entitlement that always caught me by surprise. Once, when we shopped at a grocery store, Ty insisted that we get all organic fresh produce. Although I often deferred to him, I was supporting both of us on my resident's salary and was struggling to make ends meet. At that time, going all organic seemed like a luxury I couldn't afford. I had agreed to pay for organic produce that didn't have skin and was more likely to contain chemicals, like spinach or strawberries, but told him other produce, like bananas and apples, would have to be non-organic for now. To my surprise, he blew up and yelled at me. I was uncomfortable with his anger, but stood my ground. This was the first time, but not the last, I would see a burst of entitlement and anger from him.

At the end of residency, I took a month off before beginning work. My system had been high-wired with stress and responsibility for eight years and I wanted some time to allow my body and mind to slow down. Ty and I spent the month outside of Puerto Viejo, Costa Rica. We rented a small cabin near the beach from a sweet couple, hung in hammocks while we watched sloths move ever so slowly in the trees above, woke up at dawn to the sounds of howler monkeys, ate chocolate bars made at a cacao farm high up in the hills, and read books on the beach. Occasionally, we rode a bike the two miles into town, with Ty sitting on the seat and pedaling while I stood on small bars extending out from the center of the back wheel and held on to his shoulders. In spite of the challenges and some conflict in my relationship with T, the slow pace and simplicity of life were a balm.

After this idyllic vacation I decided to move back to Charleston. The maternal, expansive ocean supported and nourished my spirit, and the marsh plough mud was grounding for me. Ty and I recognized that our journey together as partners was coming to an end, in part because of the ongoing dynamics in our relationship, and in part because he was very clear that he did not want to have children, and I knew that I did want to have a child at some point. We painfully agreed to part ways, but we have remained connected through the years and have supported each other on our individual journeys.

• • •

After my two-month retreat, when a greater identification with the "me" returned, I assumed that the ultimate goal of my spiritual path was to remain in the state of non-separation, in pure awareness, in what is "Real." I continued to pursue this state for years through meditation and with spiritual teachers. Finally, when there was nothing left in me desiring that anything be other than "what is," when all seeking and efforting dropped away, I came to see the beauty of the dance of identification. I came to embrace the paradox of the beauty of the awareness of pure presence and lack of separation, *and* the ability to be a "me."

My growing appreciation of the human experience shifted me from trying to get rid of the ego by eliminating reactivity and uncomfortable emotions to welcoming these experiences as doorways to my own heart and awakening. I realized that each experience arising in awareness is the perfect doorway for that particular moment. I discovered that if I opened to my pain, there was the possibility of a deeper opening and unfolding.

Over the years, I found my interactions with patients shifted along with my own deepening. Early on, when I was still seeking and diving in deeper in my spiritual life, I often nudged patients to go deeper. When all seeking dropped away for me, I no longer felt compelled to push patients to go deeper, but simply provided the opportunity. When I work with patients now, I often find myself checking or testing to see how deeply they can go—in a way screening their capacity. At times I find myself nudging or pushing them deeper, but only when that is being pulled forth from me by the patient—which is very different from me *wanting* them to go deeper. If, for example, a patient simply wants relief from suffering with medication or a tool that may help relieve the symptom that is causing the suffering, I provide that for them if it won't be harmful.

Even as I ask patients about symptoms, response to medication, or medication side effects and cover the left-brain, medical piece that is required of my role, there is a fluidity and spontaneity that occurs in my interactions with patients. In response to my sense of where the patient is at, at times my own energy becomes gentle or soft, or at other times a fierce energy may be pulled forward, confronting a rigid pattern or setting firm boundaries. In my work with patients, my spiritual journey has been as important as my medical training in my still-evolving capacity to be a physician, therapist, and healer.

Reflections on the Dance of Identification

When our attention in daily life is placed primarily on our personality—on our ideas about who we are; on our likes, dislikes, and tendencies; on the past and the future—we mistakenly think that the personality and body are who we are and we lose our innate connection with spirit. As we open to our difficult emotions, these contractions of thought and personality begin to unwind and our deeper nature begins to reveal itself. Our contractions, discomfort, and suffering are our own personal beacons calling us back Home.

When there are glimpses or experiences of Love or Truth, and later the identification with the individual "me" and the natural suffering that accompanies identification returns, often the mind turns *That which is real* into something to be attained again, something that someone else has that I don't have, something that I must try to get and keep in the future.

The mind projects Love and Truth out "there," separate from what I am. Projecting enlightenment as "out there"—on a spiritual teacher whom we may think is realized or "has it," or into the future as something to be attained—only delays our own coming Home. Some spiritual teachers are not only channels for truth, wisdom, and love, but are also unconsciously or consciously perpetuating this projection onto themselves out of their desire to be powerful and idealized in that role. They want to be seen as having truth, wisdom, or love to impart. Even as they are a channel for a deeper wisdom, their unacknowledged or unseen identification as a "me" that wants or needs to be a teacher is getting played out. This is all part of the dance and the role they are playing in this life for their own unfolding.

It is the mind that separates, labels, judges, and categorizes. That is just what the mind does—separates into yes/no, me/you, us/them, likes/dislikes, etc. As the idea of "non-duality" dissolves, what remains is a fluid effortless movement between and within all that the mind would otherwise label and the capacity to use the discriminating mind when it is called for. The idea in spiritual circles that there shouldn't be a "me"—that the goal is to get rid of the "me"; that there shouldn't be desires or fears; that there shouldn't be identification with thoughts, emotions, or the body; that the mind shouldn't separate; or that there are higher states to be worked towards—disappears. When the idea of "getting there" drops away, effort disappears and the ability to shift between or to experience the deeper truth of our Being *and* the individual self remains—without the mind's labeling or separation of these states of consciousness.

When the awareness of our deeper Being is in the foreground, one's personal life may seem no more relevant than someone else's circumstances or emotions. Life becomes more impersonal, even as one's personal life is lived more fully. As the energies of desire and fear that fuel thoughts, ideas, or habits of separation unwind, the compulsion of the mind to separate unwinds. This opens the doorway to merging with another when we meet them where they are at, without an agenda of needing or wanting anything from them. There is a natural sensing into the "other" person, feeling where they are coming from as if we *are* the other person. From this lens of perception, whatever is needed in the moment is pulled forth from us. We naturally respond with compassion and love from this place of deep connection. Without our personal "stuff" muddying the interaction, the spaciousness of our Being resonates with and awakens the other's Being, which optimizes the opportunity for the "other" person to remember who they really are.

PART III

Saachi

Your children are not your children.
They are the sons and daughters of Life's longing for itself.
They come through you but not from you,
And though they are with you yet they belong not to you.
—Kahlil Gibran

CHAPTER 17

For Old Times' Sake

The dark night of the soul comes just before revelation.
—Joseph Campbell

Before moving back to Charleston, I flew there for a visit. I drove straight from the airport to Folly Beach and felt myself relaxing into Amita's gentle kindness and love even before I got to her house. I was surprised to find myself turning into a neighborhood off Folly Road I had never been in before. Before I knew it, I was parked in the driveway of a small hexagonal house that appeared to be just the right size for me. It was up on stilts and the expansive marsh was visible from my car. I opened the car door and the smell of plough mud washed over me. I breathed in deeply, absorbing the nourishment into my cells. The plough mud grounded me and made me feel more present even as my awareness expanded with the spaciousness of the marsh, which seemed to go on and on forever. A rickety dock tiptoed into the plough mud of the marsh grass and provided a perch for a few birds. Off in the distance, the marsh melted into the ocean. A large mother oak tree hugged the house on one side, its strength and solidity adding to my own sense of presence and solidity. The place embraced me.

The house was for sale and Dad loaned me the down payment. I planted camellias and gardenias and a garden of white flowers and lived there for the next thirteen years, my body and spirit nourished by the marsh, the tidal creek, and the ocean.

I worked with underserved patients at a county mental health clinic. The patients at these clinics tend to have the most severe forms of mental illness and they are often in crisis, exacerbated by lack of follow-up either because they don't come to or aren't able to get to follow-up appointments, or because at these chronically underfunded and understaffed clinics it can take several months to get an appointment. The patients have significant socioeconomic issues that complicate their mental illness—homelessness, unemployment, lack of transportation, involvement in abusive relationships—and substance abuse issues frequently complicate their psychiatric diagnoses. Their lack of access to medical care also results in poorly treated or untreated medical issues; diabetes and hypertension are common. Because the patients and their situations are so complex, and because they often come in while in a suicidal, psychotic, or homicidal crisis, providers at county mental health clinics are usually overwhelmed. I often felt as if I were working in a psychiatric emergency room.

Much of medicine is driven by decisions made by clinic administrators or insurance companies with the primary goal of keeping costs to a minimum. With the boom of available psychiatric medications several decades ago, the responsibility for therapy and medication management were divided, with case managers or psychotherapists paid to offer psychotherapy, and psychiatrists paid only for medication management. Psychiatrists were given less time to see patients, with the assumption that sessions would be limited to medication management, and would not include therapy.

I found that I couldn't limit my sessions to the prescriber's standard gathering of detailed information about psychiatric symptoms and medication side effects. This was a one-dimensional approach to patients and there was so much more going on with each person. Bypassing their psychological, emotional, and psychosocial issues kept treatment superficial, while treating the whole person could bring about the healing I hoped to see in my patients. It was impossible to separate out what was happening in their lives from their psychiatric symptoms, so I took the time to learn about their internal and external lives, to support them through their grief or anger, and to schedule much-needed medical appointments. I called their other physicians when I needed information, such as medical history the patient was unable to give me, or to get the green light for a new psychiatric medication from an oncologist who was giving the patient chemotherapy. Sometimes I needed to give the other physician information, such as letting them know the patient was abusing the opioids they were providing. I called case managers and coordinated social services, such as providing a list of Alcoholics or Narcotics Anonymous groups, finding emergency funds to keep their electricity on, or arranging transportation to a shelter that night so the patient didn't have to sleep under a bridge.

I learned to be very efficient and very present with my patients; I wanted them to feel heard even within such a limited time frame. But even with my freshly-honed efficiency, I was always running late. Patients at times were initially angry after having waited in the waiting room for some time, but most soon recognized that I gave each of them the best possible care that I could and came to accept the wait.

I loved working with these patients. Those of us with privileged lives typically don't have the opportunity to engage with people who are dealing with this degree of struggle. Humbled by their suffering, I felt honored to offer them whatever support and help I could. But because of the intensity of the county mental health clinic, I decided to work part-time there and also open up a private practice, knowing that private practice patients would be much less complex. With private practice patients, I could schedule enough time for both therapy and medication management. Because of the tremendous hassle of billing insurance companies, many psychiatrists in private practice do not accept medical insurance. I attempted the medical insurance route but finally gave up in frustration and I, too, only saw self-pay patients. Most of the patients were high-functioning, and many were on their own spiritual journeys. Private practice ended up being a good balance for my work at the county mental health clinic.

During my first year back in Charleston, I got an email from my ex-boyfriend, Joel. After completing his fellowship in San Francisco, he had moved to Tampa, Florida, where he now worked doing general otolaryngology (ear, nose, and throat surgery) and facial plastics and reconstructive surgery. I was surprised to hear from him. Joel felt he had made a mistake by agreeing to break up with me and wondered if I was open to the possibility of dating again. I was stunned, as this was completely out of character for Joel. Humility was not his forte. Not only that, when he cut someone out of his life, he cut them out for good. I knew that it had taken a lot for him to contact me in this way. Although flattered, I wasn't sure if reconnecting romantically was a good idea. I remembered our old patterns all too clearly and feared they would resurface. I also knew that long distance dating would be challenging. I loved Charleston and had no interest in moving to Tampa.

We exchanged a few emails, then spoke on the phone. Having completed our stressful training years, we were now settled into our lives as practicing physicians. With that came maturity, confidence, and a steadiness that had been missing during the years of our training when we were together. On the phone, our old playfulness and shared laughter resurfaced, as did our quick banter and our ability to understand the medical world we each inhabited. Joel said he was coming to Charleston in a few weeks for an ENT conference, and I agreed to get together for dinner.

Joel and Mindy

We fell in love again, and for the time being set aside all practical considerations. We traveled back and forth between Charleston and Tampa on weekends, our attraction and romance reignited even more by the long distance relationship.

After about six months of this, Joel came to Charleston for a long weekend. He asked if we could visit our old stomping grounds at the VA "for old times' sake." I agreed, happy to indulge the romance. We drove over after supper, laughed about the potholes in the parking lot that still hadn't been fixed after all these years, and walked through the revolving door and into the lobby. Everything was just as we had left it, but it all felt different. We had changed. I felt stronger, taller, more solid. We walked through the nearly empty hallways and made our way to the quiet and dimly lit ENT clinic hall. All the office doors were closed and locked after what we knew had been a busy clinic day. We stood at the end of the hall, right where I had bumped into a younger version of Joel a lifetime ago on the first day of my ENT rotation when he had taken my breath away.

We stood silently, Joel's arm around me, each of us flooded with memories. Before I realized what was happening, Joel went down on one knee in front of me. My mind short-circuited. Joel pulled a ring out of his pocket, looked into my eyes, cleared his throat, and asked me to marry him.

Although I was enjoying the romance of our renewed relationship, I was well aware that its long distance nature kept the romance alive and prevented us from seeing any issues that would be exposed on a day-to-day basis. I was keenly aware that Joel and I didn't share what was without question the most important thing in my life—my spiritual journey. Joel was interested in spirituality and occasionally attended a satsang with me, but his interest was a mental curiosity, not the driving force in his life as it was in mine. Without this deeper connection, I didn't know how our relationship could be sustained. When I had shared this concern with him, he hadn't seen it as a challenge or obstacle, but rather thought it was good that we had different interests. This only amplified my feeling of disconnect. Different interests? My pull to Truth had nothing to do with an interest, a hobby, or something I was curious about. My whole being was pulled to Truth as if by a tremendous magnetic force. It was not just an aspect of my life—it was the most important thing in my life.

But even with this disconnect, I was well aware of a river carrying our relationship along, a force of its own that needed to be played out. I sensed that fighting this current with my rational mind wouldn't work, and I had to surrender to these karmic forces. Each of us had lessons to learn by being with the other. This all ran through my mind in a flash. I saw Joel's eyes flicker when I hesitated for a split second, his fear reflecting my doubt. In spite of having the sense that this might not be forever, I said yes.

We both loved Charleston and agreed that we would live there. Many of my closest spiritual friends lived in Charleston and I was not interested in moving away from my spiritual family. Joel assumed he could land a job with an ENT group in Charleston that he had trained with as a resident. Although he wasn't able to talk about the blow he felt when he did not get the job, I sensed his devastation. He insisted that we move to Tampa. I pleaded with him to continue to look for a job in Charleston. He was a very gifted, skilled, and brilliant surgeon—he had gotten one of the top scores in the nation on his ENT exam during residency—and I felt certain he could get a job with another group. He refused. I reluctantly agreed to move to Tampa, with the agreement that I would keep my house in Charleston in order to visit my close friends whenever I could.

I didn't realize how deeply nourishing the marsh, the plough mud, and the ocean in Charleston were to me until I moved to Tampa where the concrete strip malls and the city energy deadened my spirit. I made many efforts to find nourishment, to put down roots, and to connect with people on similar spiritual journeys. I went to meditation groups and churches and satsangs and retreats with Francis Lucille, a spiritual teacher with roots in the tradition of Advaita Vedanta, trying to build a support system for myself. Hard as I tried, I still felt alone and isolated.

While in Tampa, I worked at a VA clinic and volunteered with Hospice of the Florida Suncoast. I loved working with veterans and with hospice patients. Joel had bought a house on the water and I managed much of the extensive remodel on the house, which was in itself a full-time job. Workers were in and out of the house almost constantly. The lack of privacy and the constant loud banging of construction wore me down.

One day, after seeing several hospice patients in their homes, I was especially raw from experiencing their pain and their families' grief. I needed some time alone before Joel got home to process some of the heaviness I was feeling, but there were workers downstairs in the living room and upstairs in our bedroom, hammering, sawing, and calling out to each other. There was no escape. I sat in the stairwell and wept, my patients' grief pouring through me and opening up my own grief and sadness.

My longing for Truth had been awakened during my initial Vipassana meditation retreat years ago and had been further set afire by spiritual teachers during my residency years. Now I was experiencing an immense ache in my heart, as this longing for Truth had only grown with time. All the meditation, seeking out spiritual teachers and teachings, the retreats—all of the work on myself had been fueled by my longing for what was Real. This longing had only increased in intensity and now I was unable to bear it. I felt hopeless. It seemed what I was longing for and had been seeking was not available to me in an embodied, real way.

The workers left for the day, but the ache in my heart and the hopelessness stayed with me. I simply couldn't bear it any more. To live with such unrelenting longing was simply too much. As I stood in our bedroom overlooking the pool and the ocean beyond, I decided to give up hope of ever finding Truth. I resigned myself to living out this life, pretending that I believed in the apparent reality of the world, ignoring my deeper knowing and longing for Truth.

Giving up on Truth was utterly devastating to me. I counted the years I had left, not knowing how I could live out this life denying this deeper call. But all I had done in order to *get there*, all of the efforting to get to Truth, had burned itself out, and I had no energy left for the seeking.

For years after this "giving up," I kept all spiritual longing at bay. Submerging my life force brought with it a profound feeling of emptiness that pervaded my daily life. As time went on, Joel and I grew further apart and our relationship began to unravel. Every few months, I took refuge in a weekend trip to Charleston. As my sense of isolation in Tampa grew, these trips to Charleston became more frequent and I soaked up nourishment from my friends and the marsh and the ocean as best as I could. I didn't share my spiritual devastation with my friends, feeling that even they would not understand. Even so, being with them and being in Charleston lifted my ravaged spirit.

Eventually I was spending most of my time in Charleston. I saw the end of the marriage coming, but didn't actively consider ending it. We tend to recreate patterns in our relationships that allow old wounds to resurface. Because of my childhood fear of abandonment, I had never initiated a break-up; instead, I projected onto my partners my fear of being left. When my partner would end the relationship, I would feel the flood of childhood abandonment that had been waiting to surface. In spite of our distance and lack of connection, when Joel made the final decision to end the relationship, I was heartbroken. The pain and feelings of abandonment from the past rushed forward to blend with the grief I felt about the relationship ending.

As I drove back to Charleston from Tampa for the last time, the crushing grief of ending our two-year marriage felt like the tip of the iceberg. The shift to a new chapter in my life highlighted my spiritual devastation, the meaninglessness of living out an empty life no longer propelled by a longing for Truth. I cried silently, the tears falling down my cheeks and into my lap as I drove, until there were simply no more tears left to fall. My fingers tightened around the steering wheel as I braced myself for the rest of my life.

CHAPTER 18

You Can Have a Child

I can so clearly see that God has made love with you
And the whole universe is germinating inside your belly.
—Hafez

After the divorce, I continued to live in Charleston. I was back at work at the county mental health clinic and with patients in private practice. I wanted some extra support with the grief process after the divorce and my friend Cindy suggested her friend Kathy Donovan as a psychiatrist. Kathy saw patients in the cluttered and comfortable downstairs of her home in downtown Charleston. Her presence was loving and maternal, and I immediately sensed her healing kindness. She spoke more, shared more, and gave more advice than most therapists. We shared our love and gratitude for Ram Dass.

After telling her about my marriage and divorce, I found myself dropping into what felt like the core of my pain. I wept as I told Kathy that the likelihood was that I would never have a child. I was thirty-nine years old and had done the math. To meet someone you want to share your life with takes time, and to get to know each other well enough to know that you want to have a child together takes even more time. I allowed myself to feel my deep sadness—to grieve fully and not hold back. I was engulfed in my grief when I heard her quiet but crystal-clear words: "You can have a child if you want to."

What!? What the heck was she talking about? Didn't she know that you need a MAN to have a child? Intrigued in the midst of my grief, I stifled my sobs, blew my nose, and turned my eyes to her. "What do you mean?"

"Mindy, you can use a sperm donor." I felt a jolt go through my body and a wave of goose bumps from head to toe. There was no thinking about it, no analyzing the pros and cons, just a deep physical knowing that this was to be. It was as if Kathy was channeling the future. There was no "decision" to be made, just a follow-up on the practical details.

I didn't know anyone who had used a sperm donor. At that time, sperm donors were mostly used by couples who were dealing with infertility issues or by gay couples. It was only later that more single women began using sperm donors. I searched online and found the closest sperm donor bank, which was in North Carolina. I knew that not only genetics but also a parent's energy gets passed down to a child. What I wanted most for my child was to provide him or her with the capacity to love as deeply as possible. As I sifted through information about different donors, I looked for someone who had a heart of gold. I hardly glanced at descriptions of physical characteristics, such as height, weight, or color of hair and eyes. I searched for clues about their personalities, anything I could glean of the donor's capacity to love.

In my search, I discovered that there were basically two types of donors—"closed" donors, who choose to permanently remain anonymous, and "open" donors, who allow the sperm donor bank to identify them to the child, typically (according to sperm bank rules) when the child turns 18. I knew immediately that I wanted to use an open donor. I told Kathy, "Their motive is a part of their energy that gets transmitted to the child. I don't want to use a sperm donor that is jacking off for the money." There are many fewer open donors than closed donors, so this quickly narrowed down my choices. After reviewing over a hundred donors' profiles at the North Carolina sperm donor bank, I didn't find a single one that resonated. Discouraged, I did a little more research online and found that I didn't have to go physically to a sperm donor bank; sperm donor banks will deliver the sperm. This broadened out my search.

Shortly after beginning to review open donor profiles at the California Cryobank, I came across Donor #03768. His parents were from Russia and he was born in 1978. When asked to list his religion, he wrote "spiritual." I liked this. His father was Jewish and his mother Russian Orthodox. He majored in Dramatic Art and listed his profession as Actor. When asked about his math ability, he stated, "Math is not my favorite subject." I giggled as I read further, thinking, I have plenty of the left brain logic genes to pass on, and my child could certainly use a good dose of creativity for balance. He described his hobbies and talents as "Being one with nature, watching great films, traveling, and experiencing life." When asked to describe his personality, he said, "Multi-dimensional—deep, thoughtful, provocative, empathetic, honest and loving." He described his family as "truly supportive, kind and loving—they have taught me to be empathetic to people and to be sensitive to others' needs." In response to the question, "What makes you unique?" he replied, 'The fact that I am always myself, never pretending or trying to be someone else." Finally, he was asked, "If you could pass on a message to the recipients or their children, what would that message be?" His response: 'That I wish a safe and full loving birth to the family and to the child—know that I love you and when you are ready, contact me." BOOM.

That was it. I didn't look any further; there was no need. I knew without a doubt this was to be the biological father of my child. In an audio recording of an interview with him, he was again asked, "What would you say to this unborn child?" He said, "I would say that I love you, because I do. Contact me when you are ready." The resonance in his voice, the truth and depth of spirit that came through his voice, confirmed my choice.

I called the California Cryobank to order the sperm. I had somehow imagined that I would be sent a kit, perhaps a syringe loaded with sperm. I was told that the sperm is delivered to a fertility clinic. I was learning the process as I went along, taking the next practical step with each new piece of information. I found the Southeastern Fertility Center in Charleston. During my first appointment, I was given two options: Intra Uterine Insemination or In Vitro Fertilization. I was told that although IUI is less expensive (about $5,000 versus $20,000 for IVF), it is less likely to be successful and I was urged to use IVF due to my "advanced maternal age," which made pregnancy even less likely. If IUI was successful at all, it would almost certainly require multiple attempts, each of which takes time—time that with my advanced maternal age, I did not have. Well, I didn't have $20,000 sitting around, didn't want to have to go into debt, and as far as I knew, I didn't have an infertility issue in spite of my age. I opted for IUI.

I followed the clinic's instructions with the fertility medication and injection. My friend Christy drove me to my appointment for the insemination. I climbed up on the exam table, put my feet in the stirrups, and before I knew it the appointment was over. I was instructed to remain supine on the table for twenty minutes, but was told that after that I could walk about freely. No way in HECK was I going to walk around freely. I wanted to give those sperm all the time they needed to meet up with my eggs. I ran through the waiting room, right past the bewildered secretary waiting to check me out, shoved open the heavy glass door, ran straight to Christy's car, jumped in and lay down in the back seat, legs up in the air. Christy, who had been in the waiting room and had seen me sprint by, rushed out behind me and stood at the car door, peering at me through my legs. "Mindy! Are you okay? What happened?"

"Girl! Nothing is wrong! I've got to give these precious spermies all the opportunities they need to meet up with my eggie. Could you do me a huge favor and go back inside to that nice lady at the desk and give her my credit card?" I handed Christy my purse.

"Oh my, lordie, Mindy-loulou. What in the world are we going to do with you?" Our joy and laughter filled the car as we headed to my house. Once home, I immediately laid on the couch, again with legs up in air. Christy set me up with a table next to the couch, where she placed a pitcher of water, a glass, a few protein bars, and an apple. Before she left, I instructed her to gather all the pillows in the house and put them at the end of the couch, where I rested my now weary legs. For the next forty-eight hours, I read books and got up only to use the restroom. I giggled on the phone about what I was doing, but underneath the laughter was a resolute determination, a knowing, a forging ahead on this path.

A week later, my nipples began to tingle. I remembered experiencing this same phenomenon years ago when I was pregnant before my miscarriage. A pregnancy test confirmed what I already knew. I felt very much that the flow of a river was determining the course of my life and I was just along for the ride; my role was to bring this child into the world.

The nausea and utter exhaustion set in a week later. I was miserable. The nausea lasted 24/7 for all nine months of the pregnancy. I didn't know if I would make it through each patient at work, let alone each day, but I never called in sick—that ever-present sense of responsibility to my patients always won over my longing to stay in bed.

Near the end of my pregnancy, while driving on the interstate on my way to work, I ended up in the middle of a twelve-car pileup after a washing machine fell out of the first vehicle. A cautious driver, I never followed closely behind other cars. When I saw brake lights ahead of me, I slammed on the brakes, only to be slammed into from behind and shoved into the car in front of me. I stumbled out of my crushed car, too stunned at first to notice my gradually intensifying contractions.

I hadn't had a chance to give my story to police on the scene before I was taken to the hospital. When a police officer came to the hospital to get my story, I was told that I was the one being held responsible for the entire wreck! Struggling to control my panic and anger, my contractions began in earnest. I explained to the officer that I was hit from behind and pushed into the car in front of me. He then called the driver that had been behind me, who confirmed this, and I was absolved from being held at fault for the accident.

Kathy, Amita, Cindy, Ed, and Christy were there when I gave birth a few days after the car accident. As I pushed with all of my might, Saachi's heart rate was slowing down. My OB gave me one more chance to push before I would need to have a C-section. I gave it all I had and out she came. Saachi's skin was blue, but the love and wonder I experienced overrode my concern. I was allowed to hold her briefly before she was whisked off to an oxygen tent. Two days later, she was brought into my room, but she turned blue while I was nursing her and was rushed again to the oxygen tent. Soon after this though, she was able to breathe on her own without supplemental oxygen.

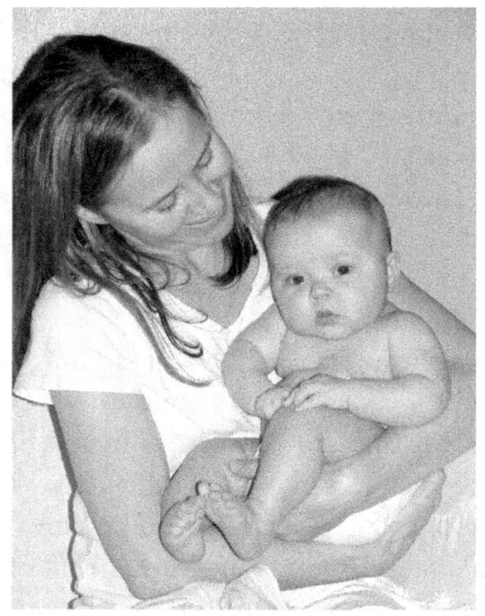

Mindy and Saachi, absorbed in the space of love

From the time Saachi was born, I sensed that she was vibrating at a frequency that I did not have full access to and that she was residing in a realm deeper, broader, and more profound than the world of my normal waking consciousness. The very space and energy that she inhabited permeated my being, and early in her life remained in the foreground of my consciousness. I sensed what felt like a paradox about Saachi's consciousness: she was completely merged with her environment and had no sense of being separate from anything or anyone around her, yet at the same time she was residing in another place completely, a realm of exquisite sensitivity of heart, a realm of pure love. I was submerged in this love.

Although it often seemed like Saachi wasn't present in this realm, at other times she was exquisitely sensitive to her environment. Every time I took her to the grocery store, or any public place, she screamed out in pain. At the time I didn't know if the pain was caused by the lights, sounds, or the energy of others around us, or all of the sensory stimulation combined. I knew though that it was a visceral pain and that she was absorbing input that most of us weren't conscious of. As a single mom, and in the era before grocery delivery, I had no choice but to take her with me to the grocery store. I tensed up before we went in, knowing that she would be in terrible pain and that her piercing cries would cut through all of us in the store. Often when I took her to a gathering of friends, she would cry out in pain. After several such attempts, I took to keeping her home as much as possible.

She was a mystery. Saachi stared down at the floor or stared through the sliding glass doors of our house out at the expansive marsh as if mesmerized, completely lost in what she was gazing at, or as if she wasn't here at all, as if she was in another realm altogether. Without realizing it at the time, I was constantly pulling her into this world, both energetically and with my interactions with her. I could literally feel my energy pulling her energy in, grounding her in the world. It wasn't something I did consciously or on purpose, it just happened. A force in me pulled her "here."

I also made great efforts to make eye contact with her, to do silly things to make her giggle, to make her smile. Saying her name loudly, laughing, kissing her cheek, tickling her toes, even jumping up and down in front of her often failed to bring her out of her deep reverie. She didn't notice. If she was staring down or staring out the window, I would sit right in front of her and smile or say her name. She would continue staring right through me as if I weren't there. I made efforts throughout the day to connect with her . . . and still, no response.

Although I knew this was unusual, I somehow wasn't concerned. The love that moved into our home with Saachi's spirit filled my awareness. During those first sixteen months, I was enveloped in the love that was her very spirit. Everything else paled in comparison, and any potential concerns were swallowed up by the love.

Because her system was so activated, Saachi hardly slept the first few years of her life. From the time she was born, her body was in constant motion. Her limbs continuously moved and jerked about haphazardly and without purpose. During her first nine months, she also suffered from severe colic, frequently crying out in pain throughout the day and night. It was as if her nervous system lacked the ability to filter out or dampen any sensory input—she absorbed everything in her environment and lacked the ability to settle down naturally after it was activated. When her consciousness was in the world and not in another realm, even the slightest sound would make her whole body jump. Years later when we went to visit a farm, one of the horseback riding instructors commented on how Saachi's body jumped with every noise, with every horse neigh, with every bird chirp. "It's as if she has PTSD," she said. I was so used to Saachi's hyperstartle reflex that I hadn't realized the extent of it until this lady's comment.

Exhausted and desperate for her to fall asleep, every day and night I spent hours rocking her as she tossed about in my arms, moving her limbs and body sporadically and randomly. When she finally fell asleep in my arms, I stood up in ultra-slow motion, walked slowly the few feet to her crib, lowered her down into the crib with nearly imperceptible movements, only to have her awaken and cry as I put her down. I would sigh in frustration and exhaustion and start the process all over again.

I read several books on techniques to help your child sleep, but none of them were effective with Saachi. The *Cry It Out* or *Extinction* sleep method, which is based on teaching falling asleep as a skill a child needs to learn, was traumatic for both of us. Determined to stick it out as per instructions, I listened for hours to her desperate cries from her crib, knowing that she had no way of understanding that she had not been abandoned. I would be in tears myself in my bedroom. Each night for a week, I called Amita in tears, my heart breaking for my daughter but not wanting to pick her up in my desperation to "teach her the skill" of sleeping. But Saachi's cries only got worse and longer over time, her hoarse weeping haunting my heart late into each night. After a week, something snapped in me. I marched into her room, scooped up her frail, weak body, and held her close. I marched back into my room, grabbed the book from my bedside table as I held her, slid my window open, and threw the book into the front yard. I didn't care if neither of us ever slept again, I didn't want anything else to do with this technique. My heart couldn't bear it.

Eventually, though, Saachi would fall asleep late at night or in the early morning hours and I would move into action, pushing through my exhaustion to cook, prep for any babysitter training I needed to do before I went to work, respond to emails, and take care of household chores. I breast fed Saachi until she was almost two years old, and also pumped milk each night so she would have a supply when I worked. Early on I had noticed that Saachi never let me know if she was hungry. She cried out in pain from the colic and cried when her sensory system was overloaded, but never because she was hungry. I made sure to breast feed her regularly, acutely aware that if I forgot, she could become dehydrated or hypoglycemic. Later, I set alarms throughout the day to remind me to make sure she drank water, her cup of water ever-present on our dining table as a reminder (it still is).

Later, when she began to eat food, I had to verbally tell her to take each bite of food and each sip of water, and often I had to prompt her many times for each bite. She didn't experience any sensation of hunger or thirst; there was nothing internal prompting her to eat or drink and her body depended on my external prompts for the nourishment it needed. She also had oral and fine motor skill delays. Sustaining attention was a challenge for her, so each meal took several hours. We spent six hours a day at the table, eating. Saachi has always been a very early riser, but back then I made sure we were up by 4 a.m. to allow time for eating and getting dressed before I left for work. I was exhausted with the process, exhausted with her dependence on me to make sure her body had the food and water it needed, and several times over the years, in exhaustion and frustration, I yelled at her, saying I just couldn't do it any more, that she would have to start taking bites on her own. This, of course, never accomplished anything.

Her complete inability to sense when her body was hungry or thirsty persisted for years. I remember clearly the first time she ever said, "Mommy, I'm hungry!" She was ten years old. I was standing in the kitchen, putting a few bags of frozen kale in our giant pressure cooker, my back to her. I couldn't believe my ears. I whipped around, a bag of chopped kale spilling onto the floor, and looked at her incredulously. "Are you SERIOUS, Saachi?" Startled by my abruptness, Saachi stared at me, eyes wide as saucers. I burst into laughter and began dancing around the house, Saachi trailing behind me, laughing and dancing with me, not understanding the cause for celebration. But before she began to be aware of hunger and thirst, the burden I carried every day to make sure that she drank fluids and ate food on a regular basis, the responsibility I carried for keeping her body alive and well without any feedback or input from her, weighed on me heavily.

During the first year, I was not only well aware of her sensitivity to sensory input whenever we went to a store or a public place because of her piercing cries, but also at home her entire body would startle and she would cry out in pain if she heard a sudden sound or loud noise. I eventually got several pairs of sound-blocking headphones and kept them in every room, in the car, and in my purse, easily available in the event of a siren, a dog barking, or thunder. The blender and the vacuum cleaner also caused tremendous pain, and whenever I could predict loud sounds like these, I placed the bright pink headphones over her ears. To this day she runs into her room, closes the door, and puts on her headphones when she sees me pull out the blender. If we are on a walk and she sees a lawn mower, even one that is not being used, she turns around and quickly walks the other way.

During Saachi's first year of life, I kept a stack of books on my bedside table—all of them spiritual books except for one, *What to Expect the First Year*. Occasionally, before I fell off to sleep, I would dutifully open the book and read a paragraph or two. From these readings, I knew that she was consistently not reaching milestones, but I wasn't worried. At six months, I made a mental note to mention to Saachi's pediatrician at her next well visit that she wasn't yet holding objects or passing them back and forth between hands, that she wasn't sitting or standing without support yet. The pediatrician was not concerned and said that all children develop at their own pace. At nine months, she was sitting with support but wasn't yet responding to her name, or babbling, or pointing, or playing peek-a-boo, or looking for things that I hid, or watching something fall, or picking up an object between her index finger and thumb. When I tried to hand her an object, she didn't reach for it and didn't understand that I was handing her something. My hand would remain suspended in front of her, her eyes not even registering the object. Still, somehow, the pediatrician and I weren't concerned. We joked about how Saachi had a mind of her own.

By twelve months, Saachi was falling further behind and I realized there was a true delay, but was only mildly concerned. When I told Saachi's pediatrician at her fifteen-month well visit that Saachi didn't understand pointing—she didn't look when I pointed and certainly didn't point herself—the pediatrician looked up sharply. Her eyes betrayed the casual tone of her voice. "Mindy, I really think she's fine, but why don't we be thorough and get a BabyNet evaluation." BabyNet is South Carolina's early intervention system for infants and toddlers with developmental delays or conditions associated with developmental delays. I scheduled the appointment and dove back in to my busy life, an unsettling feeling beginning to nag at me.

At her BabyNet appointment the next month, I was surprised and relieved that Saachi barely met criteria for a further diagnostic evaluation. We were referred to a developmental pediatrician at the Medical University of South Carolina, Jane Charles, MD. When I called to schedule her appointment, I was told that Dr. Charles' next available appointment was in nine months, and that no other doctors could complete the evaluation. Discouraged, I called my friend Cindy and shared this news with her. She told me that Dr. Charles happened to be her neighbor and friend. Saachi was scheduled to see Dr. Charles a few weeks later.

CHAPTER 19

Diagnosis: Autism

Although people with autism look like other people
physically, we are in fact very different in many ways.
We are more like travelers from the distant, distant past.
And if, by our being here, we could help the people
of the world remember what truly matters for the
Earth, that would give us a quiet pleasure.

—Naoki Higashida

During the weeks before her appointment, I became more aware of Saachi's delays, and more concerned. One day while Saachi was napping, I stood in front of our washer and dryer and looked through the section of childhood disorders in my DSM-IV (the Diagnostic and Statistical Manual of Mental Disorders). As a general adult psychiatrist, I was very familiar with adult psychiatric disorders, but not nearly as much with child psychiatry. When I got to the Autism section, I felt the blood drain from my head and extremities as the whole world shifted under my feet. I went through each symptom. Check. Check. Check. Check. Unsure of how I could carry on with all of my daily responsibilities, I intentionally shoved what had just happened as far back as I could. I recognized that I was in denial, but didn't know how else to continue to function.

April 30, 2010. After several hours of testing with Dr. Charles and the psychologist, Laura Carpenter, PhD, they both came in and sat down at the child-sized table with me. When they told me the diagnosis of autism, I initially felt numb, as if they were talking to me through an impenetrable ocean of water, their words unable to reach me. Going through the motions, I asked about prognosis and they told me it is different for each child—a child may be diagnosed initially as severe, but may lose most symptoms over time and be highly functional later on, or vice versa. They told me that early intervention was crucial, and suggested that I begin a type of therapy called Applied Behavioral Analysis right away, along with speech therapy, occupational therapy, and physical therapy. Dr. Charles and Dr. Carpenter took their time with me, answered all my questions, and held my hand when my voice shook and I fought back tears. As I reflect back on that day, I'm filled with gratitude for their presence and compassion. Their kindness helped me come to terms with Saachi's diagnosis.

When the appointment was over, I stood up, shell-shocked and overwhelmed with information. I strapped Saachi in her stroller and walked out into a completely different world.

Before her diagnosis, my own consciousness had been engulfed by hers—by the expansion, the sensitivity, the love that her spirit emanated. The diagnosis of autism triggered a tremendous fear in me and yanked my consciousness out of that expanded state. The root of the fear was for her survival—my fear that Saachi might not be able to function independently in the world as an adult, that she might not have anyone to care for her when I was gone. Although I was still aware of the depth of her spirit, this awareness moved into the background and my fears about her survival and ability to function in the world moved into the foreground. This fear fueled my life over the next several years. I went into overdrive, determined to provide her with every opportunity to function independently and "normally" as an adult, hoping that she would be one of the few whose autism would disappear.

The night after her diagnosis, after putting Saachi to bed and completing household chores, I sat down at my computer and typed "autism treatments" into my browser search bar. I was overwhelmed by all the information that came up. Researching treatment options for autism soon became a nightly ritual. Friends began sending me information about treatments they had come across and I researched those, or I scoured the internet for other treatment options. I was beyond overwhelmed by all the treatments available, but feared that I would miss an effective one. I couldn't bear the thought that I could miss something that might be helpful for Saachi and give her the best chance possible for independence. I am thorough by nature and this trait only magnified the enormity of educating myself about the seemingly infinite autism treatments out there. Finally, a bit of common sense intervened and I narrowed the scope of my research to only those treatments that I knew without a doubt would not harm Saachi in any way and that I could pay for without financially jeopardizing our present and future security.

Although I knew many treatments did not have research to back them—my scientifically-trained mind would much have preferred all options to be backed by double-blind, placebo-controlled studies—I also knew that these studies take time and that there might be many effective treatments available that were not yet backed by research. Always aware of the crucial impact of early intervention—aware of the clock ticking for Saachi—I was determined to do all that I could. Even as I navigated the overwhelming world of therapeutic interventions, I reached out for help.

My dear friends,

I am writing to share with you some difficult news. My precious Saachi has been diagnosed with autism. I have known for some time, but we finally got the formal diagnosis 1 month ago. Needless to say, there has been much deep grief and heartbreak, and in the midst of all that, quite a bit of chaos while trying to learn all I can about it, trying to get services and therapy in place (oh, the red tape!), many appointments as we are also making sure there is nothing else medical going on, weekly speech therapy, occupational therapy, and physical therapy, a million phone calls and even more paperwork—and all this on top of work, caring for Saachi, and getting the basics of life done. Overwhelmed is quite an understatement!

I first noticed Saachi was developmentally delayed when she was about nine months old. She does have global delays with motor skills, speech, and communication. She also has some of the classic symptoms of autism, including not respond-ing to her name, not understanding pointing, not being able to imitate or communicate with gestures/speech, lack of what they call "joint attention," getting mesmerized by patterns, and not a lot of eye contact.

And here is what is much more true than her symptoms: her precious, sweet spirit shines through loud and clear. Whatever is happening with her body and mind doesn't touch that one bit. Her sweetness permeates our home, and my heart, and everyone that comes in contact with her. Although I am playing the role of being her mother, she is without a doubt my Teacher on so many levels. She is also my own Heart. Saachi is the greatest gift in my life, even more so with this diagnosis. This is how I feel: I am prostrate at her feet, with a love, devotion, and gratitude so deep it cannot be spoken.

From this love is born within me a profound strength and courage. I have said several times that I will move a mountain for her if I need to—and I mean this literally. There is no way to predict prognosis with autism, and as Byron Katie [a spiritual teacher] would say, it is not my business. My business is pro-viding her with what I hope is best for her. My business is also allowing this journey with Saachi to continue to open my heart.

I want to ask for your help. I know without a doubt that visualization and prayer are very powerful, and I feel clear that this is one very important aspect of Saachi's "treatment." I

*Saachi and I both send you our love. In the midst of the grief
and exhaustion is also a deep stirring of my soul, in anticipation
of where this journey will take us. I cannot begin to imagine! We
will keep you posted.*

Love,

Mindy and Saachibean

• • •

Saachi's diagnosis of autism qualified her for Medicaid in South Carolina under TEFRA. Although I also had her on my private insurance family plan, which was considered her primary insurance, Medicaid covered the many co-insurance and co-pay fees associated with what became her many therapies. I was working part-time, three days a week, in order to be more available for Saachi and to navigate the full-time job of juggling Saachi's therapists and babysitters. I relied on the Medicaid back-up to cover some of our medical expenses.

Saachi had been diagnosed with autism several months prior to Governor Nikki Haley's announcement that there would be significant cutbacks to Medicaid funding. I first heard about the Medicaid cutbacks through a local autism parent email group I had joined. Governor Haley's promise that medically-necessary treatments and therapies would not be cut was of little comfort to parents like me, who knew that the therapies our children received were crucial for their ability to function as independently as possible in the future. There was a flurry of fear throughout the autism and special needs community in South Carolina. We had many questions, and few answers. What is defined as "medically necessary?" Who will determine what is medically necessary for my child? Will my child's services be cut back or cut off, and if so, how do I fight this?

I felt the collective clench of fear and recognized from the patients I worked with at the county mental health clinic that many parents were not equipped, either financially, emotionally, intellectually, or due to circumstances, to either understand the impact of cutbacks on their children's therapies or to fight this battle. Soon I began to hear stories about their children's therapies being reduced or terminated. I heard their feelings of helplessness and anger about their inability to ensure their children got the care they needed. I knew it was only a matter of time before Saachi was similarly affected.

Sure enough, one cold winter day I opened up the letter that told me that Saachi's speech therapy, occupational therapy, and physical therapy were all being reduced to once a week. I had worked hard to get insurance approval for Saachi to have ST, OT, and PT twice a week, instead of the standard once weekly. I wanted to provide her with as much support as possible, especially during those formative years. Her doctors and therapists had written letters supporting the medical benefit of the higher frequency of therapies for Saachi, and after many phone calls and letters of my own, ultimately my request had been approved by her insurance.

I didn't sleep that night, fear clutching at my chest as I lay in bed, a sense of utter helplessness in the face of my worst fear. I was well aware of how vital these early years were in terms of brain development. Children's brains are the most malleable and absorbent during their first several years and what is learned during this crucial period in many ways lays the foundation for skills that are developed later in life. For me, this reduction in therapies could mean the difference between Saachi becoming independent or needing care as an adult— care that at some point I would no longer be able to provide.

By morning, my terror and helplessness had shifted to determination and anger. The Mama Bear in me awakened. I knew that depriving Saachi and other children of therapies that would support them in learning how to function in this world was wrong. I knew that these children were unable to advocate for themselves, as were many parents. When Saachi's early interventionist arrived that day, I shared with her my fears and my anger about this injustice that would affect the long-term future of so many children. I asked if I had any recourse and she told me that I could appeal the Medicaid decision through Medicaid court, although it could be a costly and time-consuming process.

I debated whether or not to pursue this for several days, knowing that the legal process would consume time and energy that I did not have to spare, and that the process would also take me away from what I felt was crucial time with Saachi. By nature I was not combative or litigious and felt an aversion to any legal process. An internal battle raged between the force of anger and determination to stand up for my daughter and other children and my practical daily life, which did not have room for anything extra, especially a legal battle. As I sat with this internal conflict, I took other steps. I called Governor Haley's office and all of the South Carolina legislators' offices. I sent emails out asking all of my friends to do the same. Saachi's developmental pediatrician and her general pediatrician wrote letters stating that the therapies she had been receiving were medically necessary. I wrote my own letter outlining Saachi's detailed progress with her previous therapies and her slowed progress since the therapies had been cut back. I sent all of these letters to Medicaid.

The phone calls to legislators offices were fruitless. When I received an impersonal form letter from Medicaid in response to my letter and documents, stating that my child's case had been reviewed but she did not qualify for any more services, I decided to move forward with Medicaid court. I just couldn't stomach others who did not know my daughter, who did not know all the children in the state who were being denied services, making decisions that would impact our children's ability to function in the world. I called Protection and Advocacy (P&A) for People with Disabilities, Inc. and presented Saachi's case. I was told that they were getting hundreds of phone calls and wouldn't be able to promise anything as they couldn't represent everyone, but I was asked to provide documents for their review. I gathered doctor's letters, therapists' notes, communications with Medicaid, my own notes and faxed them over. A few days later, I got a call from Mr. Oliver, an attorney who worked for P&A, saying that they would take Saachi's case.

Mr. Oliver and I had many phone conversations over the next few months. He was kind, awkward, young and inexperienced, but attentive to details. When I arrived at the Medicaid court building on our appointed court day, I met him in person for the first time. He was pale, tall and thin, a mop of disheveled brown wavy hair covering his forehead. His voice was tight as he spoke and I sensed his anxiety. As we stood outside the building, I noticed a slight hand tremor as he reviewed a few documents with me. Somehow, though, as we walked towards the conference room where the court session was to take place, a sense of calm descended over me. I had a knowing that, regardless of the outcome, we were speaking up not only for Saachi, but also against an injustice that was harming many others. I felt a tremendous force of support behind and around us.

I expected a formal courtroom and was surprised when Mr. Oliver opened the door to a conference room. Across the large conference table that filled the room sat two men. One of the men looked up dismissively and said a terse "Good Morning," then turned to the other man and pointedly began to speak with him about the weather, clearly excluding us from the conversation. Tension filled the room as we sat down. Mr. Oliver opened his folder on the table and tilted his head down, studying his notes. I sat quietly, uncomfortable with the tension, stealing glances at the two men across the table. One was clearly an attorney. He was polished and self-assured, used to being in charge. Although not large in stature, his presence demanded a lot of space in the room. Woven into his thick Southern accent was a tone of arrogant dismissiveness. The other man sat directly across from me. Although he pretended confidence, chuckling at times with the attorney, I sensed his underlying anxiety. He sat slumped slightly forward in his chair, his navy blue suit draped over his thin shoulders, his wide red tie crooked across his chest and abdomen, revealing a line of buttons down his thin, well-worn shirt.

I shifted in my chair, aware of the harsh fluorescent light overhead, the repetitive *sh-clunk, sh-clunk* from a photocopying machine in a nearby room. The faint scent of perfume hung in the room. My neck tightened and I was breathing shallowly, tensing up against the onset of a headache.

After some time, a woman entered the room. As she sat down at the head of the table she introduced herself as Judge Brown and asked each of us to introduce ourselves, looking to me first. "I'm Melinda Edwards, the mother of Saachi Edwards. Your honor, I wish Saachi could be here today, so you could all meet her in person. She is truly beautiful and precious—and of course I am not biased in any way as her mother." I smiled as I pulled out several photos of Saachi, each in a simple clear acrylic frame. "May I put a few photos of her on the table, so that we all have a sense of who this is about today?" Judge Brown smiled and nodded. I placed a photo of Saachi's beaming face in front of each person—and felt the ice in the room begin to melt as I did so. In this way, Saachi's spirit joined us in the room and became the focal point for our court session.

After Mr. Oliver and the opposing attorney introduced themselves, the man across from me spoke. "My name is Dr. Alexander. I work with Medicaid in a variety of roles, including reviewing cases for approval of services." Judge Brown then asked Mr. Oliver to present his opening arguments.

Mr. Oliver's voice trembled as he made our case, often going off on tangents, sometimes not completing an argument. When he finished, I was given the opportunity to speak and summarized as best as I could that Saachi had made significant progress in speech, fine motor skills, and gross motor skills when she had been engaging in OT, ST and PT twice weekly, but that this progress had slowed since the frequency had been reduced to once a week. I pointed out that her own physicians, who knew her much better than a physician who had never met her, had written notes of medical necessity for her therapies. I also shared that some of my patients at the county mental health clinic who were not able to advocate for their children had disclosed to me that their children were no longer getting services they needed. I explained that often the parents of children with special needs themselves have significant needs and are unable to advocate for their children, and although this specific case was about Saachi, I hoped to also speak up for those who were unable to do so.

Next, the opposing attorney began his arguments. To my surprise, he had looked at each date Saachi had received therapies. She had missed a total of two weeks of therapies during the six months prior to the cutbacks. He pointed out that she had not regressed during those two weeks in spite of having no therapies. I was stunned at this argument, and at the time did not remember her having missed therapies, but later remembered that she had been very sick one of those weeks, and the other week two of her therapists had been on vacation. I, of course, knew that progress is measured over a period of weeks and months, not days, but was so stunned I wasn't able to put this into words at the time. Mr. Oliver was also unprepared for this argument and remained silent, distractedly looking over his notes.

Dr. Alexander reiterated Saachi's lack of regression during the two weeks she did not have therapies. He was not as polished as the Medicaid attorney and began to ramble a bit. He was clearly intelligent, but this intelligence was accompanied by a social awkwardness—a combination familiar to me, as many of the medical students and residents I had trained with shared this combination of brilliant minds and difficulty connecting socially with others. Dr. Alexander blurted out that he didn't actually remember reviewing Saachi's case, although he knew he must have because his signature was on the review.

The Medicaid attorney cleared his throat quietly, leaned forward in his chair, and put his hands together on the conference table, intertwining his fingers. Dr. Alexander, seemingly oblivious to the attorney's non-verbal cues, pushed forward with some intensity and said, "I had hundreds of cases I was reviewing, and was in the office all that weekend trying to get through them."

His head bent down briefly as his voice cracked almost imperceptibly, displaying what was left of his thin, graying hair, swept across the top of his head, scalp peeking through in pale lines between wisps of hair. I felt my eyes soften and the hard veil of my ideas about him, my mind's projection onto him, dissolve; the harshness of my fear, my self-righteousness, my judgment gave way to a receptivity, an openness to this human being sitting across from me. As my fear and anger dissipated, they no longer colored my perception of the world around me. I found myself wondering about this man's life, the hardships he had endured, his childhood. As he spoke, I studied his face, the lines on his forehead, the two sharp vertical lines between his eyebrows, describing better than any words the decades of stress, of anxiety, of pressure, of responsibility this man had endured. My heart went out to him.

I knew the tremendous pressures that we often face as physicians—the stress of the nearly impossible work load, the burden of decisions that can have tremendous impact on patients' lives, the burden of the tremendous responsibility we feel and our genuine desire to do what is best for our patients, even as we feel compromised by external structures that limit what we can do. I knew first-hand the fear we all experience, the fear that in spite of our best intentions, in spite of being as thorough as we are able to be, that we will make a mistake and that our mistake will harm a patient. I knew the fear of being sued by a patient, the fear that I might someday have to defend myself in court, the fear that I might have to defend a decision I made about a patient that perhaps I didn't even remember making. I felt for this man, imagining the position he was in, making decisions as rapidly as he could about patients he had never met—and now being asked to defend his decision about a patient he didn't remember. I felt the tragedy of the whole situation. As he spoke, he glanced up at me, and our eyes locked for a brief moment—human to human, a felt understanding and compassion with and for each other.

In a flash, I saw that each of us in the room had our own role to play in this situation. In life, no role is better or worse, right or wrong—we each play out our role, doing the best we can within our circumstances in this mysterious dance of life. This place of connection, of love, was much bigger than and more *real* than the content of the experience; it was more real than my role as Saachi's advocate. And yet it was my own fear, anger, and drive to advocate for her that had opened the door for this deeper realization, this deeper opening. I experienced directly how my life experiences as a separate individual serve as opportunities, doorways through which I can go back home, back to love, back to who I Am.

After court, we stood up and shook hands. I thanked him for coming to court and for his efforts to support our children within the constraints of a system that made it difficult to do so. He seemed relaxed, transformed, as if speaking out about the position he had been put in relieved him of some of the guilt and stress he had been experiencing. He thanked me for stepping forward with Saachi's situation and for allowing him to know her through me.

We won the case.

But this experience had a much greater impact on my life than the outcome of the case. I had experienced my own fear about Saachi's future transform and harden into determination and anger, into a hardening of judgment and ideas about the opposition—initially about politicians and the Medicaid entity, and then about the Medicaid attorney and physician. I saw how my fear not only fueled the actions I took but also fueled my own projection onto what and who I saw as "them," how I allowed this energy to harden into ideas about me being right and them being wrong.

Ram Dass used to speak about the photos on his *puja* (altar). He put up photos of all the teachers he loved and of his guru, Neem Karoli Baba. At one point he decided to add photos of those he couldn't yet love. He jokingly described how he greeted all the photos before meditating each day. He would look at Maharajji, feel his heart open wide, smile and say "Good morning, Maharajji." Similarly, he would greet Ramana Maharshi and other teachers, feeling a great sense of expansion and love with each one. Then he would get to the last picture. He would frown and say, through clenched teeth, "Good morning, President Reagan." Ram Dass had a spacious sense of humor about working on himself in order to be able to love everyone, as Maharajji had instructed him to do.

Through some form of grace, my judgment dissolved when my heart opened to the physician who had made the decision to cut back on Saachi's therapies. Through grace, I was brought into a place of love, a recognition of our common humanity.

CHAPTER 20

ABA, RDI, OT, ST, PT . . .

There is a voice that doesn't have words. Listen.
—Rumi

I knew Saachi's spirit was exquisitely sensitive, but I didn't yet understand that her symptoms were a manifestation of the contrast between her own vibration and the collective vibration of the world. My focus was to make every effort to rid her of her symptoms so that she would be able to function and hopefully thrive in the world. The medical disease paradigm of autism further fostered and supported my misguided focus on getting rid of her symptoms, on making her more "normal."

When Saachi was first diagnosed, her medical team recommended immediately beginning Applied Behavioral Analysis (ABA) therapy, the standard treatment of choice for autism. Dr. Ole Ivar Lovaas, a UCLA psychologist who studied behavior modification in children with autism in the 1960s to 1980s, was the father of ABA. He had studied under Sidney Bijou, a behaviorist who was a student of B. F. Skinner. When Saachi was diagnosed, ABA was the only research-backed therapy at that time, and was also the only therapy covered by health insurance. In the world of medicine, ABA remains what is considered the gold standard of treatment for autism. This therapy is used to shape and change specific behaviors, often using rewards such as praise, preferred activities, or food to create or increase behaviors considered "desirable" or "normal," and using negative consequences to suppress "undesirable" behaviors.

I was told to begin forty hours of ABA therapy each week, as this was the standard of care and the amount of therapy that had been shown by research to be effective. This alone was enough to trigger my fear. I was desperate to do everything that could be of help to Saachi, and knowing that ABA was backed by research spoke to my left-brain, scientific self. But because of Saachi's developmental delays, on my days off from work I was also trying to squeeze in occupational therapy, speech therapy, and physical therapy, each twice weekly, as well as weekly appointments with our early interventionist, appointments with Saachi's general pediatrician and developmental pediatrician, and appointments with a case manager. There simply wasn't enough time in the day to do it all along with Saachi's naps, which we both desperately needed—her for sleep and me to get things done. With a great deal of distress, I ultimately resorted to scheduling just twenty hours of ABA each week, as that was all I could manage.

ABA sessions made me cringe and went completely against my grain. The focus was solely on Saachi's behavior without regard to her emotions or her spirit, and the techniques were dry and cold. Initially, the ABA therapist created a comprehensive list of detailed behaviors we wanted to work on. Graphs and charts for each behavior were placed in formidable three-ring notebooks. Our ABA line therapist asked Saachi to repetitively perform different behaviors, clicking a counter she held in her hand with each response or stopping to record the response on paper. The lack of human warmth, the dry calculation, the focus on behavior and not spirit, and the time spent recording and taking notes instead of just being with Saachi and engaging with her, made my stomach turn, as did the interruption of engagement with Saachi to take notes. I did see progress in some areas, but wondered if the same progress could be made while engaging with Saachi at a heart level.

I soon began to research other techniques. I resonated with Floortime, a relationship-based technique created by Stanley Greenspan that follows the child's lead, meeting the child where they are and building on their strengths through creating a warm, interactive relationship. Although I intuitively knew that establishing this type of deep connection was crucial, my hesitation with Floortime was that it might not provide enough structure to help Saachi learn the skills she would need to function in the world.

After researching another technique—Relationship Development Intervention (RDI)—I felt it would be a good fit for us. RDI was developed by Steven Gutstein and is focused on cultivating the building blocks of social connection, including forming emotional bonds and sharing experiences with others. The technique builds on a child's internal motivation and not the external rewards used by ABA. In supporting and amplifying internal and emotional motivation, the skills become spontaneous, natural and generalizable, without being dependent on an external reinforcer.

I had been told that many children who are engaged in ABA become somewhat robotic in their speech and behavior, often without internal motivation; in essence, their interactions often aren't "real" or spontaneous since they perform these behaviors in order to get a reward. I knew that I did not want this for Saachi. I wanted her to be able to love and be loved, and felt that the ability to genuinely connect with other humans was more important than any other skill she might learn.

With RDI, parents and caregivers are trained by an RDI therapist to be the child's primary therapist. It made sense to me that as Saachi's primary person, I would be able to have the greatest impact in her life. In my research I found that there was only one RDI therapist in South Carolina, who happened to be in Charleston and happened also to be an occupational therapist. When I first spoke with Becky on the phone, I found myself relaxing into her warmth and strength, at last feeling that I could trust and depend on someone else to guide me in this journey with my daughter and that I no longer had to carry the burden of all the decisions about interventions on my own.

Becky began engaging in occupational therapy with Saachi. During her sessions, she utilized RDI techniques, teaching and demonstrating for me the tools I was to use and focus on during the upcoming week. She gave me specific assignments, which always involved planning real-life activities with Saachi in a way that supported social and emotional connection. Becky taught me to do body brushing as a tool to support sensory integration. She also taught me to do reflex therapy with Saachi—a ritual of tapping different muscles throughout the body as a means of integrating primitive reflexes. I did the body brushing with Saachi several times each day and the reflex therapy morning and night without fail.

I loved that the primary focus of RDI was genuine social connection and sharing joy, even as we worked on learning skills. I also loved that RDI was incorporated into daily life. Because the tools I was learning were woven into the fabric of our daily activities, therapy wasn't limited to sessions with therapists—Saachi was connecting and learning throughout the day.

Saachi seemed to come from another realm entirely, one completely unfamiliar with human ways—unfamiliar with how to function in a human body or how to relate to other humans. Basic human skills did not come intuitively or easily to her. Every skill had to be taught to Saachi intentionally, and with great effort. Skills that come naturally to neurotypical children were broken down into steps, practiced many times, and took a long time to learn. Teaching her to look at an object that a finger is pointing to involved initially tapping an object repeatedly with the pointed finger or blowing a whistle near the object while pointing to get her attention. When she learned to look with these prompts, I began pointing at an object with my finger a few inches from the object instead of directly on the object, and over time was able to move my pointed finger further and further away from the object. This skill alone took hundreds of practices over the course of more than a year, even as she was learning many other basic skills.

Reciprocal play didn't come naturally to Saachi; she did not know how or even understand the concept of playing together. For learning reciprocal play, we used a tool that Saachi loved and we knew she would be interested in—a ball—and began with learning to roll a ball back and forth. We sat on the floor facing each other, feet touching in a V. I'd roll the ball to her. Initially she didn't even notice the ball; she was lost in her own world, seemingly unaware of her surroundings. After some time, with efforts on my part to bring her attention back into the world, she began to pick up the ball and play with it herself. Occasionally, the ball accidentally rolled back to me and, when it did, I laughed and praised her enthusiastically. After several weeks, she began rolling the ball—not to me, but within the boundaries of our legs. A few months later, she was intentionally rolling the ball towards me in return, giggling and laughing with me. We then sat further apart and began the same process again with the added variable of physical distance. Eventually, we practiced this skill outside and in other environments, much further apart, and later practiced other types of reciprocal play.

Similarly, Saachi had no understanding of handing someone an object or of reaching for and receiving an object that was being handed to her. If I tried to hand her an object, she simply sat there, barely noticing my hand was in front of her, not understanding that I was trying to give her something. We again started by using a ball— gently opening her hand, pausing pointedly as I placed the ball in her palm, then praising her and laughing as she held it. Over time, Saachi learned to receive and reach for the ball, and later other objects that were being handed to her. She also learned to take turns, first with building blocks, then with games and obstacle courses.

In this way, by breaking skills down into simple steps, each laboriously taught and learned and then gradually generalized to different situations and environments, Saachi learned many foundational skills—skills that come naturally to most children, but for her were very hard-earned.

Among many other tools, we worked with a scooter board and sand box for her sensory and fine motor skills. Individuals on the autism spectrum tend to be very concrete in their thinking; I used symbolic play, such as pretending a banana was a telephone, to help Saachi develop the ability to think abstractly. Symbolic play, though, didn't seem to translate into the ability to consider concepts or to make or understand generalizations for Saachi. She continues with concrete thinking today, which I now recognize as a manifestation of her innocence and purity.

Saachi's energy level and her engagement fluctuated quite a bit during the day. I assessed her energy level throughout the day, using tools to increase or decrease her energy as needed. If her energy was low or she was disconnected, we used tools to increase energy, such as movement and excitement; if her energy was too high to the point of dysregulation or inability to participate in an activity, there were calming techniques, such as slowing down my movements and speech, body brushing, or swinging on the indoor therapy swing I put up for her.

After six months of intensive therapies, Saachi had a follow-up appointment with Dr. Charles, the developmental pediatrician who had diagnosed Saachi with autism. She was stunned to see Saachi looking at her and looking around the room. Dr. Charles' happiness with Saachi's progress was genuine, infectious, and encouraging. She shared that during her first appointment with Saachi, she didn't see Saachi's face at all because Saachi had stared down at the floor the entire appointment, lost in her own world. She was delighted with Saachi's progress.

• • •

During pregnancy I had developed carpal tunnel syndrome and DeCuervain's tendonitis, which never got a chance to heal because of the normal baby-lifting I had to do as a new mom. In addition to her developmental delays, Saachi had hypotonia (low muscle tone) and wasn't able to support herself sitting up until she was ten months old. Saachi's therapies during her first three years included physical therapy (PT) and working on gross motor skills, core muscle strength, and balance. She frequently fell over while sitting or crawling and often sported goose eggs on her head. After a year of physical therapy, Saachi learned to stand and then to walk, although she was quite wobbly for a few years. We then laboriously taught her how to jump, showing her how to bend her knees and push up. For months, her feet remained on the floor in spite of her best efforts to jump. Her babysitter and I threw a celebration party after she jumped for the first time. Similarly , Saachi's therapist, her babysitter, and I worked for months teaching Saachi how to walk up stairs by alternating feet, first by physically lifting each of her feet alternately and placing it on the next step, then later touching each foot to prompt her to step up.

Saachi's developmental delays and hypotonia required extensive lifting and physical support and further exacerbated my wrist issues. My constant wrist pain was an ever-present reminder of how hard I worked to take care of Saachi's physical needs, and sometimes intensified to a searing pain. I feared I might drop Saachi inadvertently when I had a bout of excruciating pain while lifting her or when she moved suddenly in my arms.

I broke down in the orthopedist's office when he told me I couldn't get any more steroid injections, as they could weaken my tendons and potentially cause them to snap (although he did give me one more injection that day). He recommended surgery, and told me I would need six weeks of no lifting after surgery on each wrist. This was impossible, as Saachi needed constant physical support with lifting, holding her upright, bathing, changing diapers, etc., all of which required both of my hands and wrists as did household chores and my work tasks. I declined the surgery and pressed on.

Despite the pain in my wrists, I continued with the first therapies Becky had taught me shortly after Saachi's diagnosis. I did body brushing, strapping on my wrist guards four to five times a day and firmly brushing Saachi's arms, back, and legs with soft plastic oval brushes, which I placed throughout the house so they would be easily accessible. Becky had also taught me to do MNRI—Musgatova Neuro-sensory-motor Reflex Integration, a type of reflex therapy designed to help integrate primary neural reflexes and to support the development of healthy neural networks. I continued to tap different muscles throughout Saachi's body morning and night as a means of integrating primitive reflexes. The pain in my wrists was continuous and for years was my constant companion. As Saachi developed more strength and coordination and needed less physical support, the pain began to ease, although to this day it remains with me in a much milder form.

Besides the strain on my wrists, I didn't realize how much extra effort—and how much time and energy—the developmental delays required from me. One afternoon, I was in the car with Christy and her son Luka, who was one year old at the time, three years younger than Saachi. Christy was driving, I was in the front passenger seat and Luka was in a car seat behind me. Luka started to fuss and Christy asked me to hand him a cracker. I undid my seatbelt, automatically leaning way back to place the cracker in his mouth. To my great surprise, Luka leaned forward, reached for the cracker and opened his mouth simultaneously. He was intuitively helping me feed him!

I was stunned at this simple gesture and at how easy it was to feed him. After giving him the cracker, I turned around in my seat and sat in silent shock, wondering how many other "little" things other children did naturally. For a moment, I glimpsed all that I was doing, all that I was juggling. I fought back tears. Christy noticed my silence and glanced over at me. "Oh, sweetie, what's going on?" she said. She turned off the CD playing in the car stereo and put her hand on mine as she drove. Her kindness and compassion melted any resistance to crying that I could muster.

Through my tears, I told her, "Christy, I just didn't know. I didn't know. I had no idea. Do you know that Luka just leaned forward to help me feed him? I have never experienced anything like that. I had no idea that kids do that and that I've been working so hard!"

• • •

Saachi and therapeutic horseback riding instructors

I told therapists to use tools or toys with Saachi, not tablets or computers, knowing that a hands-on, practical approach would connect Saachi to the world more directly. We never watched television or used technology. Instead I made a constant effort to connect with her directly through our multitude of therapy assignments and activities. Becky was in full support. She said that when children on the spectrum use technology, they tend to become even more obsessed with it than neurotypical children do. From the perspective of traditional medicine, the core symptom of autism is lack of social connection—and technology only serves to foster more social isolation and more tuning out of the rest of the world.

Because I always erred on the side of being thorough, we threw ourselves into several therapeutic interventions in addition to RDI, many of them concurrently. Immediately after Saachi's diagnosis, I implemented several biomedical interventions. I consulted with dietitians, including holistic physicians and dietitians who specialized in supplements. I shifted to a gluten-free, dairy-free diet (except for casein from breast milk—I felt the benefits of breast milk outweighed potential harm from breast milk casein). We already ate mostly organic whole foods, so the shift to gluten- and dairy-free only required a few simple modifications. I began supplementing Saachi's diet with omega fatty acids, probiotics, digestive enzymes, a multivitamin, vitamin D, calcium, TMG, folic acid, vitamin B12, coenzyme Q10, L-glutathione, and zinc cream. Later on, I also tried CBD for her ADHD—which was ineffective for Saachi—and added N-acetylcholine for her picking compulsion.

Until she was three years old, Saachi's therapists came to our home. When weather permitted, I loved to leave the sliding glass doors open to let in the nourishing humid marsh breeze, tinged with the familiar and comforting scent of plough mud. Saachi's therapists always brought with them big bags filled with activities and tools and sat on our hardwood floor with Saachi and me in our small living room. Our schedule was nuts, with therapies scheduled throughout the weekdays. Juggling our therapists' and babysitters' schedules and training babysitters to implement all of the new techniques I was being taught each week kept my system high-wired and tense.

In retrospect, a much simpler, quieter, and calmer life would probably have been every bit as useful for Saachi, and certainly better for me, but my fear was driving the show. I was on the autism treatment train, for better or worse. After long days at work and on my days off, I participated in back-to-back therapies with Saachi and her therapists. I took copious notes on therapeutic techniques and the therapists' homework assignments to be done with Saachi over the next week. Yellow sticky notes decorated the entire bar area off the kitchen, the bathroom mirror, and the walls of our bedrooms to remind me of the countless things I was to work on with Saachi. Saachi, by nature very determined and a hard worker, went along with the program, giving everything her best effort.

One afternoon Cindy called to tell me that Temple Grandin was giving a talk in town that night, and that her neighbor Dr. Charles had offered to give her front-row ticket to me. In 2010, Temple Grandin was one of the *Time 100*, one of the hundred most influential people in the world in the "heroes" category, both for her work in the humane treatment of livestock and animal behavior, and as the first autistic person to break down the stigma and shame of being on the spectrum. As she said, "I am different, not less." Cindy offered to babysit, and Dr. Charles drove me to the talk in downtown Charleston. I hadn't had an evening out since before Saachi was born, and felt a sense of joy and freedom as I found my way to my seat in the large auditorium.

Temple Grandin was beautiful and the history of her life was inspiring. I was touched by her wisdom, her purity, and her uniqueness. After the talk, she allowed parents to ask questions. I quickly became aware that each parent carried the same fear I had about my daughter's future, the same intensity and drive born out of that fear, and the same tendency to compare their children's abilities or progress to others. For some, this fear manifested in bragging about their children's accomplishments and skills, mostly in the area of technology. Although I sensed and understood that the source of the comments was fear, their boasting about their children's abilities triggered in me some doubt about not using technology as a tool in my work and therapists' work with Saachi.

The next day, I shared my doubt with Becky. She was very firm, telling me that in her experience our priority needed to be helping Saachi to connect socially and that this priority was the foundation for the progress Saachi had made and would make. Only half-joking, she issued an ultimatum that if I introduced Saachi to technology, she would no longer work with us. I laughed, relieved of my doubt, and I recognized the fragility of all parents with children on the spectrum—our wanting more than anything for our children to be able to function in the world, and our vulnerability to doubt and fear.

As much as I disliked ABA, I was too afraid to ditch it, knowing that according to research studies the technique produced results. For two years I juggled both ABA and RDI, attempting to integrate both therapies. When I had first approached our ABA lead therapist about incorporating some RDI techniques into ABA therapy, she was dismissive, stating that there was no research to back RDI, but said she would be willing to have the team work with our RDI therapist in order to integrate both therapies. But not only were the techniques at odds, I also found that when it came down to it, ABA therapists were committed to maintaining the purity of their therapy. There simply wasn't room to incorporate the RDI tools I was learning into ABA. I found myself repeatedly frustrated, and ultimately, with more than a little trepidation, decided to discontinue ABA.

The relief was quick and immense, even though doubts about my decision continued to surface for some time. Our schedule was no longer cram-packed and I was able to focus more on the therapies that resonated most. Later, when Saachi had developed a foundational ability to connect with others in a heartfelt and meaningful way, I brought ABA back in to our lives to support Saachi in targeting specific skills, such as parting her hair, telling time, sweeping the floor, reading comprehension, speech articulation, and gently loading and unloading the dishwasher (all of our dishes are chipped or broken as Saachi tends to unintentionally toss them into their place). Although I was working on teaching these skills to Saachi, I felt that with some of them I had reached the limits of my ability, and I didn't have the time or the patience to devote to teaching her all of these various skills. I also came to realize and accept that I didn't have the temperament and mindset to teach certain skills, like telling time. As for Saachi, she responds well to everyone, and doesn't differentiate between work, play, or the type of therapy she is engaged in. She is generally enthusiastic about whoever and whatever she is interacting with.

• • •

Saachi's first speech therapist was assigned to her by our early interventionist. Alex was young, pretty, and fresh out of her training. I didn't have any experience with therapists before Alex, and no one to compare her to, but even I could tell that she wasn't fully engaged with Saachi. Although on the surface she was cheerful, her heart wasn't in her work. She spent her sessions swinging Saachi on our indoor therapy swing and attempting to teach Saachi a few words in sign language. She didn't work at all on helping Saachi learn to vocalize.

After a few months of this, I mentioned my concern to our early interventionist, Lindsey. After discussing this with Alex, Lindsey came to our scheduled weekly appointment at our house and as usual sat on the floor with Saachi and me. "Mindy, I need to talk with you about something. As you know, speech therapists here in Charleston have very long wait lists. There just aren't enough of them for all the children that need speech therapy. I was able to get Alex because she was just out of school, but I don't think she is a good therapist for Saachi. I didn't want to tell you this, but I feel you need this information to make a decision. When I asked Alex why she isn't working on vocalization with Saachi, she said that it's because she believes that Saachi will never talk. Mindy, it is absolutely wrong for her to make this assumption, especially this early. But I've called every speech therapist in town that I know of, and they are all booked out for several months. Do you want to continue with Alex until Saachi can get an appointment with another therapist?"

Although the sinking feeling of devastation was by now becoming familiar, it did not make it any easier. Panic rose up. If my daughter couldn't learn to talk, how would she function in the world? How would she survive when she had so many other challenges? Unable to handle the panic, I shoved it aside and replaced it with a steely determination. "I don't want Alex stepping foot in this house ever again, or getting anywhere near my daughter." I heard my voice through my tears.

Excruciatingly aware of the crucial importance of early intervention, I began asking everyone I knew if they knew of a good speech therapist in town. One of Saachi's occupational therapists highly recommended Shelly, a therapist with whom she often collaborated at her clinic. I immediately left Shelly a voice mail, explaining that I was looking for a speech therapist for my daughter as soon as possible. When Shelly called back, she told me she had at least a nine-month wait list. More devastation. I knew that this was a pivotal window of time for work on Saachi's communication skills. I told Shelly that if she had any unexpected openings to please call me, as I was desperate to get help for my daughter. She said she would. I called her at least once a week after that to see if she had any openings. Because of my persistence, after several weeks Shelly found a way to work us into her schedule and began seeing Saachi at our home twice a week.

When Shelly walked in for our first appointment, it was like a shining light of joy had entered our home. In truth, that day an angel came into our lives. Shelly's bright spirit and laughter bubbled out of her, and she immediately recognized Saachi's spirit. Saachi basked in Shelly's light, recognizing a kindred soul. Shelly always saw Saachi's potential, always followed Saachi's lead, and always engaged Saachi naturally. Shelly's approach began with establishing and reinforcing a nonverbal connection with Saachi—a tangible connection that served as a foundation for all other forms of communication, including social referencing, language, and gesturing. Shelly told me that this foundational nonverbal connection would help Saachi develop the intrinsic motivation to engage with her before attempting to engage with speech.

She explained to me that children who learn speech before they connect nonverbally often develop hyperlexia, excessive language that isn't functional or connected with others, and that this can also lead to a big discrepancy between a child's expressive (spoken) language and receptive (understood) language—a child may be able to speak but not understand what is spoken. Shelly explained: "The child may know a lot of memorized facts, like animal names, shapes, letters, or may memorize a lot about their favorite topic. She might know all the letters but not understand that the letters make a sound and that sounds make words. She might talk a lot but only about what she has memorized, and its typically scripted language. She might recite commercial jingles or recite memorized parts of movies. The problem is that this premature language, before a nonverbal connection is developed, isn't really functional, and once it's in place, it's very hard to expand on it."

Shelly further summed this up when my friend Mary spoke with her about her son Railey's speech. Mary's son was diagnosed with autism not long after Saachi was diagnosed, and since then, Mary and I have walked through the stages of parenting a child on the spectrum side by side, arm in arm. Our children are very different, but our paths have been similar in many ways.

When our children were diagnosed, we both hoped desperately that our child would be one of the few who "got better." Our hope fueled our drive and gave us the energy we needed to engage so fully in researching therapies, hiring therapists, learning all the therapeutic interventions ourselves and implementing them in our daily lives. Over time, one by one and little by little, with each unmet goal and each unmet milestone, we were forced to grieve and to accept our children's limitations. We both have gratitude for the hope and for the motivation it gave us during those crucial formative years. Hope gave us the energy to give it all we had. We both feel that the effort we put into our children during those foundational years made a tremendous difference in their lives and in their ability to function in and engage in the world.

Using Railey's pediatrician's assessment of his language skills, Mary told Shelly how many words Railey could speak. This is typically how pediatricians measure development of speech and language. Shelly said to Mary, "Number of words spoken does not equal communication." Mary said this completely shifted her understanding of her son's autism, and changed the course of the interventions they did with Railey.

To establish a nonverbal connection with Saachi, Shelly utilized Floortime techniques, following Saachi's lead and expanding on Saachi's interests to cultivate circles of communication, back-and-forth exchanges. We started with a goal of one nonverbal back-and-forth exchange with Saachi, and over many months increased the circles of communication to the point where Saachi was often able to remain engaged for extended periods and we no longer had to count exchanges.

Autistic individuals typically and very noticeably do not engage in eye contact with others. Before Shelly came into our lives, "teaching" Saachi to have eye contact was a priority for me. As always, I worried about her future if she wasn't able to have eye contact. Most people interpret lack of eye contact as a lack of interest and lack of engagement. I worried that without eye contact with others, she wouldn't be able to make friends or get or keep a job later on. Although it took some time for me to let go of my fear that lack of eye contact would significantly impact Saachi's life negatively, I eventually recognized the truth of what Shelly told me. She said that individuals on the spectrum are so exquisitely sensitive, so deeply connected and merged with their environment and others in the environment, that engaging with another's eyes, the window of the soul, only heightened this sensitivity and was painful and overwhelming for them. She said that a few children she was working with had been able to verbalize this to her, in their own way. Shelly told me that circles of communication—verbal or nonverbal back-and-forth exchanges—were our priority for engaging Saachi, not eye contact.

I trusted Shelly implicitly, and often watched in astonishment as she engaged Saachi naturally. When Shelly first began working with her, Saachi was developing a keen interest in anything round, especially balls. Shelly used Saachi's interest in balls to develop joint attention (two people paying attention to the same thing), identifying and recognizing emotions in herself and others, social referencing (looking for emotional clues about a situation in the faces of others), and emotion sharing. Shelly used Saachi's love of balls to get her to point—she had to point to request playing with the balls—then moved from pointing to visual referencing, hiding the ball and then having to follow Shelly's gaze to locate it. These social skills typically develop naturally and effortlessly in infants but are often missing in autistic individuals. They were all skills I had never even thought about before Saachi's diagnosis, had never had to conceptualize.

I participated in all of Saachi's therapies and speech therapy was no exception. I learned from *how* Shelly interacted with Saachi, not just the activities and tools she used to engage Saachi. In my interactions with Saachi outside of therapy I began to follow her lead more and more as a means of connecting with her. As Shelly and I established our nonverbal engagement with Saachi, Shelly began teaching her basic sign language so that she would be able to communicate and avoid the frustration of not being able to let me know what she wanted or needed. We started with the signs for "my turn," "help," "open," and "all done," and then progressed to other signs. Meanwhile Shelly began helping Saachi learn how to vocalize and produce sounds.

When Shelly first began working with us, Saachi was able to say two word approximations: "mah" for mama and "bah" for ball. For six months, we worked intensively on the bilabial (two-lip) sounds of b, p, m, and w, pronouncing these sounds and asking Saachi to repeat after us. Trying to pronounce sounds and later words and sentences was (and still is) very hard work for Saachi, and Shelly always used fun activities as a means of engaging Saachi with speech. We might take turns rolling a ball to each other after we each pronounced the sound we were working on, or use other activities Saachi enjoyed to make the process fun for her. We didn't use overt rewards, like giving a treat or a preferred activity as a reward after a drill, but whenever Saachi approximated a sound we celebrated with our joy, smiles, and high-fives. In this way, the reward became the joy of the vocalization itself. This supported Saachi in furthering her own internal motivation to speak and kept her from developing reliance on external rewards.

Once Saachi was able to make the bilabial sounds, we began working on the back sounds (k, g, h), which we did for several more months, then shifted to other consonants and individual vowel sounds. When Saachi had a good repertoire of consonant and vowel sounds, we helped her make syllables for word approximations using changing vowel sounds. For example, we might ask Saachi to say Bay, Bee, Bye, Bow, Boo. Later, after Saachi was able to pronounce consonants at the initial position of words or word approximations, Saachi worked on pronouncing each consonant at the medial and final positions in words. The process was painstaking and laborious, but Saachi's willingness to engage in this work and her persistence paid off, and she made steady progress.

Shelly emphasized the importance of responding to everything Saachi said in order to encourage all verbal communication. She helped me learn how to expand on Saachi's sentences to facilitate circles of communication and more speech. Saachi often did not respond to questions because she was unaware of what a question was, unaware that a response was expected, and simply did not understand the meaning of Who, What, When, Where, Why, and How. I learned to ask deliberately simple questions and started out by placing myself face-to-face in close proximity to Saachi in order to ensure I had her attention, and to always follow through for responses.

I was encouraged by Saachi's steady progress. As she got older though, I began to notice a growing disparity between her speech and that of children her age on the playground. At three years of age, Saachi was not yet able to say a CVC (consonant-vowel-consonant) word, like "mom." Other kids her age were using full sentences, clearly and spontaneously, without any effort. I began to feel discouraged with the slow progress. Where previously my determination had kept me forging straight ahead, the discouragement now allowed doubt to creep in. I began to wonder if Saachi would ever be able to say intelligible words, let alone sentences. I was crushed by the possibility that she might never be able to communicate through speech. The doubt weighed on my heart, heavier and heavier, until I finally needed to talk about it with Shelly. By this time, Shelly had become a dear friend, often seeing me at my worst, always welcoming my tears, my frustrations, my joys and celebrations as if she were a family member.

When Shelly walked in that day, she immediately sensed the heaviness in my heart. "Honey! What's going on?" she said, her eyes full of concern, as she dropped her big canvas bag on the floor and sat down in front of me. I looked into her kind eyes, my own brimming with tears.

"Shelly, I have to ask you something, but I need you to tell me the truth. I know that Saachi is making progress, but it is very, very slow. Other kids her age are talking so well, in full sentences! Will she ever really be able to talk?" The question burst out of me with all of the pent-up emotion behind it.

As I cried, Shelly reached for my hands, still looking into my eyes. "Mindy. Listen to me. Saachi is going to talk, I promise you. I have absolutely no doubt. You know how I know this? She is very, very determined, she is such a hard worker, she is already vocalizing, and she has the desire to communicate through her voice. She is making tremendous progress, Mindy. Don't even think about comparing her to other children. She is her own precious beautiful self and she is learning to talk and learning this world on her own time line. Let go of that doubt. We are all in this together, and we will keep taking it one step at a time." She wiped the tears from my cheeks.

I wanted to believe her, but couldn't fully, not quite yet. "Shelly. Please tell me the truth. Don't blow smoke if it's not true, I only want the truth. If she's not going to talk, I want to know now, so I can face it and grieve and adjust our lives."

Shelly smiled, real big. "I love you, Miss Mindy. I promise you, I am telling you the truth. Why would I lie? You just let go of that doubt right now."

And I did. Sometimes, doubts can be like anaerobic bacteria. They need to be exposed to oxygen, to the fresh air of love and compassion, in order to die out. Years later Shelly told me that all parents ultimately ask her this question. I asked if she always tells parents that their child will talk in order to give them hope. She said, "I always help parents see the unique strengths in their child and help them realize that standard scores and developmental skills are not what's most important. As long as progress is made in some areas (gross motor skills, fine motor skills, or speech) the child is evolving. Change is happening. The sky is the limit and I would never impose limitations. What good would that do? None. It's not being unrealistic; it's knowing that a child has the desire to communicate. All people do, it's human nature!"

For a few years, Saachi worked hard to talk at home, but was silent whenever we went out. Shelly explained that this was because her system was processing all the unfamiliar sensory input outside of our home—her energy and attention were consumed with unfiltered sensory input and there wasn't any left over for putting in the tremendous effort it took for her to talk.

I have a crystal clear memory of the first time Saachi said a word out in public. My mom, Saachi, and I were at a restaurant on the Folly Beach pier overlooking the ocean. I always brought Saachi's food when we ate out because of her food sensitivities and her challenges with chewing; she couldn't swallow anything other than soft foods. I put her bowl of pressure-cooked beans and kale in front of her. My mom and I were involved in a deep discussion about my sister's family while we waited for our food to arrive. My sister Kathy's husband had been imprisoned on drug charges, to our surprise and dismay, and Kathy was now juggling work as a full-time teacher and raising her three children. During a pause in our conversation, Mom and I both heard a quiet, sweet, high-pitched voice breaking into our consciousness: "Kai! Kai!" Astonished, I looked at Saachi. "Kai! Kai!" she repeated, this time more enthusiastically. I followed her gaze out the window—where a large red-and-yellow kite billowed up in the sky, dancing joyfully with the rhythm of the background music in the restaurant. My mom and I were unable to contain our joy over this gigantic milestone.

As if on cue, the music in the restaurant shifted and I heard Madonna's "Express Yourself" playing in the background. I pulled Saachi out of her booster seat and held her tight as we danced across the room, dodging tables, dipping, swaying, and bouncing with the exaggerated moves I instinctively knew were needed in order to engage her, all the way up to the window. Her bright pink headphones bonked my forehead as I leaned in to kiss her on the cheek. She giggled and looked in my eyes. I beamed at her and pointed at the kite. "YES, Saachibean! THAT is a kite! And YOU are a rock star!"

CHAPTER 21

Give You Ball

It is after the appearance of the first personal pronoun that the second and third personal pronouns appear; without the first personal pronoun there will not be the second and third.

—Ramana Maharshi

Saachi had significant oral-motor hypotonia, or low tone of her mouth muscles, that interfered not only with her ability to form sounds and create speech, but also created challenges with chewing and swallowing. Shelly worked with Saachi consistently on chewing, swallowing, and oral stimulation exercises (such as Beckman oral motor stretches). I used a vibrating toothbrush before all meals and before she worked on speech to "wake up" her mouth and help her be aware of her cheeks, tongue, and the roof of her mouth. Over the years, with Shelly's oral-motor exercises and my follow-through during the week, Saachi's chewing and swallowing improved and I was able to gradually introduce more solid foods.

For years, I had either blended food for Saachi or cooked her food until it was soft. She often choked even on water or soft food, and several times I had to do the Heimlich maneuver. As an infant I'd flip her over my forearm, turn her upside down, and deliver blows between her shoulder blades with the heel of my hand; later on I'd perform the child Heimlich with upward thrusts delivered to her abdomen. These choking episodes terrified me, but somehow when they were over I just moved on with the task at hand and set the fear aside. The momentum of our busy lives always took over and filled the space immediately.

Pronouns took many years to teach (and Saachi occasionally still gets confused about them). Most people understand that "I" means *me* and "you" means *you*. On the surface this seems simple, until you try to teach someone who has no understanding of these concepts. I often felt like I was in a comedy routine with Saachi when I was trying to teach her pronouns.

She might say, "Give you bah!" when she meant, "Give me ball!" I would say to her, "Honey, when you say "you," it means me!" pointing to myself as I said "me." Then I would put my hand on her chest and say, "Me! This is "me!" Similarly, the idea that who the word "you" referred to depended on the user was difficult to explain and to understand. I finally decided to work on pronouns only when there were three of us present in the room—Saachi and me, with either Shelly or the babysitter—so that one of us could sit beside her and use the same pronouns that she would use while referring to herself and the other person in the room. For example, Shelly would sit beside Saachi and hand a toy to me, saying, "Here, this toy is for you," then ask Saachi to imitate.

It wasn't until six years later that I understood why pronouns were such a challenge for Saachi. My new friend Melissa, who is very intuitive, came over to our house to visit one day. She immediately sensed Saachi's expanded state of consciousness. As Melissa and I sat down on the couch with cups of hot tea, Saachi said to Melissa, "You show me your room!" Weary and somewhat frustrated with this ongoing pronoun challenge, I explained to Melissa that she was learning about pronouns and that she really meant, "I want to show you my room."

Melissa said, "Of course pronouns are foreign to her. She doesn't experience herself as separate from her environment, as separate from me or anyone else, so to refer to someone or something as other than herself doesn't make any sense to her. She is residing in a place of complete unity."

As Saachi took Melissa by the hand and into her room, the truth in Melissa's words hit me hard and pulled the rug out from under my feet. Melissa and I had both been on lifelong spiritual journeys. Our spiritual efforts and practices were all designed to dissolve the illusion of separation, to dissolve the concepts of "me" and "other" that are so tightly held by the human mind, to bring our awareness back to the Love and Unity at our core and at the core of all existence. Until that day, I had only been aware of the superficial "symptom" of Saachi's lack of understanding of pronouns, and my attention and efforts in this area had been exclusively focused on trying to teach Saachi how to use pronouns the way the rest of the world did. While Saachi was residing in a place of unity and love, I had been trying to get her to see the world through the eyes of separation—trying to get her mind to create a "you" and a "me."

This was my first "Aha!" moment with Saachi—a realization that I might have the whole thing wrong. Maybe it wasn't my job to help Saachi be more like the rest of the world. Saachi was merged with her environment—she wasn't separate from anyone else. For her, there was no "you" or "me." She experienced everyone and everything as herself. Perhaps Saachi and others like her were here to guide the rest of us into a higher state of consciousness, where we begin to live in the realization that we are one.

Identifying emotions was another area that didn't come naturally for Saachi, and we worked hard on that. For a few years her therapists, babysitters, and I made exaggerated expressions with our faces of several basic emotions to help her identify sad, mad, scared, happy. We then moved on to photos of familiar people with expressions of emotions on their faces, and then photos of people of different ages that she didn't know, adding more variability as she learned.

Saachi also experienced space in a unique way. She was prone to frequent accidents and injuries because she misjudged distances and spatial relationships. Once, when we joined Christy at a restaurant, she gave Saachi a straw. Before I could intervene, Saachi attempted to put it in her mouth but instead slammed the straw into her eyelid, cutting into her eyelid and barely missing her cornea. During a battery of tests when she was four years old, she was given several toys to play with. She attempted to put a tiny shoe no bigger than her fingernail on her foot. Another time, she tried to climb tiny stairs inside a doll house.

Similarly, concepts of time have been challenging for her. She lives in the now; not often remembering the past or thinking about the future. Because she is mostly free of thoughts about the past or future, she doesn't carry burdens of emotions of past memories, or fear or anxiety about future events. This also means that learning from past experiences and planning for future events do not come naturally to her. She is still trying to understand the meaning of before, after, morning, afternoon. For Saachi and many autistic individuals, every situation is experienced as brand new. Like an infant or a toddler, Saachi sees everything with fresh eyes, without past experience coloring her perception. She is fully present in the moment, and her experience is not clouded by a conscious or unconscious mental or emotional memory of the past or by thoughts about the future. It's a state many spiritual seekers and meditators aspire to, but Saachi doesn't need to work at it. She lacks the ability to superimpose past experience on a current experience. Similarly, her mind lacks the capacity to compare or to judge.

This freshness, this pure presence, can make it difficult to function in our world. Learning from past experience and generalizing to a new experience are taken for granted by most of us, but for Saachi any such learning is hard won. When Saachi was three, she saw a red hot burner and, naturally curious, reached out to touch it. Because she couldn't feel her body very well at the time and also had a delayed motor response, she suffered a severe burn on the palm of her hand. To this day, Saachi understands that pots and pans, and my cup of tea, all may be very hot, but her curiosity about how it might feel compels her to touch them. She doesn't generalize from her experience of having been burned by one hot object to understanding that another hot object might burn her. Building on something learned in another similar situation doesn't happen intuitively. This also makes problem solving difficult.

For each new experience that I knew Saachi would encounter, I practiced every possible foreseeable aspect of the experience with her many times prior to the actual activity. Saachi's therapists also helped prepare Saachi for new experiences. When Saachi was four years old, Shelly invited us to go trick-or-treating in her neighborhood for Halloween. For several weeks we practiced dressing up in her pink princess costume, holding her bucket, staying on a sidewalk while walking in a neighborhood (this, too, was not intuitive for Saachi, and still isn't), walking up to a door, waiting her turn, then saying her best approximation of 'Trick or Treat!" Because of Saachi's allergies and diet, she wasn't able to eat the candy, so she practiced taking just one piece of candy, saying "Thank you!" and then exchanging the candy with Shelly for a little toy.

When Halloween finally arrived, Saachi was bursting with excitement. We parked in front of Shelly's house, where Shelly stood on the front porch with her dog Tucker, who was dressed as Superman. Shelly knew that Saachi loved dogs and brought Tucker along for her. We walked with Saachi up to the first house. Saachi stood still in front of a lady standing in the front yard next to a card table with a big plastic pumpkin filled with candy. I saw that Saachi was on sensory overload—overwhelmed by the flashing lights, the colorful costumes, the children's laughter and screams around us. She stood frozen, looking dazed, as children began piling up behind her. I squatted down, giving her a gentle prompt as I put my hand on her back. "Saachi, you can say 'Trick or Treat' now." I watched her eyes perk up as she came back into this realm, alert and present. She looked up, saw the front door of the house, and before I knew what was happening she had darted right past the astonished lady with the candy, had marched up to the door, opened it, and walked into the house. Shelly and I scrambled after Saachi, apologizing and giggling as we ran to get her.

We hadn't thought to practice not going inside houses. Saachi had no concept of ownership of things—of a house or anything else. Shelly explained to Saachi that she couldn't go inside the houses and we continued trick-or-treating. Although she had initially been overwhelmed, Saachi in general loved new experiences and this was no exception. Her joy and excitement were infectious. By the tenth house, Saachi was able to go up to the house on her own, get a piece of candy, and come back to us. We left after that, intentionally leaving on a good note.

More recently, I taught Saachi how to turn on the tub water to a comfortable temperature. When I realized that adjusting the faucet each time she took a bath was too challenging for her, we marked the faucet with a blue piece of tape where she could point the faucet handle for the right water temperature. A few weeks later, I wasn't aware that the blue tape had fallen off the faucet. Saachi got in the tub and turned on the water. I was in the kitchen cooking, planning to check on her in a few minutes, when I heard her crying loudly. I ran back in the bathroom and saw Saachi standing in the tub with scalding hot water running and rising up over her ankles. She was standing in the burning water, crying loudly in pain. I picked her up and out of the tub. I was baffled and frustrated. Why didn't she get out of the tub herself, even if she didn't know how to turn down the temperature of the water?

A few days later, an adult friend of mine who is on the spectrum came over for a visit. As our children jumped on the trampoline, we sat on the patio in white plastic chairs, warmed by the sun and our children's laughter. Toni shared with me some of her childhood challenges, including one experience where her foot got stuck in a stairwell bannister. She didn't have the ability to problem solve and hadn't known to turn her foot sideways to get it out or to call out for help. She was stuck there until someone came along to help her. Similarly, she described standing at the corner of a street, frozen, having no idea how to cross the street. This was another of those "Aha" moments for me. I now understood that when Saachi had stood in the burning hot water in the tub, she had simply not known how to problem solve in order to stop the pain by getting out of the tub. What may come instinctively to many of us does not to individuals on the spectrum. Because every situation is new, coming up with a creative solution to a novel problem is a big challenge.

CHAPTER 22

Obsessions, Elopements, and ADHD

Love comes with a knife, not some shy question,
and not with fears for its reputation!
—Rumi

Saachi's love of all things round persisted for years. When she was first learning to talk, she exclaimed hundreds of times each day, "Bah! Bah! Bah!" when she saw anything that to her resembled a ball. The bah might be a plate, a button, a lamp shade, a cloud, her headphones, a pencil head, a coin, an actual ball—or anything else remotely round. Initially, I was thrilled that she was engaging in joint attention, wanting me to see what she was so excited about. Once, when a therapist arrived at our house clad in snug yoga pants, before the therapist had a chance to sit down, Saachi ran over to her and patted her bottom, loudly exclaiming, "Bah! Bah! Bah!" We both laughed, delighted with Saachi's engagement.

Over time, I became exhausted with her obsession. If I was trying to engage her in a therapeutic activity, she would inevitably get distracted by anything remotely round and begin to exclaim excitedly. She was so excited by the roundness of the object, it was very difficult to pull her attention back to our activity. I decided it was time to break her of this obsession. When she had first become interested in balls, I purchased many different balls for her, happy to have her be present in the world and expressing interest in objects. So she had an abundance of balls.

On my mission to extinguish her obsession, I first tried limiting her access, giving her a ball only after we finished a therapeutic activity. This approach did not lessen her love of balls, so next I tried removing all balls from the house for several weeks. Her obsession persisted. Next, I tried flooding her with balls. I brought more balls into the house and had them everywhere, on the floor, on the couch, in the kitchen, the yard, everywhere, thinking that overexposure might exhaust her obsession. To no avail. At some point, I realized it wasn't balls she loved, it was the shape of round. Although she was saying "bah," she didn't think everything round was a ball. She was using "bah" as a substitute for the word "round." I gave up, resigning myself to the possibility that she might be completely captivated by round objects for the rest of her life and that this obsession might interfere with her ability to function in the world.

Eventually, though, her obsession with balls began to fade; then Saachi developed a love of sports shorts with pockets. She loved the slippery feel of sports shorts and loved putting her hands in pockets. Unfortunately, this was not limited to her own shorts and pockets; she often impulsively reached out to touch others' shorts. Social etiquette is not Saachi's forte; in fact, it is foreign to her. She doesn't have to try to think outside the box; for her, no box exists. I tried repeatedly explaining to her why she shouldn't touch others' shorts, that they didn't like it, that their shorts belonged to them, not her (a concept she didn't understand). I tried giving her silky pieces of material and other objects to hold and play with. I bought her many pairs of sports shorts with pockets, hoping she would keep her hands to her own shorts. She wore her shorts all the time, including over leggings during the winter months. Nothing stopped her from impulsively touching others' shorts or putting her hands in the pockets of unsuspecting strangers.

At each school she went to, I discussed this with teachers, asking them to talk with her classmates about it and let the other students know that they could tell her not to touch their shorts. At the grocery store, she would spot someone in sports shorts and dart off towards them as I chased her, cringing at what I knew was coming. Before I could reach her, she would inevitably already have her hand in the startled stranger's pocket. Weary of trying to explain her behavior, I resorted to joking, "So sorry. I've been teaching her how to pick pockets but she's still learning!" I'd smile, pull her hand out of their pocket, and march her back across the store to our cart.

Saachi with Wilder and her Global Warming book

Saachi still loves shorts, but her obsession with them has faded as well. For now, she is keenly interested in books on global warming and carries her favorite book with her most places, including on our evening walks. I no longer try to rid her of her obsessions, although I do try to intervene if her passion results in behavior that is disruptive to others. I love her even more because of her quirks.

Understanding rules or "acceptable behavior" is difficult for Saachi. Saachi loves to play all kinds of ball and has been on many soccer teams. She is great with the ball, but doesn't understand or forgets many of the rules of the game. During her first few soccer seasons, she managed to run up to the referee (who she assumed was another ball player) and kick the ball out from under his foot. Another time, she grabbed the ball from the ref's hands. Occasionally, Saachi kicks the ball into the wrong goal.

I find myself giggling and at times all-out laughing at the beauty of the inability of rules to contain her spirit.

Not long after Saachi's diagnosis, I asked my friend Melanie over, planning to share the diagnosis with her. With a heavy heart, I told her Saachi had just been diagnosed with autism. Melanie's eyes lit up and she blurted out, "She's so lucky!" Surprised, and sensing that her remark was genuine and spontaneous, I asked what she meant. "Mindy, because she now has that label, she will have permission to not abide by the rules of society. She can completely be who she is!" Her response was so unique that it stayed with me. As Saachi grew older and I became aware of the social norms imposed on children, I understood more and more the truth of her words.

• • •

As I parked the car at a grocery store one day, I watched astonished as a mother turned her back briefly on her toddler in order to reach into the car and get her purse. I assumed she was negligent, until I saw another mother in the grocery store, speaking animatedly with a friend she had encountered and not paying any attention to her young son, who stood at her side throughout the conversation. I couldn't believe that these kids didn't dart off the second their mothers let go of them, and couldn't believe how relaxed the children's mothers were. They certainly weren't on high alert at all times, trying to anticipate potential danger. On the playground, I followed Saachi around constantly, frequently averting an injury and sometimes not able to do so in spite of my proximity and best attempts. I noticed other parents sat on nearby benches, using the time to relax, socialize, or text on their phones. My astonishment in seeing parents relaxing and not on high alert with their children has still not diminished.

One day on the playground, Saachi wanted to climb up on the play set with the other toddlers. I helped her climb up the stairs and reluctantly let her loose, fearful that she might harm herself or unintentionally harm another child, or that her unsteadiness would cause her to topple over if another child bumped into her. Unable to follow her up the equipment myself to offer her guidance and support, I was tense, standing nearby and watching her closely, unlike the other parents who were chatting together on a bench further away.

I saw it coming but couldn't reach her between the bars. I watched as she looked at another child standing in front of her, the child's back to her, a bright pink hood perched upside down like a handle where it draped on the child's back. I saw Saachi look at the hood, watched frozen as she reached impulsively for it, grabbed, and yanked down. The girl fell backwards, hitting her head on the metal floor of the play set. She screamed out in pain as her mother rushed over, yelling at Saachi and yelling at me. "Why the hell is your daughter trying to hurt my baby? What a monster!"

Horrified, I apologized. As soon as I could get to Saachi, I helped her off the play set. I scolded her as we walked down the stairs together, knowing that she didn't understand—knowing that she had seen what looked like a handle and had pulled on it. She hadn't known that a girl was attached to the hood, hadn't known that she would hurt someone. The girl ended up being fine, but my heart was heavy. I felt helpless to explain the world to my daughter when her perspective so often didn't match up with what worked in this physical reality. She wasn't able to generalize from learning something specific to other similar situations, so I was trying hard to teach her about every possible situation I could anticipate. How could I ever imagine and teach her one-by-one the millions of things that could come up in the world, like not to pull on a child's hood?

Elopement, or impulsively running off, is another tremendous safety issue for many autistic individuals, and Saachi was no exception. From the time Saachi was able to walk, she would often dart off, even more so in public places where her system was on overload from all the sensory input. Sometimes Saachi dashed off towards something she saw that she was interested in. At other times, her body ran off impulsively, seemingly without a destination in mind. Whenever she ran off, she did so with lightning speed.

Although I quickly developed a keen hypervigilance, more than a few times she was nearly hit by cars in parking lots, and several times I lost her in stores. I kept her in the grocery cart seat as often as she was willing; when she grew too big for that, I put her in the cart with all of our groceries. I dreaded the stress of shopping, and each time we went to a store I had to give myself a pep talk before getting out of the car. When she refused to sit in the cart, and eventually grew too big to fit in the cart, I held her hand with my left hand while I pushed the cart with my right. Inevitably, though, I would have to let her hand go briefly to get an item, to open a refrigerated door, or to unzip my purse and get my credit card out of my wallet to pay. I quickly became very adept at watching her like a hawk while I grabbed whatever I needed—but a split second after I let go of her hand, off she went, sometimes heading straight out the door and into the parking lot. I would chase after her, leaving everything behind. Often, by the time I finally made it to the car and had Saachi strapped into her car seat and groceries loaded in the trunk, I sat in the driver's seat, my head resting on the steering wheel, exhausted and unsure how I would make it through the rest of the day.

At home, I was on high alert with Saachi at all times, always in fight-or-flight mode, rushing to complete household tasks all the while keeping a close eye on her. One afternoon when Saachi was three, after attending to the pressure cooker in the kitchen for a minute, I rushed into the living room, only to find her . . . nowhere. I called her name loudly and frantically looked through our small home. I rushed out the front door. Terrified, I ran down the stairs, calling, calling for her. Soon I found her next door, exploring a balcony that was under construction, no rails in place. I hadn't known Saachi was even able to open a door. After this, I installed an indoor lock at the top of the door, well out of her reach.

I noticed over time that when our home environment was not cluttered and was relatively organized, Saachi's system was more regulated and she was less impulsive and less hyperactive. She absorbed chaos in her environment, at home or outside the home, and expressed the chaos through her behavior. Taking my cue from my friend Mary, I organized Saachi's toys and therapy tools in bins and did my best to keep the house uncluttered. When I played or worked with Saachi, I put everything away except whatever we were playing with or working with.

• • •

One sunny but cool winter afternoon, Saachi had a follow-up appointment with Dr. Charles, her developmental pediatrician. After getting into the car to leave for the appointment, I forgot to lock the car doors. As I parked the car in the garage parking lot, Saachi unbuckled her seat belt and slipped out of the car door, darting off into the other parked cars. I threw open my car door and ran after her, catching her by the arm and yanking her back as a large SUV backed out, nearly slamming into her. Heart racing and shell-shocked, I pulled myself together as best as I could and held her hand tightly as we walked to the clinic.

When Dr. Charles looked at me with her kind eyes and asked how I was doing, I broke down, sharing with her what had just happened and telling her we had had many such near misses over the years. "I do the very best I can, Dr. Charles, but she is so quick. I'm so scared she'll get hit by a car."

"Mindy, Saachi needs a handicapped sign so that you can park in handicapped spaces. I'm going to give you the paperwork. You'll go to the DMV to get the sign for the car." I had not considered this option before, assuming that handicapped parking spots were reserved for those with physical limitations. Now, with the handicapped sign, we park in a handicapped spot right next to wherever we are headed. I'm still right there as Saachi exits the car door, blocking her from wandering into the parking lot, but we don't have to walk across the parking lot. We haven't had a single near miss since we've had the sign.

271

• • •

After Saachi's diagnosis, I researched service dogs, knowing that her love of animals would augment all the practical benefits a service dog would provide for her. I found several companies online, many of them with fees of $20,000 or more for a service dog. From my research, Canine Companions for Independence looked like a very good company, and because of grants they received, they were able to provide service dogs to applicants without any fee. From my research I also found the CCI application process was very competitive and most applicants were not approved for a service dog. I had to wait until Saachi was five years old before I could even apply. The wait list was also very long—typically two years after the rigorous application process. I waited patiently and filled out the lengthy application as soon as Saachi turned five.

Over the next two years, we completed the application process, including telephone interviews with me and with Saachi's providers, and on-site visits to Canine Companions headquarters. Saachi and I were beyond excited when we made it to the last step of the process—a two-week training boot camp at the Santa Rosa CCI headquarters. When we were matched with Wilder as our new family member, we were overjoyed.

Wilder is an old, old soul, calm and alert. When he came into our lives, I had no idea that one of the biggest services he would provide was elopement prevention. CCI provided us with a vest with an attached harness. When we are out, I hold Wilder's leash and Saachi holds onto his harness. She doesn't leave his side. When we grocery shop, I hold Wilder's leash with one hand and push the grocery cart with the other. Knowing that Saachi is safely holding on to his harness, I can reach for items without the stress and fear of her running off. Even now, with Saachi as a young teenager, I have Saachi hold onto Wilder's harness mainly for safety reasons, but also because "walking beside" someone doesn't come naturally to her. Without Wilder's harness to hold on to, inevitably she wanders ahead, or lags behind, especially in places that are less familiar. Wilder helps with many practical things, including getting Saachi a glove when she is picking at her skin. His calm, gentle nature permeates our home, and she and I both absorb his love and his quiet strength like sponges. Saachi has said that Wilder will come back as a human in his next life; she talks to him throughout the day, explaining excitedly to him everything that she is learning about being human and how things work in this world.

Saachi's impulsivity, her enduring lack of understanding of or ability to sense danger, and her hypotonia and tendency to choke early on created in me a hypervigilance and hyperstartle that bordered on PTSD symptoms. When she was an infant, one time I found her in her crib, on her stomach, face down and buried in her mattress. When I turned her over, she was pale and breathing very shallowly. She lacked the natural instinct or ability to turn her head or to turn over to get more oxygen. For months after this I slept in the room with her, terrified to fall asleep, afraid she would somehow end up face down again and I would sleep through it. She often fell or toppled over and injured herself because of her challenges with balance and coordination. Out of necessity I watched Saachi like a hawk every second, never turning my back on her, keenly aware of how quickly she could impulsively and accidentally harm herself. I was on high alert every moment she was awake, and found that I couldn't turn off this activation of my nervous system even when she slept. I am still astounded when I see toddlers walk around without toppling over, or when they reach for food or a bottle, or eat without assistance, or stay by their parent's side without their hands being held.

When Saachi was almost two, my mom and sister came into town to visit and both spent the night with us. Saachi still was not sleeping well and often woke up in the middle of the night crying. I knew that when she woke up, if I didn't get to her quickly to rock her back to sleep, her system would only get more and more activated and she would be unable to return to sleep for the rest of the night. This, of course, meant that I would not be able to sleep the rest of the night. By this time, I was beyond sleep deprived and utterly exhausted. I needed every precious minute of sleep I could get. That night I woke up immediately with Saachi's first faint cry and ran from my room to her bedroom, swiftly picking her up and dropping into the rocking chair, desperately hoping she would drift back off to sleep before she fully woke up. I thought nothing of my rapid shift from sleep to being wide awake.

My sister, though, had been reading in the living room when I had rushed to Saachi that night. The next morning she said, "Mindy, you really need to calm down. You don't have to run to Saachi at night. She'll be fine." I tried to explain, to tell her that if I didn't get to Saachi immediately, her cries would quickly intensify and then she would be up all night no matter what I did. I saw the skepticism in her eyes, her fixed look. I knew my sister wanted only the best for me and that she was speaking out of concern for me. I also knew that it was impossible to convey how exhausted I was, how desperate I was for sleep, and how I feared I couldn't keep our world afloat, couldn't keep juggling everything all day long if I went another night without sleep. I didn't have the energy to try to help her understand, didn't think she or anyone else could understand. "You're right, Kathy," I said as I looked away, feeling alone and defeated in my attempt to share my world with anyone else.

My friend Mary understood. She recently said, "I still have hypervigilance and hyperstartle all these years later, even now when elopement is much less of an issue for Railey. For Coco [her daughter, who is not autistic], my hypervigilance looks like preference. It's not that she thinks I don't love her. But the hypervigilance has created jealousy—she is always trying to get my attention because my vision is always first going to Railey to make sure there's no danger. When she was two and Railey was four, I would tell her to stay here while I ran after him. At five or six, when Stephen and I were distracted at an airport for a few seconds, she would be furious and terrified that we weren't watching him." Even though her daughter understands the need for vigilance, and in fact prompts her parents when more vigilance with her brother is needed, the equating of attention with love happens at an emotional level, not a mental level, and Coco's jealousy has persisted in spite of her conceptual understanding.

For the first seven to eight years of her life, Saachi was constantly moving, except when she was sound asleep. When she began to walk and climb at two years of age, her hyperactivity combined with her impulsivity became a big concern. I had to be with her at all times, as she was prone to impulsively engage in dangerous behaviors. I had to cushion off all sharp edges in the house with foam.

One day, Saachi was in the kitchen with my mom. Nobody else was as alert to her impulsivity as I was and this was always a concern for me. Although I told everyone who cared for her that they literally needed to watch her every second, it's impossible to imagine the need for this and to muster up the energy to do so. That day, when my mom turned to get something out of the refrigerator, Saachi impulsively put her hand on a hot burner and suffered a severe burn that took months to heal, the healing process complicated by her impulse to pick scabs.

But her impulsivity and distractibility were not limited to dangerous behaviors. She was unable to sustain attention enough to attend to any task without constant prompting. I would have to guide her into the bathroom for bathroom breaks, as she couldn't make it the three yards to the bathroom without getting distracted by a fuzz ball on the floor or a nail in the wall, which she would reach for and completely forget her original mission. She required one-on-one guidance all the time. I became more and more exhausted with the level of attention and effort required just to keep her safe.

I knew that Saachi met criteria for ADHD, but did not want her to begin medication as I tend to be very conservative with medication; I also feared it would alter the development of her brain. When she was four years old, I came across a research study done on the brains of children with ADHD. The treatment group had received medication over a period of time; the control group had not. The brain scans revealed that the brains of the treatment group had normalized over time, while the brains of those without treatment had not. I was shocked. It had never occurred to me that by withholding treatment,

I might actually be preventing Saachi's brain from developing. After speaking with her developmental pediatrician, Dr. Charles, we decided to try Adderall.

I picked up the prescription from the pharmacy that afternoon. The next morning I gave Saachi the pill, which she chewed as she was unable to swallow pills. I watched closely, not knowing what to expect and concerned about possible side effects, such as cardiac issues. To my great surprise, in about fifteen minutes Saachi marched over to a bin that contained markers, pulled out several markers, then reached for a piece of blank paper from another bin, took these items over to a table, sat down, and in her fine motor-challenged way, drew the most beautiful flowers I have ever seen. Never before had she been able to sustain her attention enough to walk anywhere in a room to get something on her own, let alone intentionally get items and complete a task. I was so excited I felt I might explode.

At breakfast, I realized I had forgotten to put Saachi's utensil on the table. I decided to test her, almost pinching myself, to see if her ability to focus was really real. "Saachi, can you go get a spoon, please?"

Saachi marched into the kitchen, got a spoon and sat down at the table. "Mommy, why you cry?" she asked.

"Oh, honey, I'm just so proud of you."

Saachi has been on medication for ADHD since then. It's not perfect. There are side effects—the stimulants, which are the most effective, decrease her appetite and exacerbate her picking compulsion.

Earlier in her therapy, after months of fine motor work in OT sessions and outside of OT, Saachi developed a pincer grasp. This was an important development as it allowed her to pick up small objects, like small pieces of food, and laid the foundation for us to begin working on other skills, like using cutlery, buttoning, and zipping. Soon, however, she began using this skill to pick; she picked scabs, mosquito bites, fingernails, and skin tags until they bled. Eventually, she picked her fingers almost down to the bone.

Her picking compulsion also increased my hypervigilance. We used a hundred Band-Aids a week, finger cots, every type of glove imaginable, and myriads of fidgets. Unfortunately, when she began taking stimulants for ADHD, the medication exacerbated the picking compulsion. Over the years we have adjusted her medication to balance out the tremendous benefit she gets from the medication with the exacerbation of the picking. Sometimes Saachi is able to get herself a Band-Aid or a glove when she starts picking, but often the picking is unconscious or such a strong compulsion that she is unable to stop.

But medication makes it possible for her to function in this world, makes it possible for her to do some things independently, and makes it possible for her to learn new things. Without medication, she would certainly not be able to be mainstreamed at school, or to read, or to focus enough to ride her bike.

I know others who are anti-medication, including friends who believe medication dims children's spirits. It can, especially if the dose is too high or if the child has an adverse side effect to the medication. Saachi has tried many different medications, and for now we have found what works best for her—the combination that causes the fewest side effects and doesn't sedate her or diminish her spirit. In truth, I always err on the side of under-medicating. But for those who hold a rigid belief that medication will harm all children, that no child should be given medication for ADHD, I would ask for them to soften, to listen, to hear what a profound difference medication has made in Saachi's life. She is able to have friends, to do some things independently, to learn new things, to read, to engage in this world in ways she otherwise would not have access to. Medication may not be appropriate for all children with ADHD, but for some, it can make a tremendous difference.

CHAPTER 23

Public or Private School

We see the figure of the child who stands before us
with his arms held open, beckoning humanity to follow.
—Dr. Maria Montessori

Before Saachi was born, I researched Montessori education and decided to educate my child in this type of setting. Maria Montessori, one of the pioneers of early childhood education, developed an educational system that recognized children's natural periods of curiosity about different subjects, or "sensitive periods." With Montessori education, these windows of opportunity are used to honor, support, and harness a child's curiosity to not only learn but also to foster a love of learning—as opposed to the one-size-fits-all approach of more traditional education. Kindness, respect, and inclusion are a foundation of the Montessori school environment. Peace, honesty, equality, compassion, and community are values that are instilled in students. For me, the environment and values instilled at my child's school took priority over other considerations.

It was only after Saachi's diagnosis that I learned that Maria Montessori had begun by teaching students with special needs—many who likely would have been diagnosed with autism today. After Saachi began RDI therapy with Becky, I recognized that Montessori education would be in full alignment with the RDI approach. In many ways, RDI seemed to be an extension of Montessori, and when Saachi was three years old, I enrolled her at Sundrops Montessori, a private Montessori school. Knowing that she needed constant monitoring for safety reasons, and a lot of support in order to engage with her environment, I provided a babysitter that worked with Saachi as an aide while she was at school. Becky and Shelly, her occupational therapist and speech therapist, also worked with her at the school.

Saachi was at Sundrops for a year and a half. At that point, due to cutbacks, class sizes were increased, the school environment became chaotic, and Saachi became more dysregulated. She was no longer learning much or making much progress socially. With some ambivalence, I decided to enroll her at another private Montessori school. While interviewing at schools, I was surprised when Charles Towne Montessori informed me that they would not be able to accept Saachi because of her diagnosis. They had not yet met Saachi and did not ask me about her symptoms or her ability to function in a school environment. This was the first time I had experienced any doors being closed to Saachi because of her diagnosis. After the initial shock, my heart ached as I realized that she would face many such challenges during her life. Ultimately, when she was four-and-a-half years old, I enrolled her at Trinity Montessori, again accompanied by her babysitter. One day, because of her inability to feel her body and to know when she needed to use the restroom, she had a messy accident at school. I was told that she could no longer be there.

I next enrolled her at Unity Montessori. I had attended Unity church several times and was excited about her beginning school there. While many Montessori schools actively recruited a racially-diverse student body, Unity took it a step further, intentionally and actively recruiting racially- and socioeconomically-diverse students. One day, Saachi's babysitter Laura told me she needed to share something with me. "Mindy, there is a student that yells at Saachi every day and the teacher does nothing to stop him. You know that Saachi isn't able to talk at school yet, so she isn't able to speak up. She also doesn't know how to walk away. She stands there while he yells at her, and she cries." I asked the babysitter how long this had been going on. "From the beginning, for the past four months. I have a hard time speaking up and I haven't known how to deal with it."

My heart ached for Saachi, that she had endured this for so long without an advocate to stand up for her. At the same time, I was still shaken by my experiences at Charles Towne Montessori and Trinity Montessori, and had developed a perpetual fear that Saachi's disabilities would cause her to be kicked out of school and that I wouldn't be able to find another Montessori school for her. The next day, we happened to have an appointment with Dr. Charles. I asked for her advice before discussing it with Saachi's teacher.

After sharing with Dr. Charles what had been relayed to me, she said, "Mindy, this is bullying. Every school by law should have a formal process to report and deal with bullying. Ask the school what their process is for this. I would ask for a meeting with the principal and her teacher." I was stunned by her use of the word bullying. It's a strong word—and again my heart ached that my daughter was experiencing this at such a young age.

When I spoke with the principal by phone, the principal said, "I'm sure there has been a misunderstanding here. I very seriously doubt there has been any bullying. Saachi's teacher would have intervened and would also have reported it to me." She did agree to meet with Saachi's teacher, her babysitter, and me the following week. Because of her own history, Laura was terrified by confrontation and asked me if she had to attend the meeting. I told her that for Saachi's sake, I needed her to share with the teacher and the principal her observations, especially considering the principal's initial disbelief that the bullying had actually taken place.

At the meeting, I immediately sensed that the principal and the teacher were on the defense. As soon as the teacher sat down, she crossed her arms. The principal carried a clipboard with a page of handwritten notes that she brought into the room, clearly prepared with her points. I tried to diffuse the tension, letting them know that I was hoping that as a team we could come up with a solution so that Saachi would not be yelled at. I told them that I was not an educator and had no idea how these things were normally dealt with but that I was sure there was a constructive approach that would support not only Saachi, but also the child who was yelling, as there was likely more than the yelling going on with him. The teacher then spoke up, stating that she did not believe that Saachi was being yelled at. She said that she was in the classroom most of the time and claimed she had not witnessed Saachi being yelled at. I looked to Laura, who was trembling with anxiety. Laura looked down at her shoes, and said quietly, her voice shaking, "Well, Miss Johnson . . . well, I see him yelling at her almost every day . . . even when you are right there."

At this point, it was Laura's word against Miss Johnson's. I knew that Laura had no reason to fabricate this. In fact, speaking out and standing up terrified her and she was doing this as a last resort out of her concern for Saachi. The principal said firmly, "I have no reason to believe that what Laura is claiming is happening. I have spoken with the other student and he said he does not yell at Saachi. As far as I am concerned, there is nothing to be done here." Her face was hard, her tone angry. There was no room for discussion. Stunned, I thanked them for their time and told them I would call later after I processed our meeting.

As a private school, Unity was not required by law to have a bullying policy or a means of addressing bullying. Even if they had, I didn't want my daughter attending a school where she would not be protected—and where now her teacher and principal were on the defense. I knew that Saachi would sense their energy and their attitudes towards her. Although I didn't have another option in place and feared I was running out of school options for Saachi, I decided to pull her out of Unity. Although grateful that Laura had ultimately come to me and told me about the bullying, I realized that her terror about speaking up had kept Saachi in harm's way for several months. I spoke about this with Laura and began interviewing for a new babysitter.

I had run out of private Montessori schools that Saachi could attend in Charleston. Two others had refused her admission as they didn't feel they could accommodate her special needs, or didn't want to. But then I heard about a new private school for autistic children, Trident Academy. I was not excited about the school, but after what felt like so many failures with private Montessori schools, I decided to give it a try. I knew I wouldn't be able to afford the $20,000 annual tuition, but grants made it possible for Saachi to enroll.

I was concerned that Trident was a step backward for Saachi. She had been mainstreamed up until then and I was now placing her in a class for children on the spectrum. Saachi often imitated other children's behavior; in a mainstream class, she typically imitated her peers' healthy and developmentally-appropriate behaviors. I feared that at Trident, she might begin to imitate maladaptive behaviors. Trident also utilized an all-ABA approach and I had tremendous reservations about ABA. Nevertheless, I felt that Trident was my last resort and reasoned that perhaps since mainstreaming her hadn't worked, being with staff that were familiar with autism might be best for her.

It turned out that Saachi was much more social and spontaneous than her peers at Trident, but her academic performance was behind her peers and her grade level. She began imitating some of her peers' behaviors with hand flapping and yelling. One afternoon, the school held an outdoor gathering for parents and children. I saw that on the playground with her peers, Saachi initiated interactions with them, but they often did not respond. Saachi's ability to connect with others was much more important to me than academic performance or the ability to do tasks, and I became concerned that she would regress socially or even stop initiating interactions without the engagement of peers.

By the end of that first semester, I was also exhausted from juggling the long commute to her school and the even longer commute between her school and my work. At my end-of-semester meeting with school staff, I felt my heart ache as they updated me on Saachi's progress. Their reports were all about academic achievement (or in

Saachi's case, lack thereof) and progress with tasks. There was no mention of her spirit, her joy, her mischief, her delight. There was no laughter or expression of delight in Saachi. There was no warmth or love. The staff was seeing her through a very narrow behavioral model at the expense of seeing her spirit. After that meeting, I called Becky, our RDI therapist, and wept. I couldn't keep Saachi in an environment where her spirit was not recognized.

By the time Saachi was five years old, she had attended four schools in the past two years. After Trident Academy, I was out of private school options for Saachi. Utterly devastated, I resigned myself to enrolling her in a public school. Having never attended a public school myself, I had never considered public school for Saachi. My parents had wanted their children to attend Christian schools, and as a teenager in the U.S. I had been taught that public schools were full of students and teachers without any values. Unconsciously, I still carried a prejudice that public schools were somehow inferior, that teachers at public schools weren't very good and didn't care much about the students. I had assumed that my vulnerable daughter would be bullied and uncared for, and that her special needs would not be attended to.

I could not have been more wrong.

In researching public schools in Charleston, I was surprised to find that there were several public charter Montessori schools. Several years prior, Charleston County School District had intentionally converted several traditional grade schools in lower income neighborhoods into Montessori programs as a means of fostering racial and socioeconomic integration. Over the years Montessori schools had become education for the elite, typically attracting middle- and upper-income students, and often lacking diversity. CCSD's hope was that these public charter Montessori schools, placed in low-income neighborhoods, would also draw middle- and upper-income students. The model has been very successful and today South Carolina has more public Montessori programs than any state except California. Most students in South Carolina's public Montessori schools come from low income homes, and forty-five percent are racial minorities.

I was very happy to know about this diversity and determined to enroll Saachi at James Simons Montessori, a public charter school in downtown Charleston. The application period had just opened up. After applying, I was told Saachi was at the top of a long wait list, and that most likely she would get in. She did, and her class was a beautiful blend of African-American, Asian, and Caucasian students. They all wore uniforms, and in typical Montessori fashion were instilled with values of community, honoring and supporting each other, and harnessing each child's own innate curiosity as a guide to learning.

Mrs. Kraft and Saachi, preparing for a Montessori 'work'

The summer before her enrollment, I was beyond surprised to hear that the principal, vice principal, and Saachi's teacher all wanted to meet Saachi and me. They were kind, supportive, and compassionate, and clearly wanted what was best for Saachi. Her teacher, Mrs. Kraft, met with Saachi several times before school started so that Saachi could familiarize herself with the classroom and establish a bond with her teacher before she would be overloaded with the sensory input of all the students in the classroom.

Mrs. Kraft came to our home the first time she met Saachi. I showed Saachi pictures of Mrs. Kraft before she came, letting her know that this would be her new teacher. I was nervous, not knowing if Saachi would engage with Mrs. Kraft, knowing that a bond with her teacher was crucial for Saachi's success in the classroom. When Mrs. Kraft knocked on the door, I cracked the door open, greeted her and only opened the door fully when I saw she was ready to step in, ever vigilant of Saachi's tendency to dart outside. I noticed Mrs. Kraft was nervous. Her voice shook a little as she greeted me. I tried to put her at ease, telling her how grateful I was for her visit.

However, as soon as Mrs. Kraft saw Saachi standing behind me, she dropped to the floor, no longer nervous and no longer aware of my chatter. She smiled at Saachi and greeted her quietly. Curious, Saachi walked up to her and touched her hair, then took Mrs. Kraft's purse from her lap. I told Saachi to put it back, that this was Mrs. Kraft's purse. Mrs. Kraft waved her hand at me, telling me to let Saachi explore. I stepped back, reining in my tendency to teach Saachi the rules of what is socially acceptable and my own habitual anxiety that her behavior would make people not like her. Mrs. Kraft helped Saachi unzip her purse and Saachi began to take out the contents, one by one, exploring each item. Occasionally, Mrs. Kraft would show her what she used an item for, like her lip balm or package of tissues. Saachi then pulled out a roll of stamps. I tensed up, fully aware of Saachi's love of stickers, having seen her remove pages of stickers and put them all over her body. She peeled a stamp off and put it on her shirt. Unable to restrain myself, I said, "Mrs. Kraft, she will peel all of them off. Let me take the stamps away from her; I can get you all some stickers to play with."

"No, no, this is perfect! Let her explore, please!" Mrs. Kraft laughed as Saachi continued to remove the stamps, alternately placing them on her shirt, then Mrs. Kraft's shirt, then Saachi's cheek, then Mrs. Kraft's cheek. Mrs. Kraft joined in and began removing stamps and applying them to Saachi's shirt and her own shirt. Saachi looked at her and they giggled together. I felt a hot tear slide down my face, deeply touched by this woman's love and kindness with my daughter. I felt my whole system relax for the first time, knowing that I could fully trust this woman, knowing that this woman was good and pure and that she already loved my daughter. (Later, I asked if I could please buy her more stamps. She refused, but I mailed her some anyway.) For Mrs. Kraft, clearly the value of following Saachi's interests and sharing a connection was worth much more than the stamps.

Mrs. Kraft fell in love with Saachi, as did the rest of the school. They all helped to lay a foundation of connection and success in the school environment that has impacted all of Saachi's life. This was the first school where Saachi's spirit was fully seen, appreciated, and loved, which was more important to me than anything else.

I was told she would need an IEP. I had never heard of an IEP, an Individualized Education Plan, at the private schools Saachi had attended. I was happy to know that her challenges and special needs would be addressed in this plan, which was a legal document, and that the school took supporting her needs very seriously. I couldn't believe it! In addition to being part of her mainstream class, she would have her own school occupational therapist, speech therapist, autism itinerant (an autism specialist), and special ed teacher. How had I not known about this? The public school system was completely set up to support my daughter! And they were trained to do so!

No longer would I need to be in charge of Saachi's learning; no longer would I need to come up with an academic and social program that worked for her; no longer would I need to guide her teachers in every area; no longer would I need to have Saachi's private OT's, ST's and babysitters come to the school and coordinate her school program with them. I hadn't even known how overwhelmed I had been by all of it until I realized I would be able to hand over much of her academic program to professionals who did this for a living.

However, I was still very concerned about her safety. I feared she would elope if she was left unattended. I was terrified that she might leave the building and get hit by a car or kidnapped if she did not have an aide watching her at all times. At our initial IEP meeting, my primary fear for Saachi's safety trumped everything else, even the comfort of knowing how deeply Mrs. Kraft cared for my daughter. I wanted to ensure that the school would provide her with a 1:1 aide for her safety.

The principal, Saachi's teacher Mrs. Kraft, her special ed teacher, and her OT and ST attended the meeting. They were all very kind, but the principal told me that a 1:1 aide was considered the "most restrictive" environment and that by law they needed to provide the "least restrictive" environment for Saachi. I felt panic rise up in my throat. This was my last option in a school and, if they weren't willing to provide a 1:1 for Saachi, it could literally mean life or death for her. I tried to explain how quick Saachi was, and that her ability to dart quickly, combined with her impulsivity and with the fact that her classroom happened to be right next to the exit door, which led outside to a street, could be deadly for Saachi.

They didn't seem to hear me. I sensed in their kind, tempered responses their years of experience with frightened parents, who always requested or demanded more than children needed or would benefit from. They were responding to me from this paradigm, seeing me through the lens of their past experiences with parents, and I didn't know how to remove their biased perspective. I was unable to get them to understand the very real danger this would be for Saachi. With two teachers responsible for twenty-three students, it would be impossible for Saachi to be monitored every second. We discussed alternate ways of providing safety. I had no choice. Terrified, I did my best to surrender to the circumstances.

As we ended our first meeting, I thanked our new team, breaking down as I described to them our journey with private schools, the burden I had been carrying as I tried to oversee every aspect of Saachi's education, and the immense relief I now felt that they could take over much of this for me. Each of them teared up with me, their compassion a balm on my heart.

Mrs. Kraft put a large red piece of tape on the floor in the doorway, instructing Saachi repeatedly not to go past the red tape. She also put a cow bell on the door so that it would jingle any time someone came in or out. These measures did nothing to allay my terror. I knew how quick Saachi could be and that a busy street lay just a few quick steps away from the classroom. In desperation, I purchased an electronic wrist tracker, knowing that it couldn't prevent her from running out the door or prevent imminent danger, but at least it would help me find her if she survived eloping from the school.

Each day Saachi went to school, I feared for her safety. I felt helpless, knowing that no one else was capable of the hypervigilance needed to keep her safe, and unable to protect her myself. At night, I had nightmares about her escaping from school and getting hit by a car. I feared that she would run off in the parking lot during school fire drills, that her teachers would not watch her every second. Although I didn't typically resort to prayer, I prayed fervently for her safety. I am sure that there were close calls, and incidents I was not informed of. But Saachi's team at James Simons Montessori ended up being right. With extra support and a few minor mishaps, Saachi ultimately rose to the occasion. We joked about my initial panic at subsequent IEP meetings. I thanked the staff for their insistence that Saachi did not need a 1:1. After all, I didn't want her dependent on an aide. My goal was always for her to be as independent as possible.

At IEP meetings I knew that if I kept my focus on their love of Saachi and their recognition of her beautiful spirit, they would be motivated to provide what was best for her. Saachi has been at schools where the team has a genuine desire to support her, and I harness their love of her into practical supports. For instance, when her peers weren't understanding her when they came over for play dates, I assumed that her peers didn't understand her at school, so I nudged them to provide an extra speech therapy session each week. When Saachi began to take an interest in handwriting, I told the team that I wanted to take advantage of this "window of opportunity" or "optimal period" (Montessori terms) by adding more OT time each week to work on handwriting. I went out of my way to express gratitude to her teachers for recognizing her spirit, not just her challenges, keeping love and goodwill in the foreground.

But practical things mattered. At each IEP meeting, I told her teachers and staff that they had to prompt her to eat and drink; she was prone to hypoglycemia and she became overheated and dehydrated easily. No one fully understood the importance and dangers of this, and teachers were very busy monitoring all the children in the class. Many times over the years she came home from school pale and weak, barely able to speak, her lunch box and water bottle untouched all day. As soon as she was hydrated and had eaten, her energy and demeanor shifted dramatically and she was back to her energetic and enthusiastic self.

I worried about the potential effects of severe hypoglycemia, including the possibility of brain damage, and spoke about my concerns in IEP meetings. Once Saachi came home weak and pale, with dark circles under her eyes. As I peered in her lunch box to see if she had eaten or drunk anything at school, I heard a thud. My head jerked up, and I saw her crumpled and limp on the floor. She had passed out, dehydrated and hypoglycemic. Once she came to and her physical needs were taken care of, I called the school nurse.

Nurse Julie had become a friend, as Saachi had played with her daughters outside of school several times. I explained to her that Saachi has hypoglycemia and that she is often unable to sense when she is hungry or thirsty, especially in a busy and distracting environment like school. "Julie, I don't know who else to talk to about this. I have been battling this for years, at every school that Saachi goes to. No one ever understands this or takes this seriously even though I explain the dangers. I'm scared to send her back to school. Could you talk to the staff and educate them?"

Julie said immediately, "Yes, I will talk with them, Mindy, but what Saachi needs is an Individualized Health Plan. I'll take care of this. She can eat lunch with the other kids in the cafeteria, but after that she will come to my office each day to finish eating, so that I can monitor her food and fluid intake." I thanked her, my voice cracking with relief and gratitude. Until then, I hadn't even known there was such a thing as an Individualized Health Plan.

My engagement with Saachi's schools is a rich and ongoing education for me. I continue to learn how to navigate school challenges—and I continue to experience a deep gratitude for all the staff and students who offer their love and support and who see and respond to her spirit.

CHAPTER 24

Saachi's Spirit

Look, Wilder!
God is in my salad!
—Saachi Edwards

Left: Izzy and Saachi at Saachi's first Surfer's Healing.
Right: Saachi and Izzy

When Saachi was eighteen months old, she began participating in Surfer's Healing, which she has enjoyed every year since. Surfer's Healing is a day-long surf camp that brings professional surfers to beaches around the world to surf with autistic children. That first year, Saachi surfed with Izzy, the founder of Surfer's Healing, who himself has a son on the spectrum. The photos of her surfing that year still bring tears to my eyes, transporting me back to the gentleness, the spaciousness, the love that Surfer's Healing creates and manifests. Each year, when I step out onto the beach in the midst of all the surfers, volunteers, participants and families, I feel I'm stepping into another realm. The whole world softens, and there is a palpable sense of love permeating the space. Children are free to be completely themselves, and parents are unconstrained by social expectations for their child. In this space of love and complete acceptance, remarkable transformations often occur. Our speech therapist, Shelly, who helps organize the Folly Beach Surfer's Healing, has shared with me that one of her patients spoke for the first time just as he finished surfing.

It is that space of unconditional love that connected Saachi so deeply with Neem Karoli Baba, Ram Dass's guru, from the time she was a baby. She reached for a photo of him often, long before she could hold it, and later carried his picture everywhere. The photo became so tattered I eventually laminated a new one and even this became worn out. She was pulled to anyone connected to Maharajji and loved listening to Krishna Das's chants, at times weeping deeply when she was moved by a song. Krishna Das, like Ram Dass, had been in India with Maharajji.

One day, our dear friend Bub was in the car with us when Saachi suddenly began to weep. Bub became concerned and asked why she was crying. I told him she was moved by the Krishna Das song that was playing. He said, "Oh my God, she knows!" He wanted to turn off the music because she was crying. I knew instinctively the importance of allowing her to experience fully the movement of her sensitive heart, and gently explained to him the value of allowing this heart-felt recognition of love to come forward.

Saachi holding Krishna Das's hand and holding her photo
of Neem Karoli Baba, as Krishna Das greets others

From infancy on, Saachi had a deep connection with Krishna Das. From the time she was a baby, I took her to his kirtans and retreats, where she would invariably give him a photo of Neem Karoli Baba or try to climb up on the stage to be with him. During one kirtan at a large church in Atlanta, she ran up on the stage before I could stop her, just as KD was getting ready to begin singing—to his delight and everyone else's. I scooped her up laughing and ran off the stage, holding her back as she tried to get up on the stage throughout the rest of the kirtan. Krishna Das came to know her. He recognized her spirit and at one retreat spoke of her closeness to God. After another retreat, she stood next to him and held his hand while he greeted a long line of participants. I was astonished. Up until then, Saachi's body had been in constant motion from the moment she was born. I had never seen her stand still, let alone for that long.

When Saachi was three, we took part in a kirtan led by Shyam Das. I had not heard of him before but heard that a Neem Karoli Baba devotee who sang kirtan was coming to town. The kirtan was beautiful. After it was over, Saachi and I shifted back into our busy lives and didn't mention him again. Over a year later, Saachi was still learning how to talk. Out of the blue, she began to say, "Shah dah! Shah dah! Shah dah!" In spite of my best efforts, I was unable to understand what she was saying. She persisted, and continued to insistently repeat this every day.

After about a month, I finally figured out that she was saying Shyam Das. I knew Shyam Das lived in India, and said, "Honey, he is in India, we can't go see him." She looked intently at me, and again repeated, "Shah dah!!! Shah dah!!!" Tired of her repetition, I thought to look on the internet to see if he might be coming to the U.S. any time soon. Perhaps I could take her to his kirtan, if nothing else to try to dissipate her obsession with his name. I typed "Shyam Das" into the search bar and pressed return.

Shyam Das had died in a motorcycle accident a month prior. Everything went silent—all the busyness of my daily life vanished. I turned slowly to her and looked in her eyes. "You knew, honey. You were trying to tell me. He has left his body. I know now." I took her by the hand and we went into our backyard, where Saachi picked a bright pink camellia. We climbed the stairs and put the flower at the feet of our statue of Neem Karoli Baba. She hasn't mentioned Shyam Das again.

• • •

When Saachi was three, we traveled to Maui for a Ram Dass retreat. With her deep connection to Neem Karoli Baba (also known as Maharajji), my own connection with Ram Dass and Neem Karoli Baba, and her connection with Krishna Das, I wanted to take her to the annual Open Your Heart in Paradise retreat so she could meet Ram Dass. I knew that she would feel at home with a group of people who were also deeply connected with Maharajji—with what felt to me like our soul family.

The trip was a huge undertaking and I began preparing Saachi several weeks ahead of time. The trip involved three long flights each way; she would have to stay in her seat during the flights and be in loud, busy airports between flights. I would need to pack most of her food for the entire week because of her food sensitivities, change her pull-up several times in a tiny airplane bathroom, and be fully present for her throughout the trip while juggling all the practical necessities.

We visited the airport several times beforehand. I made sure Saachi had her hot pink noise-blocking headphones on, and spoke with her about the airport ahead of time in an excited voice, telling her how much fun it would be. The airline staff allowed us to walk on an airplane and practice sitting down in the chair and fastening our seat belts. Shelly created a social story about the trip, using simple sentences to describe the trip from Saachi's perspective, accompanied by pictures. "My name is Saachi and this is a story about how I will be going on an airplane for the first time. Mom will be with me the whole time and will hold my hand in the busy airport. I will get on the airplane with mom, sit down in my special seat, and put my seatbelt on. The plane will make a loud sound when it starts to fly. I will have my headphones on and it won't sound loud to me. It's so beautiful to look at the clouds out the window...." The story went on to describe the hotel we would stay in and other aspects of our trip that would help prepare Saachi for the journey.

We arrived at the retreat right before the first evening gathering. About seventy-five pairs of shoes lined the entrance to the gathering space, which was open to the balmy air. Some people were still milling about, others were already seated on zafus on the floor or in chairs. I held Saachi on my hip, looking for a spot near the entrance in case she wasn't able to be still enough and we had to step out of the room once the session got started. As someone walked by, Saachi wriggled in my arms and reached out. I turned, looking towards where she was reaching, and saw a woman nearby. She saw Saachi reaching out to her and walked up to us. Saachi leaned towards her and placed her forehead on the woman's forehead, their noses touching. The woman took Saachi from my arms; they smiled as they looked in each other's eyes.

"You know about *honi*! What is your name, precious?"

Saachi was silent and still, unable to speak. I answered for her. "Her name is Saachi. What is your name? Saachi has such a strong connection with you!" Lei'ohu explained to me that honi is an ancient and traditional Hawaiian greeting where two people greet each other by touching foreheads and noses. The foreheads touch at the third eye, or the intuitive center of the body. By touching forehead to forehead, greeters connect deeply and intuitively. While touching noses, greeters exchange breath. The ha, or divine breath, is held in each person. When greeters exchange breath, they are exchanging the part of themselves that comes directly from Spirit—the breath of God.

Saachi bowing to Ram Dass

Lei'ohu and Saachi on stage at the
Open Your Heart in Paradise retreat

Then Ram Dass came into the room in his wheelchair. Saachi walked right up to him and rested her head on his knee. Ram Dass placed his hand on his heart, then on her head, his face shining with love. My heart filled with joy. Their meeting and connection felt like a completion, a coming full circle.

A few minutes later, Lei'ohu opened the retreat. She took Saachi up on stage with her and held her in her lap as she spoke. I felt myself tense up, knowing that the lights, the sound of the loud speakers, and all the people would be overwhelming for Saachi. Lei'ohu spoke about Saachi's spirit, about her purity, innocence, and openness, and with her words and Saachi's presence we all dropped into that place within ourselves. I relaxed into the sweetness. Saachi looked out at the crowd of people, her sweetness, her gentleness, her vulnerability permeating the whole space.

After some time, she started to cry, touched by and overwhelmed with all of the input. I stepped up to the stage as Lei'ohu handed her to me and I held her close. Lei'ohu then spoke about the unconditional and pure love of the Divine Mother. I was stunned and embarrassed when she spoke of me as the embodiment of the Mother. I had spent the last three years feeling that I wasn't doing enough for Saachi, feeling guilty for the times I had lost my patience, for the times I wasn't fully present with her. I knew Lei'ohu had seen the depth of Saachi's spirit, but I figured she had gotten it wrong about me.

The next day, Saachi and I stepped outside during one of the talks. Our friend Bubbie was standing outside. Once again, rows of shoes lined the entrance and the path in front of the entrance. While Bubbie and I spoke, Saachi began trying on shoes, each pair swallowing up her feet. With each pair, she clopped along for several steps, then abandoned the pair she had just walked in and tried on another pair. I tried to stop her, realizing that the owners wouldn't be able to find their shoes when they came out. I knew from my own experience that at retreats with a large group of people, it was hard enough to remember where I had left my shoes during the chaos of everyone exiting and putting on their shoes all at once. But Saachi was on a mission and not easily stopped. Bub told me to let her be, to let her enjoy the shoes. "It'll be good for everyone to come out and find things are different than what they expected!" I burst out laughing, imagining the scene, and let Saachi play shoe dress up. She tried on every single pair of shoes, and moved all of them to different places. I made sure we were gone before everyone came out.

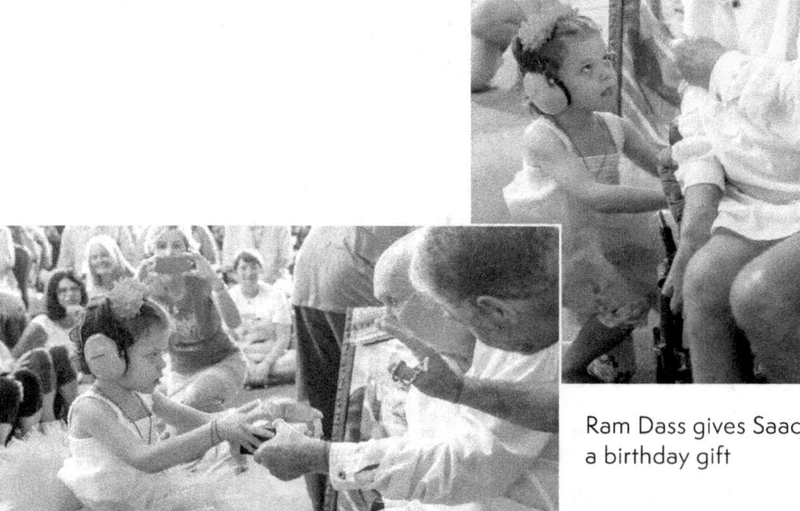

Ram Dass gives Saachi a birthday gift

Saachi's birthday fell during the retreat. We had a birthday party in our hotel room and the hotel staff made her a giant birthday cake. Later, at the closing ceremony, Ram Dass gave Saachi a small Hanuman statue. After opening the gift on the floor, she gazed up at him, looking into his eyes. Ram Dass held his hand on his heart as they beamed at each other. For everyone else, this was a beautiful moment. For me, not only was my heart brimming over, but I was also surprised to see how present Saachi was, astonished that she was looking into someone else's eyes when this was not something she normally did, and stunned that she was sitting still. Her connection with Ram Dass cut through her usual symptoms.

After the retreat, we returned home, basking in the love and spaciousness, in the sense of having been home with family. The next day, though, I jumped right back into my rigorous schedule of work, therapies with Saachi, babysitters, and household chores. The busyness of my life soon clouded my awareness of Saachi's spirit.

My life was set up within the traditional medical paradigm of attempts to ameliorate Saachi's symptoms. I didn't have a place to put my awareness of her spirit, didn't know how to shape our lives around that, but I was aware that something was missing. An email I wrote to my friend Mary reflected that: "I am usually so busy with the practical day-to-day instead of resting in the deeper spiritual knowing, which is by far most important to me… There is a mismatch with what I know deeply and where most of my attention/ energy is. I would so love to reside and rest in the heart and soul, while doing all the rest."

• • •

Not long after Saachi began speaking, she began to make strange sounds with her voice. This was another intense fear-trigger for me. The sounds were so bizarre, so strange—so other-worldly—that I feared Saachi would scare away anyone who might be interested in connecting with her. Whenever she began to make sounds, I interrupted her, often harshly, and told her to use her words, not sounds. Just as she did when I yanked her out of her merged state of consciousness during her "zoning out" episodes, Saachi often cried when I interrupted her sounds. As she learned to use her voice, the sounds became more and more frequent, intensifying my fear.

Years later, my friend Toni, who is also on the spectrum, shared with me that as a child she, too, made unusual sounds. She explained that the sounds attuned her body, sort of like tuning up a musical instrument, and helped her come into her body more. Crushed and humbled yet again by the ignorance and pain my fear had caused, I sat Saachi down, looked her in the eye, and apologized for the countless times I had been so harsh with her when she made sounds. I told her that I now understood that it was very important for her to make the sounds and explained that while it was probably best not to make those sounds while she was with others, here at home she could make them any time without my interference. Later, another friend who is very intuitive and works with individuals on the spectrum and their families suggested her theory that Saachi and others on the spectrum are communicating in another language with other beings or realms.

I also came to understand Saachi's sensory issues in a context deeper than the traditional medical paradigm of defining autism in terms of symptoms. Whereas traditional medicine may define a lack of awareness of body sensations or an exquisite sensitivity to sensory input as "sensory issues," I came to understand these symptoms as manifestations of Saachi's sensitivity and openness of spirit, of her state of consciousness. As with many individuals on the spectrum, Saachi's body was extremely sensitive in so many ways but, paradoxically, in other ways she was completely unaware of her body. Her profoundly heightened sensitivity to sound and light, and the way she absorbed the emotions and energies of others around her often overwhelmed her system and caused her great pain.

As my eyes opened to the depth of her spirit, I came to understand that her symptoms were a reflection of her spirit's sensitivity, and sensed that her system was vibrating at a frequency much more subtle than the rest of the world's. The tremendous discrepancy between her frequency and the more gross frequencies of the world made it impossible for her to inhabit her body fully and completely. The body is where the spirit and the world meet, and it was almost impossible for her to tolerate the harshness of the world. It was too painful. As time went on, her spirit was better able to integrate the energy of the world, and she was better able to inhabit her body.

Saachi came into the world in a place of unity. She identified as spirit and didn't identify with her body or think that "she" was located in and limited to her body. This also explained her inability to sense hunger or thirst. Her consciousness was expanded far beyond the confines of the body. In realizing Saachi's depth and breadth of spirit, I saw that energetically she and others who share this sensitivity of spirit are forging a path for the rest of us. Where they reside is where the rest of us are evolving towards—a place of unity, love, and no separation. They come to us from a place beyond this realm, and in bringing themselves here they refine our energy by their very presence. My energy becomes more subtle and more sensitive because Saachi is here. Her spirit pulls me into love.

Saachi and Mindy

I recognize that one of my roles is to support her in coming more fully into her body, in integrating more fully into the world. But while this used to be in the foreground of my consciousness—when my fear that she wouldn't be able to function in the world drove most of my interactions with her—my role in helping her learn to be in the world is now in the background. Who she is and her role here is much deeper and much more profound than her ability to function in this world. By their very presence in the world, she and others like her are guiding all of us back to the love that we are.

Infants and children open our hearts because of the innocence and purity that they embody. We recognize in them the very qualities that are at our core. Over time, as children develop their sense of "me" and identify with their personalities, their innate innocence fades into the background. Their natural sense of oneness, of unity, of wonder and awe, and their spontaneity begin to fade as their sense of "me" crystallizes and they learn about the way things work in this realm. Individuals on the autism spectrum are born in this unity, permeability, and oneness, and they experience their environment as not separate from themselves. Unlike others, they retain the childlike openness and transparency that arises from living in non-separation.

When Saachi feels joy, it flows from her completely uninhibited and is infectious. When she experiences a tenderness of heart, for instance when a song moves her heart, she weeps openly, the tenderness flowing through her without any inhibition or self-consciousness. Similarly, she experiences and expresses sadness fully, without thought dampening the experience. If Saachi is sad, and she is asked why she is sad, she often doesn't know. She is just fully in the experience, not attaching a mental reason or cause to what is happening. She doesn't have the drive or need to understand her experience or to interpret it. The energy/emotion moves through her system and then it is complete. She is present in the moment with whatever arises.

Saachi is completely herself, incapable of pretending or faking anything. Like a child, she is spontaneous and uninhibited, without the ability to imagine what someone else might be thinking about her, without the ability to superimpose ideas about what may or may not be socially acceptable, and without the ability to compare herself or anyone else to another person. She never developed self-consciousness. She is who she is, and she is incapable of judging others. When we go for walks, she stops to watch others; she is fascinated by them, without understanding that this may make them uncomfortable. She is present with whatever arises in the moment and responds spontaneously to the entirety of the situation. Her presence and spontaneity bring out the best in others—love, joy, the impulse to help, and their own innocence and purity.

Saachi doesn't understand the concept of a stranger. I have explained it to her many times, worried that because of her innocence she may be taken advantage of. Because she experiences others as herself, the concept of a "stranger" is foreign to her and she is fascinated by it. I have heard her explaining to her dog Wilder many times that a stranger is someone that you haven't met before—processing this concept in her own way, and as she says, helping to prepare him for his next reincarnation as a human being. To her, not having met someone, not having spoken with someone before, doesn't translate into lack of familiarity. When a "stranger" is crying, she goes up to them, sits beside them, or hugs them.

Similarly, Saachi struggles to understand the concept of ownership. If you don't experience yourself as separate from others, and if you experience yourself much more as energy/spirit than as body/matter, something belonging to you and not to someone else would be impossible to understand. Because of her inability to understand the concept of ownership, when we are on walks, Saachi doesn't understand that she shouldn't explore others' yards. She never went through the childhood stage of "Mine!" Sharing is not a concept to her; it happens spontaneously because she isn't able to impose the idea of ownership onto objects.

Saachi and Mindy

For Saachi, the wonder and awe she expressed as a small child has not faded at all. She is equally in wonder of a mosquito as she is of a giraffe. One day, Saachi's teacher emailed and said that Saachi had found an ant in the classroom, named the ant Jeb, and insisted on finding it a good place to live. The whole class became involved and the school nurse prepared a cup with some food. Recently Saachi watched in wonder as a small gnat flew about and asked, "Mommy, can I pet the gnat?" It's as if she is experiencing everything on Earth the way someone from another planet might—fresh and full of wonder.

Throughout the day, every day, she explains to Wilder what it's like to be human. As she learns the rules of this realm, she explains them to him. "Wilder, when you are a human, you use your voice to say words." "Wilder, see, if you are unkind, it hurts people's hearts." "Wilder! You have to wear your helmet when you ride a bike or you could get hurt!"

By breaking social norms, those on the autism spectrum show the rest of us how we unconsciously follow all the rules, even the ones we aren't aware of. They think outside the box—because their mind doesn't have a box to begin with.

The way Saachi uses words reflects this lack of restrictive mental structure. One morning during breakfast, she suddenly said, "Mommy, kind words hug the soul." Recently, after sitting cross-legged while playing cards for some time, her leg tingled from having fallen asleep. When she stood up she said, "Oh my lands! My leg has some hoarseness!" Her friend Adam, who also has a diagnosis of autism, recently emailed her to thank her for a tie-dyed shirt she made for him. He said, "Dear Saachi, That makes my heart bloom up. You are the best ever. Love, Adam."

Saachi has difficulty remembering rules—whether they are rules of a soccer game, rules in our home, or societal norms. Some people on the spectrum experience the opposite—a fixation with or over-emphasis with rules. These are opposite sides of the same coin. When a being is residing as spirit, as energy, and the grosser world of matter is in the background, an over-emphasis on rules can serve to make this realm of matter and the concrete world more real. Working to harden concepts can bring the world into the foreground and in this way make it less difficult to function here.

Wilder and Saachi dressed up in hair bows

Although Saachi explains to Wilder the "rules" of being human while she learns about this world, in her daily life she is often unaware of norms and others' expectations. She stirs up energy wherever she goes, shaking things up and leaving a bit of chaos in her wake. This might be uncomfortable for me—like when she touches a strangers' shorts—but my greater sense is that even though in my role as her mother I try to contain the chaos, shaking energy up and breaking up some social norms is good for all of us. Breaking out of our normal state of consciousness even momentarily can expand our capacity to be present with and inclusive of aspects of others and ourselves that we may otherwise not have opened to.

Saachi often asks me what something that does not have a voice would say if it could speak, or she gives voice to it herself. "Mommy, what is the water saying?" "What does the trampoline say when we jump on it, Mommy?" Last night, she had a pain in her leg and asked, "Mommy, what is the pain saying?" Sometimes she asks me what something says and instead of answering, I ask her what she thinks it says. One day, she asked, "Mommy, what does life say?"

"I don't know, honey. What does it say?"

Saachi said, "It says, I want to love."

What I see as revelations of the depth of her state of consciousness carry no more weight to her than anything else she might say. Everything is equal because for her there is no "deeper," no comparison to another state. Everything just *is*.

• • •

The shift of my primary focus from amelioration of Saachi's symptoms to the recognition of the depth of her spirit did not happen all at once. There were many "aha's" along the way, where seeing her state of consciousness pierced my habitual, fear-driven efforts to get rid of her symptoms. Layers of grief and acceptance continued to emerge, each layer dissolving yet another veil of fear. This juxtaposition of fear and grief with the recognition of her spirit was often uncomfortable, disconcerting to my system and bewildering to my mind, but as the acceptance dissolved the fear, and more and more space opened up to allow me to truly see her spirit, her spirit then moved into the foreground for me. The real transformation happened at a cellular level, from the inside out. In this way, my recognition of her spirit was a spiritual path back to my own heart.

With all spiritual paths, although a mental concept or paradigm can be useful in conceptually understanding where the transformative process is heading, the real transformation takes place at a deeper level—at a level where habitual patterns of thought, emotion, and energy shift in a foundational way. As the veil of my fear about Saachi's ability to be in the world dissolved, space opened up in my system for a deeper truth to reveal itself. The hallmark of every spiritual path is the dissolution of contraction, of fear, which is the source of separation and suffering. When fear dissolves, that which is deeper and truer than fear emerges. When fear and separation dissolve, love remains.

In realizing the depth of my daughter's spirit, how do Saachi and I live our lives together? On a very practical level, it remains hard for her and others on the spectrum to function in this world. Do we abandon efforts to try to make those with autism more "normal," to try to make them more like us so they can better function in the world? With the shift in my understanding of my daughter, the way I hold her uniqueness and challenges has changed. I'm no longer trying to make her more normal. I open myself and my spirit to hers, thereby opening to the purity, innocence, sensitivity, and love that is the birthright of each of us. But in my role as her mother, I continue to support her in learning how to navigate this world as much as possible—in speech articulation that will help her communicate more clearly, fine motor skills, and other skills that support her towards independence. These efforts, though, are no longer fueled by fear, and no longer take front and center stage. The practical things we do are just what we do to help her be in the world. Meanwhile, I'm aware that we are all evolving into residing in the place she inhabits—the space of love.

A note on "normal"

Western society has firmly defined boundaries around what is considered "normal" and acceptable behavior. Any behavior outside of those boundaries is typically pathologized when seen through the lens of the traditional Western medical paradigm—symptoms needing to be fixed or made more "normal." But what is pathologized in Western cultures is perceived very differently by other societies in which an individual is viewed primarily through the depth of their spirit—their connection to God.

Within this context, non-conformity with social norms or the inability to function in "normal" society is interpreted as a reflection of one's spiritual state of consciousness, and these individuals are seen as visionaries or mystics. They are honored and revered for their insights, sensitivities, and gifts. In these cultures, if someone is regarded as a holy person, they are supported by the rest of society when they cannot meet their own basic needs. In India, sadhus or holy men or women are given food by others. While the medical paradigm is still available and utilized when needed, the societal paradigm is broader and deeper and allows for a larger context within which to hold all expressions of humanity.

Ramana Maharshi was an Indian sage and guru who was considered an enlightened being. As a teenager, he fell into a deep samadhi, or meditative state, and was completely unaware of his body. He was so unaware of his body and his surroundings that others had to put food in his mouth to keep him from starving. Later, he was recognized as one of India's greatest saints. In the West, Ramana Maharshi would likely have been diagnosed with a psychiatric disorder. The traditional Western medical paradigm tends to view all uniqueness or variations from the normal curve as pathology, as symptoms that need to be gotten rid of or fixed. Because of this, many spiritual experiences or openings are misinterpreted and suppressed, and many individuals who come into this world with a depth of spiritual sensitivity are not seen for who they are.

Shifting into a broader paradigm of autism, which includes recognizing the spiritual sensitivity of these beautiful beings, broadens and deepens the spiritual awareness and sensitivity of the entire society. By recognizing and becoming more sensitive to the divine in others, we realize it in ourselves. The divine, by nature, is not limited to individuals; it is within all and gives birth to all. When we recognize the divine, whether our minds attribute it to another or ourselves, we are realizing it within our own human form. As we all become more sensitized to the divine, the world naturally shifts to ways of being that are more supportive of that sensitivity.

Meanwhile, even as we recognize the state of divine consciousness and the depth of spirit of autistic individuals, we have to continue to support these individuals in learning to be in the world as it is now; to help them navigate the "normal" world with their sensitivities. The shift is that our efforts to help them adjust to the world—a world that does not share their awareness and sensitivities—moves to the background, and seeing their spirits remains in the foreground. We are not trying to "fix" them. In fact, we recognize and honor the depth of their spirit and we aspire to develop our own spiritual sensitivity. But we see the tremendous challenges a sensitive being faces in functioning in a harsh world that has not yet evolved to unity consciousness, and we do what we can to support them in learning to navigate the world. We do what we can to help the world see more deeply. We do what we can to open to our own sensitivity, to the unity and love that is at our own core, that is at the core of all creation. And ultimately, Love Itself, the love that is at my core, at your core—the love that we are—is seen, is known, is realized by our own individual consciousness.

PART IV

Spirit

It is love alone that gives worth to all things.
—St. Theresa of Avila

CHAPTER 25

The Fire Reawakens

Isn't it time to turn your heart into a temple of fire?

—Rumi

I loved my daughter deeply and recognized the depth of her spirit. Even so, a feeling of emptiness and a sense of the meaninglessness of life had been my near constant companions since I had given up on Truth. My life was bursting at the seams on every level, but ever present beneath all of the busyness, beneath all of the joys and stress, was the utter spiritual devastation that had been with me since that day in Tampa when I could no longer tolerate the intensity of my longing for Truth. All hope and spiritual seeking had died that day.

When my friend Vanesa started talking enthusiastically about a new spiritual teacher she had met, I was quietly skeptical. Vanesa was uprooting her whole life and moving across the country in order to live in his spiritual community. As she went on about how he was "the real deal," I internally rolled my eyes. I had been with so many spiritual teachers, and was done with them. Even if I resonated with their teachings or felt a transmission in their presence, none had helped me fulfill my deepest longing for Truth. I had given up on Truth and teachers. Not only that, I had no time to read his website as she kept urging me to do.

Six months later, in 2015, exhausted and ready to collapse into bed, I found myself watching a video of this teacher and felt something awaken deep within me. He spoke of Truth, of his own awakening, and said that the realization of Truth was possible in this life if you had a spiritual teacher who could guide you. I felt an unmistakable current of energy, an awakening of my chakras, as he spoke directly to me. What the hell was happening? Satvata felt so familiar to me, and I was experiencing the force of the very Truth of which he spoke. Even his name meant "the devotee of Absolute Truth." By the end of the video, I was on fire.

I emailed him that night and, to my surprise, he emailed back a minute later and scheduled an online meeting in two weeks. As soon as I saw him on screen, I became aware of a current of energy between us. Satvata looked at me and around me and said, "You seem to be quite spiritually open; you've had quite a saturation in your system with Ram Dass. But it hasn't been integrated, and so it can't complete." It was as if two things were happening at once— this current of energy was in the foreground, and the words we exchanged in the background.

I shared openly with Satvata my intense longing for Truth and how I had come to a place where I could no longer bear it and had given up. I wept, sensing that he was fully receiving and understand- ing the utter devastation I had been living with. After asking me about my life circumstances, he said, "I'm here for this—my job is to take people where they can't go by themselves. The glimpses you've had can't take root until the vessel has been processed more. You couldn't be doing a more effective *sadhana* (spiritual practice) to take you to Truth than what you are doing right now. The burning, the longing, is the last stage. This inner fire consumes that in us which is not Truth and Love."

Satvata instructed me to simplify my life, and to restrain my tendency to get involved. He said I was allowing myself to get over-involved with my daughter and at work. "As long as you are as invested and identified as you are with your daughter, you're standing in the way of her forming her own identity. All your devotional energy has needed an outlet and has been channeled to her. If instead you channel it to a realized being, you merge in realization. You are already a high being and are working from a high consciousness. You need to simplify in order to have time to be with God and Truth. Your highest dharma is to go to God and Truth. Your other dharma is to take care of your daughter and to work. Now that we've met, something can start happening that hasn't been able to happen before."

He went on. "When you're a dry log and you roll up next to the bonfire, you start burning. So cozy up and you'll be consumed in the flame that I am. Just keep getting connected to me and this will keep pointing to what's left in you. Coming out of your personal self and strengthening your spiritual self is the process."

I could hardly believe it. After all these years, after having given up hope, I was now being told that he would help guide me to Truth. "Thank you for coming into my life," I said, with a depth of gratitude and relief. I asked him if he had any other suggestions besides simplifying my life.

"Meditate for two hours each day." I laughed out loud. I had no idea how I could find ten minutes to meditate, let alone two hours. With this fire reawakened in me, though, I knew I would find a way. "When you meditate, sit silent and still. If you think of me, the capacity will continue to expand because I am meditation personified."

And with that, my whole life changed. My circumstances didn't change much for some time, but my whole life did. The fire within grew and intensified. My path was clear now, and my compass was Satvata. He awakened in me the possibility of fully realizing Truth in this life.

There wasn't much I could do to simplify my life, but I did the best I could. I was determined to meditate two hours each day as instructed, so I stayed up an hour later and woke up an hour earlier to do so. This meant getting three to four hours of sleep each night. I was on fire, though, and didn't feel tired. Instead of devastation and emptiness underlying my entire life, this reawakened fire and longing were my constant companions.

I was filled with gratitude. The gratitude soon shifted into devotion and a longing to be with Satvata. Western culture tends to value autonomy and independence; there is little space for or understanding of devotion. In Eastern cultures, where gurus and spiritual teachers are woven into the fabric of daily life, devotion to a teacher or guru is a natural and important part of one's life. I felt as if I had been waiting all my life for a living teacher to guide me to Truth, and the transmission of energy I was receiving from Satvata seemed to break a dam and fan the flames within my heart all at once.

I experienced an intense longing to merge with the Truth and Love I recognized in him. I felt free to share everything with him, either through emails or Skype meetings—my spiritual experiences, challenges, and insights—or to ask for guidance. He offered guidance, encouragement, and affirmation. I joined in by phone for Satvata's weekly talks, each time feeling the burning fire inside intensify.

In group gatherings, I could see that all of his devotees or students were responding to a deep inner call, but many were also vying for Satvata's attention and approval. Igniting a deep spiritual longing for Truth and Love also activated a personal desire for love and approval in many who wanted to be special to him. Whenever Satvata praised someone, speaking highly of their spiritual attainment or their higher spiritual qualities, some in the room experienced jealousy so thick it could be cut with a knife. I saw clearly that by praising students' spiritual experiences or attainments, he was simply boosting their spiritual egos. I didn't understand how egoic spiritual achievement was any different from any other type of attainment in the world, and didn't understand why he was stimulating our egos in this way, but assumed it was a tool to bring us closer to Truth and Love.

Sometime later, while standing in line for lunch at a weekend retreat, I overheard Devi, Satvata's wife, tell another student that Satvata "is always infatuated with new devotees and their spiritual potential, but like in romantic relationships, it always wears off." I was alarmed to hear this, but shoved aside my discomfort. I wondered if Devi was jealous of his relationships with his devotees, as I certainly would have been if I were in her shoes. I assumed that if what she said were true, Satvata had a long-term plan for the devotee's spiritual development and his decreasing engagement with students who weren't new wouldn't be coming from his own egoic boredom or disappointment. I didn't believe he was capable of self-motivated behavior.

Meanwhile, all my old issues of fear, jealousy, and reactivity were being activated and magnified. Satvata explained that these were old *samskaras* (the subtle impressions of old actions) that were being transformed by the fire of the force of Truth that he transmitted; over time, this fire would burn up these aspects of the individual ego. Ultimately, this fire of Truth would burn up the illusion of the separate self—the cause of all suffering. Each time I heard him speak, the fire in me burned brighter. Each time I was around him, even virtually, the energy in my system was magnified. He told us he was the transformative Vortex of Truth that would purify our systems and bring us to Truth and Love. Experiencing this vortex, this massive energy of Truth, was an important part of our purification and transformation process.

Early on I had no reason to doubt him. Not until much later did I understand that the vortex was not "his"—this energy was and is the life force in all beings. An intensification of this life force energy can be cultivated by anyone through meditation, and is also intensified by the attention and projection of others onto a teacher. In my case, my projection onto him was not only a mental idealization but also an energetic projection, fueled by the power of my sincere longing for Truth. Even the assumption that this energetic vortex was closer to enlightenment, or to Truth, was simply another mental concept. The effort to cultivate this energy was another attempt to "get *there*"—somewhere other than right here and now. Energies come and go, and experienced energetic stimulation or flow is never the absolute Truth.

But I wouldn't come to this understanding until later. I initially attributed this intense energetic force to Satvata and assumed it was my direct path to Truth. I longed to meet Satvata in person. Soon I was preparing to attend a weekend retreat, piecing together a 24/7 babysitting schedule. At the retreat, the energy intensified, as did my longing. When Satvata finished his talk and opened up the room for questions, my hand shot up in the air. He called me up to the front of the room to the "hot seat."

I knew that in order to purify my system, I would need to meet all of the contractions in my system and allow them to burn up in this fire. Exposing my issues would serve to move that process along. The longing in me was so great that I wanted to expose to the light every obstacle, like my jealousy and my desire to be special to him. I said bluntly, "I only want Truth, Satvata. AND I want to be your only student! I don't want there to be anyone else." I laughed as I gestured towards the audience. I heard them and Satvata join me in laughter. He told me I was destined for Truth, but that he could see that there were hard-wired contractions in my system that would need to unwind. He gave me a few more instructions, then cut our conversation short.

I soon discovered that exposing my human desires prompted him to trigger those very issues. I presumed he did this as a means of clearing them out. He began limiting my contact with him, knowing that would kick my jealousy into gear. He limited me to one Skype session every two months and told me not to attend retreats. The old childhood terror of not going to heaven resurfaced in a different form—the resurgent fear that I would not come to Truth. Satvata told me I was very sensitive to his transformative force and didn't need much contact with him—virtual or in his presence—for the transformation to continue. Nevertheless, my jealousy and fear overrode any feelings of being "special" because of my spiritual sensitivity.

On one retreat, I shared with others the difficulty I was having with the fear and jealousy that was triggered by Satvata's limits on my contact with him. Devi, his wife, was sitting nearby, and said, "If you want more contact, pretend like it doesn't matter to you. He's limiting your contact because he knows it will trigger you." I was surprised and disconcerted by her advice. Any idea of trying to manipulate Satvata in order to avoid my own issues was at odds with the whole thrust of my life. Her advice was out of alignment with my intention and my integrity, and I set her words aside.

In addition to intentionally triggering my fear and jealousy, Satvata told me I needed to slow down the transformative process to protect my nervous system and be able to care for Saachi. He often told me of the importance of fulfilling all of my worldly duties, including caring for Saachi and working, even while I engaged in this intense spiritual journey. He said, "You cannot get there any faster. Now that you have found me, your progress is assured. I am feeling your connection to me. This means you are in the boat and being carried to your goal. Have faith in this process and continue to follow my instructions."

I had no intention of not fulfilling all of my responsibilities. I appreciated Satvata's understanding and respect for my life circumstances and responsibilities, but in spite of his instruction to slow down the process, I was still on fire. I wanted to dive straight in. I feared I wouldn't get to Truth with his imposed limits on my direct participation with him. There was no way I was going to try to slow down the process! I was determined to follow all of Satvata's guidance and his many instructions—with the exception of slowing down the process. If I followed his instructions, surely my spiritual progress would be faster.

In addition to meditating two hours each day, he instructed me to copy one chapter each day from the *Bhagavad Gita*. After returning home from work, caring for Saachi, putting her to bed, cooking and taking care of household chores, late at night I meditated and handwrote a chapter from the Gita. Satvata also told me to cut all caffeine, sugar, and chocolate out of my diet. I had been eating a bar of dark chocolate each day as a means of boosting my energy. I didn't know how I would give it up, but I determinedly returned ten bars of chocolate to Whole Foods, gave up the black tea that helped get me going in the morning, and began to read food labels religiously to ensure there was no sugar.

Later, Satvata told me to exercise vigorously for a total of four to five hours each week. I told him I didn't know how I would squeeze it into my day. I was only getting three hours of sleep each night as it was and I was managing all the practical aspects of my life as efficiently as humanly possible. He told me I needed to figure out how to fit it in. I was in complete surrender and had been following all of his instructions, but with this direction I felt desperate. I didn't know how I could possibly fit more into my day. It felt as though the circumstances of my life were preventing me from realizing my deepest longing!

At the time, I was working five days a week at a clinic. I saw one patient after another for thirty-minute appointments, and often ran late. I typically spent my scheduled lunch break working, trying to catch up. But this lunchtime "break" was the only time I could find in my day that I might be able to exercise. I started to work out in the clinic gym during my break, doing my best to get in a forty-five minute workout each day. Then I would rush back to my office, wipe the sweat off, and change back into my work clothes.

Satvata had awakened in me a powerful desire to surrender, and I assumed this surrender would dissolve my ego self. All my ideas or normal ways of engaging with others and the world began to crumble and the fabric of my personality began to dissolve. The longing to surrender overrode any resistance to Satvata's instructions. When resistance arose, I intentionally surrendered further.

Although I followed all of Satvata's instructions, not everyone did, at least not all the time. One of my friends was told many times to leave her husband and her sixteen-year-old daughter in order to live in the Satvata community and devote the rest of her life to Truth. Satvata told her that he had left his wife and sixteen-year-old daughter to be with his guru. When my friend told him she felt she needed to be there for her daughter, he laughed and said, "My daughter was sixteen when I went to be with my guru, and after I left she declared herself an emancipated minor." At the time, my friend believed she didn't have the commitment it took for a true spiritual journey because she chose to stay with her family. However, when he instructed her to leave her psychiatric practice to join him for a two-month retreat in India, in spite of significant anxiety and many practical obstacles, she did so. Satvata told another friend that he would need to leave his wife and daughter, move to the community, and turn over his money to Satvata if he wanted to be enlightened. This enlightenment would then benefit his wife and daughter in the end. I found such instructions Satvata gave to his devotees troubling.

When one devotee was in India and emailed Satvata that he was experiencing chest pressure, Satvata told him it was spiritual energy and did not require medical attention. I knew this person had a history of hypertension and expressed my unease. I felt that Satvata was over-stepping his authority by giving medical advice and was concerned his students' health would suffer as a result. Later, a young man with a history of psychosis, who had been diagnosed with schizoaffective disorder, came to live in the community. He was a very sweet, gentle man, and had profound spiritual experiences. With Satvata's support he began to taper off his antipsychotic medication. Soon he was sleeping very little. He became manic and then psychotic. Satvata assumed that the power of his own force had caused this imbalance. He believed it was a kundalini awakening in response to his energy, not understanding that Mark had a biochemical imbalance that required treatment with medication.

While I found some of his psychological, psychiatric, and medical advice suspect, I resonated very much with Satvata's teachings about working on our individual samskaras as a means to dissolve the ego in order to realize divine universal Love and Truth. I had seen how my willingness to work on my own issues served to open my heart more to Love. I loved that Satvata actually taught what I had experienced about the importance of meeting whatever was arising in life. He seemed to understand that our human psychological self was part of our spiritual path.

Satvata spoke about the ways to approach Truth in a somewhat traditional Hindu model. An individual with a vigorous mind and intellect might traverse the path as a *jnani,* using inquiry and dis-crimination. The *bhakti* path—the path of devotion—suits those whose emotions are more vigorous. On the jnani path, one's awareness expands and expands; a jnani moves through states of profound detachment and expanded awareness into states of transcendence, silence, and stillness. On the bhakti path, spiritual experiences increase, such as bliss and ecstasy. Ultimately, both paths lead to the same place, where all separation disappears—All becomes One and One becomes All.

Satvata taught us what he called the four stages of spiritual attainment, which he had learned from his guru and described as the Gita path: (1) Ego—self-awareness; (2) from Ego to Self—a disengagement from identifying with one's life story, situation, beliefs, points of view, and habits, and enhancing a natural connection with Presence/Being/Existence; (3) from Self to God—moving from duality to the non-dual; the loosely-held ego becomes capable of holding and transmitting universal forces, leading to an arising knowingness in the body or heart or intelligence of what is true; and (4) from God to Truth—when an individual becomes a universal being. All that is left is Truth, the I AM, the eternal Reality. The universal being is a vehicle for the transmission of light, truth, love and wisdom into the world. At this final stage, all seeking comes to an end.

Satvata said that for those who surrendered their egoic will to a fully-awakened, realized teacher like him, the stages of spiritual attainment were accelerated. He asserted that when one was ready to go from the Self to God or Truth, the guru appeared in your life. "Without the link with one who has merged with God or Truth, the intensive forces needed for the final transformation cannot occur." He told us that the further along we were on the journey, the more sensitive we would be to the transmission of his energy. It was a compelling setup. Each of us felt special because Satvata had appeared in our lives, and we were easily swayed by his intense energy transmission to believe that he was the key to our spiritual progress.

CHAPTER 26

Out West

The question 'Who am I?' is not really meant
to get an answer; the question 'Who am I?'
is meant to dissolve the questioner.
—Ramana Maharshi

A few months after I first met Satvata, he began referring to himself as a *satguru*—a true guru, an enlightened being, a physical manifestation of Truth. He often referred to himself as Krishna, boldly insinuating status as an avatar, the highest form of incarnation on the planet. In retrospect, such a claim should have been a sobering eye-opener.

In true guru fashion, he occasionally bestowed spiritual names on some of his students. This was done with some fanfare and showering of praise for the devotee's spiritual attainment, qualities, or contribution to his community. This acknowledgement was treasured dearly by devotees who were given a spiritual name; it was seen as reinforcing one's detachment from the individual identity, the "I" or the ego.

However, such "naming" also set up a hierarchy in the community—those *with* names being higher on the ladder—and provided more opportunity for me to encounter my jealousy.

Satvata attracted some interesting and impressive students. Many were professionals—doctors, lawyers, psychologists— and others were successful in business. Most were long-time seekers who had decades of experience with the *Who's Who* of spiritual teachers in America and India. Some, having been disheartened by guru scandals, were engaging in another opportunity with Satvata. Being in such good company made it possible for me to ignore Satvata's hyperbole.

My capacity for discrimination had also been subdued by his power to impact my subtle body and my *chakras*, or energy centers. For myself, and for many who came to him, this blast furnace of energy was proof enough that something was happening.

Satvata spoke of engaging with beings on other planes of existence, and said he could influence world events that were battles between dark and light forces. For example, he told us he was engaged in such a conflict before the U.S. election in 2016, and later he spoke of how he would avert the climate crisis with his energy. I noted that anyone who heard him speak about these things could think he was an egomaniac, but because I was personally experiencing the force he transmitted, and because I was surrounded by intelligent, insightful, and big-hearted people, I discounted these thoughts.

With Satvata now formally identifying himself as a satguru, his relationship with his students followed more closely along the traditional line of guru-devotee relationships, with surrender to him an important part of the spiritual journey. This meant that his students sought his advice and asked his permission about their life circumstances. Some asked him about the smallest details of their lives, like what should be done with a collection of plates one had inherited. Others stuck with spiritual instructions.

I felt such a pull to be in his presence that I very much wanted to move out west to be part of his community. I needed his permission to do so, and I asked him every time I spoke with him. To my frustration, he kept refusing my request, endlessly triggering my jealousy and fear of spiritual failure.

Each year Satvata took many of his devotees to India for one or two months. Late one night, I had a Skype session with him while he was in India and asked him again if I could move to his community. I told him I had found a job opening for a psychiatrist at a VA clinic in a town near his community, and a public Montessori school that seemed very similar to the one Saachi was currently attending. I had already put her on the wait list for enrollment that fall. To my surprise, he agreed that I could move. I decided to wait until Saachi finished out the school year, which would also give me time to let my patients know I was moving and to say goodbye to them.

I was ecstatic. I felt that through this move and by being in proximity to Satvata, I finally could devote my entire life to Truth. I would be able to attend group gatherings and meditations frequently, and would be in the presence of his energy often. Saachi and I had good lives in Charleston, but my longing for Truth trumped everything else. I went through all our belongings, down to every last paper in my files, and prepared to sell our house in Charleston. I was leaving family and close friends behind without any reservations, letting go of all identification with the past. As I packed, the image of cutting an umbilical cord kept rising up in my mind.

Satvata insisted that I rent rather than buy a house, that renting would be best for my spiritual development. This did not make financial sense to me. I also felt that Saachi and I would feel much more settled in our own home, but in my state of surrender I was willing to do whatever he said. A month before our scheduled move, I met with Vicky, a realtor that one of Satvata's devotees recommended. I felt an immediate resonance with her. When I mentioned Saachi, I felt she immediately "got" her. Vicky felt I needed to look at a house that was for sale, as she sensed it was just right for Saachi and me. As soon as I walked into the house, I knew it was our new home. The energy was clean and *sattvic* (pure), the lines and modern simplicity of the house reflecting its energy. When I told Satvata about the house, he again instructed me to rent.

However, after I returned to Charleston, Vicky told me that a couple wanted to purchase the house soon, but she still felt that the house belonged to Saachi and me. Vicky shared with me that she and "Timothy" (Satvata's name before he gave himself the name of Satvata) were friends; they both had lived with the same guru in India for several years. She wrote Satvata a lengthy email, describing the house and the practical reasons she thought it would be a good home for Saachi and me. Ultimately, he agreed and I purchased the home.

Because of Saachi's elopement tendencies and to keep her safe during the transition, I traveled out west with our belongings a few weeks before our final move. I shared with Satvata at that time that I was not looking forward to taking on a full-time job at the VA clinic. I worried that I would have little time left to attend satsangs and meditations. Satvata suggested that I look into the possibility of working at a Native American clinic. I called the clinic and spoke with Valerie, the director of mental health, who told me they were looking for a psychiatrist. We felt an immediate connection, and she shared that her son was also autistic. She offered me the job on the spot, letting me know that I could decide how many hours I worked. Satvata's instruction to look into working at the Indian health clinic only served to confirm my faith in him.

I flew back home, worked at the VA in Charleston for another week, said goodbye to friends and family, and flew back out west with Saachi. Our flight arrived in the middle of the night. I put a very sleepy Saachi to bed, kissed her on the cheek, and whispered that I would show her the house in the morning.

I was awakened at dawn by squeals of laughter and joy. My system was startled awake with a rush of adrenaline, fearing that Saachi was in some kind of danger. I rushed out to the kitchen where I found Saachi standing at the large window, gazing out at the majestic and mystical mountain that overlooked our home. Its silent presence permeated our home and the surrounding neighborhoods. I opened the sliding glass door and ran across the back yard after Saachi as she laughed and pointed, saying repeatedly, "Mommy, the mountain! Mommy, the mountain!"

Over the years, Saachi had gradually become more and more present in the world. She had fewer periods where she seemed to "zone out"—staring off into space with almost nothing I could do to get her attention or bring her back into the world—and we had ruled out a seizure disorder as the cause. Occasionally, though, to my dismay she still had an episode, and as always I made great efforts to bring her back "here." In our new home, these zoning-out episodes typically occurred when we were eating at our small round kitchen table, next to the large window that overlooked the mystical mountain. Saachi would be fully engaged with me, carrying on a back-and-forth conversation, until she looked out the window. She would then suddenly go silent, staring out the window, firmly planted in her own world. I was often unable to reach her, unable to get her attention even if I spoke her name loudly, blew a whistle, or waved my hands in front of her.

These episodes triggered great fear in me, as I always thought to the future; if these altered states continued to occur, maintaining friendships, jobs, or any other "normal" activities in life might not be possible. Whenever she was tuned out, I made great efforts to bring her consciousness back to the here and now. When I finally succeeded, she would weep in sadness and pain. I didn't understand her weeping, but always comforted her. At the time, I believed that even though pulling her back in to the world was upsetting to her, it was for her own good.

• • •

Several weeks after our move, I met with Satvata for an individual session. I had decided to share everything with him, especially the things I tended to keep private, as a means of undoing any egoic structures. Although normally very private about my finances, I reviewed my financial accounts with him. I shared my constant struggle to save for Saachi's future, as it was likely that she would need support for the rest of her life, and the fear this responsibility triggered in me.

Satvata listened quietly and then asked if I could donate $65,000 to his nonprofit organization, which he said would be used for the residential program and to hire an employee to assist Devi with the business side of the organization. I told him I would need to think about it; my first responsibility was to my daughter and I was concerned about saving for her future. Later that week I found out that the sale of the house in Charleston had cleared exactly $65,000. I took that as a sign that Satvata must have somehow known I would have this amount available. I had heard him say that any financial gift to the guru was a direct gift to Truth, and served our own spiritual progress. I threw all caution to the wind and wrote out the check, having full faith that this would ultimately be best for myself and for Saachi. I was also responding to my concern that failing to make the requested donation would negatively impact my relationship with Satvata.

The realtor Vicky and I quickly became close friends. After some time, when I shared with her some of my doubts about Satvata, she told me that back when she and Satvata had been in India, his desire to become a guru had been well known among the other devotees. At one point, he read a book entitled *How to Become a Guru*. When asked why he was reading the book, his response was along the lines of "That's the career path here, isn't it?" Vicky was not surprised that he had begun calling himself a satguru.

Learning of his desire to become a guru was unsettling to me—after all, he taught us that ridding ourselves of desires and fears was the means of dissolving the ego and making progress on the spiritual path. How could he really be enlightened, or as free of ego as he claimed, if his whole scene was created and fueled by desire? I was also seeing that any effort to change myself, others, or the world was arising from my desire or fear—the very foundation of the ego, the separate self. I didn't know how to reconcile his claim of being fully awakened with his desire to be a guru, his need to direct the details of others' lives, and his desire to change others (even if to a more "advanced" spiritual state). It seemed to me his teachings were just another religion—another person's desire to change others and the world. But who was I to judge? I sensed that the subject of his desires was off limits, and I set my doubts aside as best as I could.

Over time, as I watched him posture, manipulate, and make demands of his students, I was unable to silence my increasingly persistent doubts. What was driving his need to be a guru? Why did he want to change anyone? Why had he created a spiritual community? Everything seemed to be about him—his power, his force, his mission, which seemed to be about increasing his influence in the world and making himself a world teacher. Were his students only means for supporting his ambition?

If all was One, and an expression of the Absolute, why did he need to influence dark and light forces? If he had realized the unreality of this realm, why did he want to play a big role in this world of *maya* (illusion)? Why did he need to define things in terms of dark and light forces, when in my experience it was all just energy? Why did he need to direct the smallest details of his devotees' lives, such as having to ask permission to talk to their children, or visit family, or have a pet?

As my own contractions unwound, I began to lose all desire. I was moving into a place of neutrality where there was no motive for any action, no need to change anything. Each day, I was simply putting one step in front of the other and meeting all the practical responsibilities of my life. This neutrality was dissonant from what I saw as his desire to change his devotees and expand his influence in the world. During an individual meeting with Satvata, I finally confronted him and said, "All of this, everything you have created, is born out of desire. Is what you're doing any different from anything else in the world, from any other religion or ideology?"

From his response, I saw that he either didn't understand my question and had not experienced the place it was coming from, or he intentionally side-stepped the question. He told me that when the Vortex of Truth comes through an enlightened being, it is used for the purpose of bringing others to Truth, even if outwardly it looked imperfect to others. The implication was that since everything that came through him was from Truth Itself, he could do no wrong.

I was uncomfortable, to say the least, with how this belief self-absolved him of being responsible for his words and actions—especially since his words and actions had such a powerful influence on those who were with him. Later, in discussions with other former students who were psychiatrists and psychologists, we were chagrined by our failure to see the classic signs of a narcissistic personality. He was grandiose, believing that he was a fully realized being; he had a sense of entitlement and an intense drive to set himself up as a world teacher with many devotees. He couldn't see outside the tight box of belief he had created, and he took advantage of others to achieve his own ends.

Despite Satvata's claim that he was a fully awakened being offering a direct path to Truth that other teachers were not able to offer, some devotees parted ways with him and left the community. Perhaps they felt they were ready, perhaps they disagreed with his instructions or teachings, or perhaps they had become disillusioned with his ability to guide or help them. Satvata tried to pressure them to stay. "You are giving up the opportunity for awakening in this life." He told the rest of us that the departed devotees "just weren't ready yet. Not everybody can handle the intensity of the fire."

Ultimately, a fissure opened up in my faith in his guidance. But it took two years before I could fully acknowledge these issues and unhook my pull to his energetic transmission so I could part ways with him.,

• • •

When I first moved out west, I was surprised to see how Satvata interacted with his wife. At that time, Satvata sat in front of the room during gatherings while Devi sat in the audience with the rest of us. Satvata seemed almost to disdain his wife; he ignored her comments and turned away from her. Since I believed that Satvata, as a guru and fully-realized human, operated only from the place of what was best for all of us—not from any of his own hang-ups, which I assumed he did not have— I figured this must be what was best for Devi.

It was no secret in the community that her ego was quite large and that she had a need to exert her control over others. Devi was neither warm nor affectionate, although she was always friendly with me, at least to my face. Later, a community member told me she had heard Devi yell at Satvata that I and another woman should not have been allowed to be there. I also found out that she had influenced Satvata to prevent me and several other women from participating as fully as we would have liked.

Devi's primary interest was the business aspect of Satvata's mission; she ran his non-profit foundation. Not infrequently, Satvata agreed to certain approaches or actions for the organization, only to have his decisions and promises overruled by Devi. She loved to travel and took great pleasure in planning the retreats abroad. Those who worked with her said she was driven by a desire for power and control, less interested in awakening than in the world. Once, when she was furnishing a bedroom in a house used by visitors, she gleefully chanted something like "I love to spend other people's money." Nevertheless, she added a grounding to some of his teachings, at times providing real life, concrete examples to elucidate his more abstract teachings.

Over the course of the two years that I lived there, Satvata's attitude towards Devi shifted. He began having her sit next to him in front of the room. She would often pipe up with comments, attempting to teach us alongside him. I resented her position, feeling that her very visible blind spots in no way gave her the authority of a teacher, or even an assistant teacher. Soon though, Satvata began to refer to her as "the Mother," and spoke of her as his equal. In the West, we limit our definition of *mother* to someone who has had children. In the East, the Mother symbolizes unconditional love, the embrace of Universal Love, and to embody the Mother is revered as an ultimate attainment. By referring to Devi as the Mother, he was upholding her as a fully-realized divine being. This didn't match up with my experience of her, nor were those around me convinced. It was disturbing that this person who was controlling and showed little empathy towards others was being held up as an expression of divine love.

Devi was known to be demanding, almost abusive with some organization volunteers, and fiercely protective of the primacy of her relationship with Satvata. Satvata's elevation of Devi as his equal precipitated the departure of Satvata's closest student, as well as others. One, leaving the satsang for the last time, said, "She's not my guru!"

· · ·

The energy in my system continued to intensify, and in spite of my emerging recognition of Satvata's limitations, over time I felt less and less separate from him. I felt as if I was dissolving into him. I experienced the immensity of the force of energy both in him and in me. When he spoke, I knew the words he was saying even as he spoke them; sometimes I even found myself mouthing the words as he was speaking them. I was fully aware each time he was emailing me. The intensity of the energy I was experiencing became difficult to bear, but I believed that this vortex was my direct path to Truth, and did not want to diminish the energy in any way.

During one group session I tearfully described my sense of dissolving into him and told him I didn't understand what was happening. He seemed very happy about it, and spoke to the group about me for some time, explaining to them that I was going through the "merger process."

Someone asked him, "If it's something good, why is she crying?"

Satvata said, "Because the experience of merger is so intense, it's almost impossible to bear."

The merger with the energy he transmitted, which I later came to understand as the life force of all beings and not personal to him, continued to intensify and created a sexual longing for him. I sensed that he and Devi were not sexually engaged and remained married as a matter of convenience. During one of our private sessions, I flat out asked him, "Would it be possible for us to have a sexual relationship?"

He smiled gently and said, "The merger is so intense that it affects every aspect of your being, including your sexual chakra. I understand you wanting to merge on that level, but that's not possible. That would prevent you from going to the next level, into love itself." He shared with me that he had experienced a sexual component when he was merging with his guru. He said, "If you think it's hard for you, imagine how confusing it was for me in a heterosexual male body with a male guru!"

To my knowledge, Satvata never engaged sexually with any devotees, although he once shared stories of his early years as a teacher, when some female students would engage him in intense spiritual discussions. In his naiveté, he did not realize until later that they were primarily motivated by sexual desire, which is common to experience with a spiritual teacher.

I emailed Satvata often about the intensity of this merger with him, but he didn't respond to these emails. Finally, in one email I asked why he didn't respond to any of my questions about the merger process I was experiencing. He emailed the following response: "You are merging with the form of the guru. This is activating your relationship and lower chakra issues. This is more rapidly taking you to your Divine nature than anything else that you could be doing. This is a wonderful grace. This process will continue to settle in, quieting and becoming more steady. Stay true and steady with the process. Of course, it will be the end of you as you know yourself to be. So this is the good news."

Meanwhile, I continued to experience a nearly intolerable burning in my system, all the time. At one point, I began burning up with questions: *Who Am I? What Am I? What is here when the body is not?* Each time I sat down to meditate, my whole being would burn with these questions; I was not seeking an answer in the mind, but the questions themselves served as a piercing fire.

I did everything I could to ground myself, including exercising and eating meat. My attention was swallowed up by the immensity of the fire I was experiencing. I stopped meditating and intentionally pulled my attention outward as much as possible, but the fire continued to intensify. My biggest concern was being able to function in order to care for Saachi.

At one weekend retreat, I raised my hand when he opened the group up for questions. It was hard to be in the hot seat, but my desire for Truth outweighed my fear. I wanted to ask him what else I could do about the intensity of this force. I was concerned that my system was close to being dangerously overloaded, and that the intensity of the energy could damage my nervous system.

As I sat down in the seat beside him, he recognized the Truth force in my system even before I spoke. He smiled at me, and said that everyone in the room could feel it. He spoke for some time about how wonderful it was, then asked for my question. I explained my fears that the energy in my system might be more than I could handle. Satvata gave me some basic grounding instructions—things I had already been doing. He seemed very happy about the intensity of the Truth force in my system, and I didn't feel he was hearing my alarm and concern. I returned to my chair, feeling a mounting fear that Satvata could not help me with this.

The drive back home was intense. It began to snow heavily and my car was slipping around on the icy roads. The burning in my sixth and seventh chakras intensified to the point where I became concerned that my chakras would blow out. I had heard stories, including about Satvata's brother, where kundalini overloads caused permanent damage. For the first time, my one-pointed longing for Truth was overridden by self-preservation, and the fear that if this continued I might not be able to care for my daughter. As the energy burned over the next few days, I realized I was on my own with this, and that in order to preserve my ability to function I had to disengage temporarily with Satvata, with meditation, with all spiritual pursuits. After a few weeks of withdrawal, the energy lessened to the point where I no longer felt my system was in danger and I gradually began meditating and attending gatherings again.

The recognition that Satvata was unable to help me when I had reached a point of real danger was a turning point for me. Even though he claimed to know us better than we knew ourselves, I realized he did not have all the answers. I began to give more space to my doubts about him, to look more closely at the red flags I had ignored in the past. I began to question some of his teachings and some of what he told me individually. Nevertheless, I still believed he was my direct path to Truth, and continued to seek his guidance and support. I couldn't deny the intensity of his energy and mistakenly equated that energy with Truth.

Any untruth—or intentional avoidance of truth—made my system shudder in discomfort. I always sought the resonance of truth at every level. I didn't do well when there was a pink elephant in the room . . . or in the community. The Devi pink elephant—the unspoken dissonance between how Satvata was presenting her as the Mother and my own experience of her—began to build in my system. I tried to ignore it, knowing full well that it was completely taboo even to question her revered position with Satvata. At retreats, I was astonished to see newcomers touch her feet, which she seemed to enjoy. The departure of some of the old devotees and the whispered complaints of residents in the community about Satvata's elevation of Devi to the position of the Mother bothered me. Why weren't we talking about this out in the open?

Several other issues were also shaking me up. One of Satvata's favorite devotees was a good friend of mine, Stella. She was very devoted to Satvata and to his mission, and served him tirelessly. He often spoke of the purity of her devotion and service and had given her a spiritual name. She was wealthy and had given a significant amount of money to him. He often met with her individually and seemed to treat her differently. Once on a retreat, she and I roomed together. After a midday hike, when I returned to our room, I found Satvata and Stella there, engaged in animated conversation. It was unheard of him for him to meet with someone in their room, let alone have an unscheduled visit with someone. I quickly backed out, closed the door, and went on another hike to be with the jealousy that was shooting painfully through my system. Later, I found them again deep in discussion in the community room. I couldn't help but wonder if the desire for money motivated his special treatment of her, but quickly brushed those thoughts aside, still hoping he had more integrity than that.

Later, I learned that Satvata had promised Stella several times that she would have a "major role" in his work. He had promised her a position on the Board of Directors of his nonprofit, a role helping with finances and committees, and involvement in his residential wing of the community. But Devi disliked Stella, and other than accepting the money she gave, Devi undermined all that Stella offered. Devi often overtly ignored her, and would not allow her to have any of the "major roles" Satvata had promised. Stella was in full devotion to Satvata, and continued volunteering in the community whenever she could, while doing her best to navigate Devi's dislike of her.

Rather suddenly, after securing hundreds of thousands of dollars in donations from her, Satvata suddenly turned on Stella and harshly criticized her during a community gathering. Stella wasn't there, as she had been asked days before to leave the community for an indeterminate time. Satvata and Devi accused Stella of being treacherous, involved in secrets and lies, and bringing in forces that were not divine. Devi added that dark forces had entered into Satvata's mission through her and affected his work. He claimed that his "misplaced compassion" had been fooled by Stella's egoic structure, and that he had sent her into seclusion in order to begin the necessary remedial transformation. Many of us saw the hand of Devi, convincing Satvata to distance himself from a devotee she found to be a personal threat.

My own experience of Stella was that she was the embodiment of service and sweetness. She spoke openly of her very human desire for Satvata's approval and love, which she related in part to the loss of her mother as a young child and to a deep longing for God. I didn't sense any treacherous or non-divine forces in Stella. I was stunned and confused by Satvata's harsh criticism of her, which went way beyond his usual pointing out of egoic structures in his devotees. Satvata recorded every satsang, every retreat, and every individual session he had. I knew Stella must be heartbroken from having been banished from the community, and would be further devastated when she listened to the recording of that gathering. The whole thing festered in my heart.

In addition to the Devi pink elephant—her elevation as the Mother when we were fully aware that this title did not match up with her spiritual attainment—and Satvata's treatment of Stella, several other issues were also gnawing at me. I couldn't understand the aura of entitlement that Satvata and Devi carried. They assumed that by giving money to them, students were furthering their own spiritual journey. Satvata and Devi didn't express gratitude; rather, they encouraged devotees and retreat participants to "give until it hurts" as a spiritual practice. Years later, I learned of his manipulation of several students' finances and demands for "donations," always framed as a great spiritual blessing for the student to serve his world mission.

Satvata's ability to merge with us, and for us to feel a profound sense of connection when he did so, was a testament to his intuitive and psychic abilities and a reflection of our openness. He was able to sense into the energy behind our egoic structures and manipulate these structures, which he said was for our own spiritual unfolding. He spoke sometimes of "manipulating *prakriti*" (the primal substance of reality), which translated into manipulating his devotees. I began to wonder if his own egoic structures might be co-opting his psychic abilities, using them to fulfill his own desires or to avoid being with his own unmet aspects. I couldn't deny the power of my experience, but also couldn't deny any longer the red flags I was seeing.

Each of Satvata's resident devotees met with him on a regular basis for private sessions. I was relegated to private meetings once every two months, in which I shared everything with him, heart and soul. Satvata recorded these sessions and sent us the recordings. We assumed that these were private sessions. Later, however, I learned that they were shared with other members of the community and with Devi. After I had given to Satvata all the money I made on the sale of our home in Charleston, to my surprise another devotee approached me and asked me for money, saying that he had been told to do so. Another devotee who was beginning to go through her own disillusionment with Satvata shared with me that he had forwarded to her many of my email exchanges with him. I was stunned that Satvata had shared with others things that I had shared with him in confidence, and felt a sense of utter betrayal.

I sat with my own pain and feeling of betrayal, wondering if perhaps my wish to have some things kept private indicated there were aspects of myself I wanted to keep hidden from others. I had experienced a sense of freedom when I had intentionally shared with the group everything I could find in me that I didn't want to share because of fear, embarrassment, or shame. Maybe this was the same. But I couldn't shake the feeling of betrayal, and the feeling that something was amiss.

The dissonance I was experiencing literally felt like a tremendous force that had to come up and out of me. I fought this feeling for some time, not wanting to bring all of this forward, knowing it would likely be met with the harshness of denial and resistance. Finally, with a great deal of anxiety, I resigned myself to knowing that I would have to speak these things in the group, to bring them out into the open, to pierce what felt like the group's blanket denial.

A group meeting was scheduled for that Saturday. Satvata and Devi were in Europe, but I knew that this session would be recorded and sent to Satvata. Before the group, I felt my upper three chakras burning, burning, burning. After the babysitter came, I drove to the community, hands shaking on the steering wheel. I did not want to do this, but felt there was no choice. We started with a silent meditation, during which I feared others would hear my anxious breathing. When the bell rang at the end of the meditation, I stood up immediately, walked to the middle of the circle, and reached for the talking stick. As I returned to my seat, I heard a few chuckles as someone said, "Wow, you must really have something to share." I was not smiling.

In our group circles, the person speaking was given five minutes to share, during which group participants were to remain silent. I cleared my throat. "I have some things to share that feel as if they are out of alignment with my system. The first is about Devi." I took a deep breath. All eyes were on me, intently. "Satvata has started referring to her as the Mother. She is very dedicated and capable in running the organization, but she does not embody the Mother to me. I hear many of you also speaking of this to each other, but it is somehow taboo for us to bring this out in the open." I noticed Prisha, one of the group leaders and the person who was the closest to Satvata and Devi, tense up, her eyes big, her face rigid.

"Another thing that is dissonant for me is Satvata's treatment of Stella. I don't understand what is behind how he has been treating her, but it doesn't feel in alignment with truth. And last of all, I understand Satvata's belief that not keeping anything private will help undo the ego. But to go behind our backs and secretly share with others what we believed was private doesn't make any sense to me. In my experience as a psychiatrist, and as someone who has been a patient in therapy, I know the value of holding a sacred space, where someone can share their most intimate heart and know that what they share will stay right there. I know the healing power of this sacred space—and treating everything as public information feels like a violation of the heart to me. It's the opposite of love. At times, a tender and sacred space is needed for a vulnerable heart to open and to heal. My system can't handle the veil we as a community have laid over all of these issues." The bell rang as I finished speaking. Hands shaking with the energy moving through me, I handed the talking stick to the person on my left.

What I had just done was completely taboo; it broke all the unspoken rules in the community. The weight of it filled the room. In turn, each person spoke out against what I had exposed. Not one person mentioned Devi; no one was willing to say anything aloud about her in the group, knowing we were being recorded. When Prisha spoke, her face contorted in rage. "No one here has any right at all to contradict Satvata. Each of us has basically signed on the dotted line that he is our guru, that what he says and does is true, and that we will surrender to him, even when we don't like it. It is up to him to make the rules around here. And there is much more to Stella's story that you all are not privy to." And then, it was over. I got up silently, put my shoes on, and drove home, aware of the vast expanse of stars. My being was permeated and engulfed by the intense force of Truth, and by the immensity of the aloneness—not only my aloneness within the community and in the world, but within all of existence.

I had never experienced much support from the community; unlike Findhorn or other communities I had engaged with, individuals in this community were there exclusively to work on themselves and to further Satvata's mission, not to support each other or to create a sense of community. I was feeling less and less connected with Satvata, and now I was the black sheep, on the outs for not conforming to the program. The acute awareness of my human aloneness within the community only highlighted the aloneness of existence that now accompanied the force of energy I was experiencing, all day, every day.

CHAPTER 27

Aloneness

Your very being is the Real.
—Nisargadatta Maharaj

This profound sense of emptiness and aloneness went well beyond any normal human boredom or loneliness or any depression I had experienced in the past. I felt devoid of all meaning, of all motivation. There was no point in anything. Even moving my body became difficult. As the experience of ego-based desires and fears dissolved, so too did the sense of a "you" or a "me." With the realization that no one actually exists, including "me," the only thing that kept me going was my sense of responsibility to my daughter. I shared this with Satvata, thinking that he could help me. Maybe the deep love I had experienced from him in the past was the antidote for this overwhelming aloneness and emptiness.

Instead of love, he became more and more distant, and less and less engaged with me. He rarely agreed to meet with me individually and didn't allow me to attend retreats. Whereas previously he had responded to all of my emails, often at length, he now responded briefly to only some of my emails. He often treated me harshly in satsangs. I wondered if I was no longer new and shiny enough for him. My intuition also told me that Devi had something to do with his disengagement.

When I finally did meet with him, he told me that we were already merged, whether or not my mind recognized this, and that this stage of the spiritual journey had to be traveled alone. I told him that I felt I needed his guidance and support now more than ever, and that this utter aloneness and emptiness, although perhaps a stage on the spiritual path, were also activating my past feelings of childhood aloneness; his disengagement and distance was reactivating and fueling my human pain. I told him that kindness and love would help this heal, but instead he was retraumatizing my old emotional wounding. He disagreed, and again said that I had to travel this stage alone.

I became more and more engulfed by the profound sense of aloneness. With the realization that the "me" and "you" or anything "other" didn't really exist, I felt I was living in a dream; nothing felt real. It was as if I were watching actors in a play. The aloneness was so much more real than any experience in the world.

No one else in the community was speaking about this and I didn't know anyone else who had come to this state. They were operating as if the world was real, as if they and others existed as individuals, and seemed unaware of the illusory quality of ordinary life. Satvata often spoke of the bliss he experienced and other spiritual teachers spoke of oneness and love. I hadn't heard anyone speak of this emptiness in the way I was experiencing it. This realization of aloneness was worse than any nightmare I could have dreamed up. I faintly remembered a teacher speaking of how the ego embarks on the spiritual journey, thinking it wants to get rid of itself. But the actual dissolution of the ego is the ego's worst nightmare. Satvata alluded to this, telling me that the suffering I was experiencing was the ego's last grip. But that understanding did not change my experience.

The reality of the world was crumbling around me, and there was nowhere else to go. This realization was more real than anything in the world—more real than any teachings, more real than anything Satvata could tell me, and from what I could tell, more real than anything he had realized. How could he guide me through this if he had not realized it himself?

The sense of utter aloneness made it very difficult to function. I did my best to be there for Saachi, going through the motions of meeting her physical needs and her emotional needs. If she were sad, I went through the motions of putting my arms around her, feeling completely empty, not able to muster up any warmth or empathy. She, of course, was aware of my emotional distance. Once as I lay on the floor doing a puzzle with her, I was barely able to muster up the energy to raise my head from the pillow periodically to engage. After some time, she said to me innocently, "Mommy, do you not like me?"

This cut through my heart. I pulled myself up to a sitting position, tilted her chin up to look into her eyes, and said, "Saachi, I am so, so sorry. I love you with all of my heart, and I love being with you. What is happening with me has nothing to do with you. It is a part of my spiritual path right now, and I will get through it, I promise." I didn't see how I would get through this, but I did my best to project confidence and to reassure Saachi. My heart ached knowing that my realization of aloneness was causing her sadness.

I was experiencing two very different aspects of aloneness: the absolute aloneness of consciousness without "an other" and the individual sense of aloneness of being a self isolated from others. By far the most profound was the realization that "you" and "I" don't actually exist, that there is only an undivided One—alone in itself. This profound realization was activating the stored remnants of traumatic human aloneness I experienced as a child and exacerbating the human aloneness I was experiencing in the community. But absolute aloneness and human aloneness were very different. Even though I was engulfed by the profound realization that no experience was real, experiences, including the activation of my old pain body, continued. In spite of my realization, my very human samskaras continued to unwind.

I despaired that Satvata was not helping me through this. I sought help from a few other teachers in Skype sessions with them, but they were unfamiliar with my state. I felt less and less hope that Satvata would be able to offer me helpful guidance, but continued to attend satsangs, not knowing where else to turn. Satvata had further cut me off, not allowing me to schedule individual sessions with him. Finally, I attended one last Satvata retreat. As I watched him speak, it was as if I were watching a body of flesh move. There was no person there. I realized that nothing in this realm was real and that every experience is a dreamlike projection of the mind. From that point on, there was no turning back. I had seen through the illusion.

Not long after the retreat, Satvata told me during a satsang that there was a dark force rising up in my *shushumna*, the main energy channel of the subtle body. Satvata had spoken at times of dark and light forces, and now he said that I was being taken over by a dark force. I was stunned. What was he talking about? All I was experiencing was the intense fire of Truth. Even so, I sat with what he said for a few days, looking for a "dark force" inside. I found only this force of Truth. Meanwhile, the community members distanced themselves further from me still, taking his words to heart that I had been taken over by a dark force.

I had an individual session with him a few weeks later, the first in several months. By this time, the force in my system and the realization of the unreality of the perceptual world were hard to contain. When I sat down in his office, I exploded. "This is all BULLSHIT! NONE OF IT IS REAL! INCLUDING YOU! Everything you are doing—it is all just another religion! You are doing what every other religious leader does, trying to change a world that doesn't even exist! You aren't even real!"

Satvata sat still, with an almost-smile on his face. "You are right; this is Truth. I was wrong about the shushumna energy, I misinterpreted it. You have come to Truth." His acknowledgement disarmed my anger, but not the force within. "Okay," I said. "But thanks a lot for turning the whole community against me!" I left the meeting feeling even less connected with Satvata; whatever realization he had come to was different from my own. I knew that I could no longer turn to him or anyone else for guidance or affirmation. My human disillusionment with Satvata and the deeper realization that nothing in the world was real dovetailed together into a profound and ever-present sense of utter aloneness.

Over time, the devastation of the aloneness and the starkness of the emptiness became less intense, as did the loss of Satvata. I was no longer able to project Truth or authority onto him, or anyone else. All devotion, inspiration, joy, and gratitude had long since disappeared, as had desire and fear. I was going through the motions of life, even as the force of Truth remained in the foreground. There was nothing left to motivate me on the human level, except caring for my daughter. I didn't feel depressed. I simply knew through and through that what I was seeing in life was an illusion.

There was no longer anything left to keep me out west. I felt no connection with Satvata or the community, but I also felt no connection with anything, anyone, or anywhere else in the world. There was nothing pulling me. I continued caring for my daughter and working, but I was no longer involved with Satvata and the community. Without a doubt, I knew that no one else could tell me what was real. I had come into my own authority, fully and completely. There was no longer any seeking, no impetus to move outward or inward. There was nothing to get, no spiritual attainment or enlightenment to be reached.

That winter, Saachi came down with a fever and cough. She recovered in several days, but then I came down with the same symptoms. I was still working at the Indian health clinic as the only psychiatrist there, and was booked out for over two months in advance because there were so many patients in need of psychiatric care. Many of them were suffering greatly, and I felt that missing a day of work because I wasn't feeling well wasn't an option; any patients I didn't see because of my absence would not be seen for months. Many were in crisis—some suicidal, psychotic, or even homicidal—and I knew they must be seen. I dosed myself with ibuprofen and acetaminophen and continued seeing patients.

As the days wore on, I became weaker instead of getting better; I was more and more short of breath as my cough progressed. I finally saw my primary care physician, who diagnosed me with Influenza

Type A and sent me home to rest. The next day, breathing became more difficult and I drove myself to an Urgent Care clinic. After a chest X-ray, I was diagnosed with bilateral multifocal pneumonia (pneumonia throughout both lungs), sent to the emergency room, and admitted to the hospital. As I hovered between life and death in the hospital, my two concerns if I didn't survive were my daughter's care, and the pain she would feel with the loss of me. I had done some planning for her future, including creating a Last Will and Testament and a special needs trust, but promised myself that if I survived, I would make sure everything was set up for her to the best of my ability.

Once I was well, I met virtually with Hal Wright, a financial advisor and author of a book entitled *The Complete Guide To Creating a Special Needs Life Plan.* I also met with another financial advisor. From these meetings, I realized the immensity of trying to save enough to support a child for the rest of her life—and saw that what I was doing wouldn't be enough. Both of them told me that at the rate I was saving, I would have enough for retirement but none left over for Saachi when I could no longer care for her. I regretted having given Satvata the $65,000 I had earned on the sale of our house, realizing that it could have provided years of care for Saachi. I crunched the numbers, and saw that it might have grown to $375,000 by the time I was eighty years old and to $2.3 million by the time she was seventy. I looked at residential communities for adults with autism and other disabilities; at the time they ran about $40,000 per year for housing and activities. Saachi's expenses for a caregiver, food etc. would likely be an additional $40,000 per year, so I estimated her annual expenses at $80,000 per year. I had no idea how I would be able to provide for her care, and was overwhelmed with the responsibility.

I had not attended community gatherings or had any contact with Satvata in some time, but decided to ask if he would be willing to return the $65,000. I thought that his desire to fund his organization had clouded his ability to recognize my financial responsibility for my daughter and that if I explained my responsibility to him, perhaps he would be willing to return the money. I presented some of the information I had gathered from the financial advisor in an email to him.

A week went by without a response from him. I knew he was involved in a legal dispute involving a former student's donations, and wondered if he was getting legal advice before responding. Finally, he wrote "I appreciate the challenges and difficulties of your journey and understand Saachi's needs, but neither myself or my organization have the resources available to help with your request. The money you gave was spent to address the specific need it was meant to support. Thus these funds no longer exist. I am grateful for your timely and effective support. But the organization is a charity and, as such, a donation is not a purchase and thus cannot be refunded." The tone of the email confirmed for me that he had gotten legal advice on his reply.

I persisted, telling him that I was asking *him* to return the money, not his organization. He responded by instructing me to meet with him.

No longer compelled to follow his instructions, I was bemused by his assumption of the guru role and his confidence that I would meet with him. Ultimately I did decide to meet with him in case there was any chance he would return the money for Saachi. I was also curious to see how I would feel when I met with him now that I had seen through the whole guru circus, and through the dynamic of my projection onto him. When I arrived at the house where we were to meet, Devi met me at the door. I spontaneously gave her a hug. After we spoke briefly, Satvata came in the room. It was taboo to hug him, but nevertheless I found myself spontaneously also giving him a hug. He was friendly and, as we spoke, I realized how different I felt talking with him now that I no longer saw him as my teacher or my guru. We were equals, sharing human to human.

We sat down at a table on the back porch. I looked in his eyes. "Satvata, I'm not asking your organization to return the money. I'm asking you. I gave the money to you in full devotion and surrender. You know I never resonated with the mission or the work of the organization. I gave the money to you. You instructed me to write the check out to your business, but I gave it to you."

I saw him prickle. I had never seen Satvata angry before this. He raised his voice. "You are asking me to take responsibility for Saachi. I am NOT responsible for her! And you chose to give that money." He went on for some time, agitated and activated. In his agitation, he described the weight of the responsibility he carried with his organization, including the financial responsibility. I sat back, somewhat astonished to see this side of him, and surprisingly amused. I wasn't upset or afraid. I watched the whole thing unfold.

"Satvata, I am responsible for Saachi. You are not. As her mother, I am responsible to provide for her as best as I can, for the rest of her life. And out of this responsibility, I am asking you to return the money." I listened as he cited the reasons he could not return the money. I offered him possible ways that he could return the money, but he stood firm. At the end of our meeting, I noticed him pull a small rectangular box from his lap. The recorder! He recorded all meetings, and this was no exception. Only this time, the recorder had been hidden on his lap instead of in plain view on the table. I looked up to his face, and he smiled sheepishly. "You can have a recording of our meeting if you'd like."

I left the meeting with a surprising sense of neutrality and freedom, and a sense of strength, my own two feet planted firmly on the earth.

That night, I felt a profound gratitude for the role he had played in my life's journey. This was a different gratitude than I had experienced before with Satvata when I was in devotion and surrender. This gratitude was imbued with compassion, and was a tender gratitude that recognized his humanness and his continuing struggles.

The next day I wrote him a final email.

• • •

Reflections on spiritual teachers

The relationship with a spiritual teacher is by its very nature one of projection. We resonate with the truth of their teachings or the truth of what they embody, and attribute the qualities or teachings we are recognizing to the teacher. Actually, the teacher resonates with us because they are mirroring a truth or aspect of being that is already within us. We project it onto the teacher, assuming the teacher "has it" and we don't. Projection is what the mind does and, in fact, the mind and projection are what create the entire world. The opportunity offered by the process of projection/idealization and the inevitable disillusionment that follows is the possibility of recognizing the Truth and Love within us—the possibility of coming into our own full authority.

With projection, we typically idealize a teacher, only seeing the higher qualities apparently within them, the qualities that are trying to come forward within us. A teacher can be very useful on the spiritual path, first opening our consciousness to the very existence of these truths, and then bringing forward our own knowing. Most teachers are in some way identified with their role as a teacher, and are often unconsciously invested in keeping that role going; in order to be a teacher, one has to "know" something that can be imparted, and one needs students who don't yet "know" in order to keep the whole thing going. Teachers don't typically disabuse their students of the students' idealization of them. Some teachers, though, do share their humanness and their own challenges; this openness and vulnerability can minimize the projection and idealization of students, and allow the qualities the students are resonating with to be recognized within themselves instead of being projected onto the teacher..

Typically, what goes up must come down. Idealizing a teacher, a romantic partner, a politician, or anyone else, is most often eventually followed by disillusionment, a recognition of the teacher's very human qualities, blind spots, or undeveloped aspects. The greater the idealization—and the more the teacher keeps the dance going—the greater the disillusionment will be, including grief, anger, heartache, and feelings of betrayal. These emotions must be allowed to wash through in order to complete the process of disillusionment. But if we remain stuck in the emotions of the disillusionment and maintain a focus on the "flaws" of the teacher, we stay stuck in the role of victim and miss the opportunity that the disillusionment offers. Alternately, we may find another teacher to idealize and thus keep the whole process going. In many ways, maintaining the emotions and negative thoughts about the teacher, or finding a new teacher to idealize, are easier than taking the next step—coming into our own full authority.

With the end of idealization and projection, we are left standing alone, in our own knowing, without anyone to turn to "out there" for wisdom, knowledge, or affirmation. The buck stops here, with me. There is simply nowhere else to turn, because the untruth of projection is seen through. The thrill of idealization and the ability to take the suffering victim role both disappear. There is nothing left to get, and nothing left to resist or judge. There is no one left "here," and no one "out there." This realization can trigger a very dark night of the soul, as the mind may interpret this as utter aloneness. The mind's interpretation of Aloneness is the ego's last hiccup, its last attempt to cling to identifying with a "me"—a "me" that is painfully alone.

But the starkness of Truth/Aloneness is the flip side of All Oneness. The realization that there really is no "me" and no "other" is born out of the starkness of Truth, and from Truth can come the realization of Love—the transformative realization that there is no separation, that "you" are not separate from "me" or from the rest of creation. Absolute Truth reveals unconditioned Love. Not love in the way our minds would think of it—loving someone else—but Love as the experiential realization that I Am All.

The efforts of the individual "me" cannot bring about the realization of Truth and Love, as the very notion of "me" is the basis for the whole illusion of separation. Efforts to get rid of the "me" on the spiritual journey keep the whole illusion going; in truth, all effort is a perpetuation of the "me." The dissolution of the "me" just happens—or more accurately, seeing through the falsity of the "me" just happens—and the miracle is that from this place, where there is no me or you, emerges the ability to dance in the world as a point of consciousness in the vastness of space and time, and the perception of the ordinary world shifts to the lived experience of the fullness of all of life as a manifestation of divine Love.

CHAPTER 28

Full Circle

I have disappeared,
and only the dance has remained.
—Sahajo

Although I had no reason to stay anymore, I hadn't planned to move and was surprised when I found myself packing up some belongings and making arrangements to move back to Charleston. The Indian health clinic asked if I could see patients via telepsychiatry after I moved to Charleston, at least until they were able to hire an on-site psychiatrist. I was happy to continue working with my patients and the staff at the clinic, and happy that I would be able to work from home in Charleston. My dear friend Vicky, the realtor who had coordinated the purchase of our house, was now looking for a house of her own. We both felt a sense of flow and ease for her to purchase the house from me.

I wanted Saachi to attend a public Montessori school in Charleston. I was told by staff at James Simons Montessori, the school she had previously attended, that their Upper Elementary classes (which she would now be in) were still making the transition to Montessori and the environment was somewhat chaotic in those classes. The staff knew Saachi well and feared that because of her special needs she might get bullied. They suggested that I consider Murray LaSaine Montessori, another public Montessori school in Charleston.

When I walked into Murray LaSaine for a visit, I first noticed the *Namaste* sign over the water fountain. Written on a wall nearby was a quote from Gandhi: *Be the change you want to see in the world.* Principal Wallace and Ms. Frasier, the special ed teacher, were both open, kind, and friendly. The goodness, the sense of community, and the love were palpable. I knew this would be a good fit for Saachi.

My dear friend Melanie was preparing to sell her house in Charleston as she was moving to Virginia. Her house happened to be in the Murray LaSaine school district zone. Saachi and I were familiar with Melanie's home. We had often come to visit and have dinner with Melanie in the past. I liked the working-class, down-to-earth families in the neighborhood. Most importantly, buying this house would allow Saachi to attend Murray LaSaine. I didn't look any further.

Saachi and I settled into our new lives. Saachi's life was full with school, soccer, speech therapy, and therapeutic horseback riding. She bloomed like a spring flower at Murray LaSaine. Her teachers and classmates saw her spirit, and loved, welcomed, and delighted in all of her uniqueness and quirks.

Mrs. Stullenbarger, her general ed teacher, often texted me to share heart-warming stories about Saachi. She sent a text the day after Saachi had attended the annual Surfer's Healing at Folly Beach. Saachi had surfed and then dressed up for a dinner with the surfers that evening. Mrs. Stullenbarger wrote: *"I wanted to tell you of the most beautiful moment we had yesterday. I pulled up the pics you sent* (from Surfer's Healing) *and invited Saachi up to tell about herself and the pics during our class meeting. She was SO proud. She told the class, I have autism and love. The way she described each photo was the best. My favorite was when she said—"This is Saachi! In a dress!!! It was great!!!" The class was enthralled in all she had to say and they were almost as proud as she was with surfing. It was a beautiful moment and I had to fight back the tears of love."*

That year, Saachi happened to be the featured surfer for Surfer's Healing. A video was made about her Surfer's Healing experience. Mrs. S. showed the video to the class, then texted me. *"The class is watching for the second time. They all love it and have requested to watch it over and over. Saachi said it was 'good.' She then told the class we can't watch again because of the EMF's [electromagnetic frequencies] being bad for your brain but we can watch it again tomorrow. I love your child."*

One time Saachi did a report about dogs. Her teacher wrote: *"I love Saachi's report. My favorite part was when she wrote that dogs eat dog food. She did a tremendous job with her presentation. I just love how comfortable she is with her friends and how she helps me keep everybody in line. They listen to her better than me. I have already had a parent send me a text this afternoon about what a positive impact Saachi has made on her son."*

Mindy, Wilder, Saachi, and Saachi's classmates
during our autism presentation to her class at Murray LaSaine

After she presented her report about dogs, Wilder and I joined Saachi at school. She and I spoke to her fourth grade class about autism and service dogs. We shared with them that autism means that someone has a really, really sensitive spirit, and that this often means that his or her body is also very sensitive—sensitive to sound, light, touch, and energy. We spoke about how Saachi's heart is so sensitive that she feels what everyone else is feeling—even when it looks like she might not be paying attention. Her classmates asked a lot of questions, and they loved watching Wilder obey a variety of commands and taking turns shaking his paw.

Saachi loves clothes, and loves putting on different clothes frequently throughout the day. When she discovered the Lost and Found box at school, she would often put on clothing she found in the box. Her teacher texted: *"Yesterday she really wanted a visit to lost and found—her favorite. I told her it was pretty warm and she probably didn't need a jacket. She said she was sure she did and proceeded to ask me to go outside with her to check the weather again. I love this girl. You know they say people are put in our paths for a reason. I'm positive Saachi was put in mine to keep my heart full of smiles and laughter daily!!"*

A few weeks later, all of the Upper Elementary students put on a show where they each created a poster about someone from history. The students all stood side by side in front of the long tables in the cafeteria, dressed up as their characters with their posters behind them. Parents and students came to each "booth," pushed a pretend button, and the characters came to life, giving a presentation about themselves. Saachi dressed up as Lao Tzu, with a long white beard and wrapped in a white sheet. On her poster she had written several quotes from the *Tao te Ching*. In the midst of the quotes, she had spontaneously written, "I love you." She read her Lao Tzu quotes and the words "I love you" to each person that pressed her button.

Another time at school, her class was having circle time. Each student was asked to share something about themselves. When it was Saachi's turn, she said, "I am Love."

Saachi as Lao-tzu

I was fully engaged in our lives, but in a neutral way that I was still getting used to. While Saachi was at school, I did telepsychiatry work from home, first with the Indian health clinic, and then with the South Carolina Department of Mental Health. I was also happy for Saachi to be reconnected with her grandma, aunt, uncles and cousins, who all lived in the Charleston area. I felt somewhat detached, but participated fully in whatever presented itself. My mind no longer categorized things in terms of "spiritual" or "not-spiritual"; all experiences were equal. All seeking had disappeared. There was nothing to "get," nothing to "become." I wasn't trying to get to Love, or Truth, or to a place where there was no ego or no reactivity. There were times of expansion and times of more contraction. Sometimes I felt as if I were the ocean, and sometimes I was a wave splashing on the shore. It didn't matter; I was no longer trying to be one or the other. The longing for Truth had disappeared out west, and now even the Emptiness and Aloneness had disappeared.

In interactions with others, I often felt I was pretending that this world was real—and that there actually was a "you" and a "me." Sometimes in the midst of conversations I wanted to giggle, knowing somehow that we were all in on this huge cosmic joke—all "making believe" our separate identities were real. When I did feel any sadness, or joy, or frustration, it was often accompanied by a sense of gratitude for the experience of the juiciness of life, the stickiness that makes the world seem more intimate and personal.

My consciousness flowed between the impersonal and personal. There were no longer any ideas that it should be one way or another. Speaking with friends about spiritual matters was no different than speaking with my patients about their symptoms or medications, and no different than teaching Saachi how to do laundry. It was all the same. Without any impetus to make anything different, or to attain anything spiritually, there was no longer an impetus to maintain a regular meditation practice, or to read or listen to spiritual teachings. There were no longer any ideas remaining about working on myself, unwinding egoic structures, or purifying my system. There was nothing left to get, and nowhere else to go but *here*.

During this time I was flooded with spiritual insights, apparently meant to be included in a book someday. I jotted down dozens of notes in the middle of the night, in the middle of a card game with Saachi, in the middle of household chores, even at stop lights while driving. They kept coming through and I felt compelled to write them down.

I wrote about the nature of contraction, the illusion of the "me," the illusion of separation, and how whenever we identify with a position or take a stand, the words or actions stemming from this very contraction create suffering. I wrote about how suffering itself is the doorway to our awakening—how each experience is a perfect entry-way to our own hearts, tailor-made for us, in that particular moment. I wrote about opening to pain and the possibility of a deeper opening and unfolding; and how turning away would cause pain to eventually come knocking again, only louder. I wrote about Truth and Love, the source of everything, and how we are all being pulled back to That, even as we participate in the dance of separation. I wrote that through seeking or longing born out of our Being, we are led to Love and to the truth of Oneness. I wrote that the suffering of separation is itself our way Home.

The insights that were coming came from my own lived experience. I was aware that sometimes my life didn't seem to match up with the realizations that were coming through, but I had no impetus to try to change this. The idea of being fully cooked or enlightened had disappeared. I was participating in life as a human being, with the limitations and proclivities that came with my particular form, including the tendency towards transparency, the tendency to expose everything.

My system is so oriented to truth and transparency that I often find myself "telling on" myself, exposing anything that feels out of alignment with my deeper knowing. Somehow, exposing all to the light of awareness in this way serves to pull back into Itself the human aspects that are not yet fully aligned with Being, with Truth, and with Love. I notice that Saachi does the same thing, perhaps because we are both Sagittarians, primed for truth. She, too, tells on herself. Recently, after a vigorous game playing ball with Wilder, she climbed up on the bar stool as I grated carrots on the counter across from her, "Mommy, I'm sorry I pushed Wilder."

"Thanks for sharing that with me, pumpkin. How about if you tell Wilder?" I said.

She jumped off the bar stool, plopped down on the floor next to Wilder, where he lay panting, and buried her head in his neck as she wrapped her arms around him. Wilder thumped his tail rhythmically, delighted to bask in her love and attention.

Compassion for my own human limitations is still in process. One night not long ago, I was tired. It was past Saachi's bedtime and I was rushing to get her into bed. Saachi was brushing her teeth. We've been working on independence with teeth-brushing for many years, and it's often a trigger for me. She brushes her teeth in the morning before her ADHD medication and at night after the medication is out of her system, when we are both tired. Her distractibility requires constant verbal prompting with each brush stroke in order to stay on task. In the past, when I was tired and frustrated, sometimes I would lose my patience and speak harshly or even yell during this tooth brushing ritual.

Then I had the idea to get a small digital recorder and made a recording of my voice prompting each brush stroke and when to move the toothbrush to the next part of her mouth. "Upstairs right, 1 and 2 and 3 and 4 and . . . upstairs middle, 1 and 2 and 3 . . ." and so on until she hopefully brushed all three "upstairs" sections of teeth and all three "downstairs" sections of teeth. The recording is fun and animated, with lots of laughter and encouragement to keep her engaged. Saachi loves it when I give voice to inanimate objects, and on the recording I speak for the bacteria she is brushing away, laughing loudly when they think she may miss a tooth, crying even more loudly when she has brushed them away. Her teeth also speak out, relieved and grateful that she is taking such good care of them. This recording has worked pretty well, taking me mostly out of the loop and allowing her to brush her teeth on her own, except for the fact that she brushes her teeth *hard* and chews on the electric toothbrush as she brushes. I have to replace the toothbrush head about once a week. When I'm tired, my mind might loop into thoughts about the long-term effect of hard brushing on Saachi's gums, the cost of the toothbrush heads, the impact on the environment of recycling all those toothbrush heads, and on and on.

That night I stood in the cramped bathroom with her as she began brushing, and felt myself tightening up. My voice tight, I admonished her to brush very lightly, pulling the toothbrush from her hand and demonstrating (yet again) how to brush her teeth gently and slowly, in time with the recording. She, of course, was aware of my tension. Every force has an equal and opposite reaction. As I launched into my tense lecture, Saachi yelled out, "STOP!" Feeling my frustration intensify, my mind piped up, warning me that I should step away immediately. I did not. I felt a rigidity set in and shifted into parental authoritarian mode, telling Saachi in a stern, calm voice that being disrespectful is not okay. I gave her a consequence for her "disrespect," telling her she needed to change into *biker* shorts.

You may recall that Saachi LOVES *sports* shorts with pockets. When she does things that she shouldn't do, or that she is trying to learn to do differently, usually we talk about it and she agrees to not do it again or to work on it. She often forgets these conversations, and her impulsivity leads her to repeat unhelpful or harmful behaviors again and again. For behaviors that are harmful or potentially dangerous—like leaving the house without permission, trying to touch exposed electrical wires during a remodel, or mischievously throwing Wilder's ball into a thick patch of poison ivy that she knows to stay away from—I use consequences that I know will upset her in the hopes of preventing the behavior in the future. There are two consequences I use: a mild consequence of sitting on her bed for a short period of time for less potentially harmful behaviors, and a more serious consequence of telling her to put on biker shorts instead of her beloved sports shorts. I don't like using that option, but having tried everything else in the books, I occasionally use it because it can curb the dangerous behavior. When the consequence is provided from a place of neutrality, in spite of her sadness and anger, she senses that it is being held consciously by love. Whenever I have moved into parental authority from a place of contraction, as I did that night, I am acting from my own frustration. Saachi knew this and told me to STOP. I wish I had listened.

Brushing her teeth too hard did not qualify as a dangerous behavior that needed this kind of intervention. Nevertheless, fueled now by anger, I had pulled this consequence on her. I repeated myself. "Saachi, being disrespectful is not okay. You need to put on biker shorts."

She began to cry immediately, yelling out again, "STOP!"

I yelled, my voice hard, "You need to get your biker shorts on RIGHT NOW!" And then I took things to the extreme—I gathered up all of her sports shorts from her drawer and put them in a bag. Saachi is very attached to these shorts and she began to weep uncontrollably. The feedback loop of pain and suffering was now literally crying out to me, undeniable. My anger began to soften and my mind again asserted itself, working to rein me in. "Stop, Mindy, you're going to regret this."

I asked Saachi to sit down on her bed, told her that I would sit with her so we could talk. I straightened her sheet, my eyes sweeping over the hundreds of lavender hearts imprinted on it. Her lavender quilt, displaying blooming daisies, lay on the floor. I picked it up and placed it at the end of the bed, giving my system time to calm down, waiting for my aching heart to melt the residual hardness. It didn't take long. I sat beside Saachi, my heart aching with her pain. I told her that I was not taking her shorts away, that when we were done talking I would put them back in her drawer. I started by explaining, in a soft voice, that I had acted from tension, that I was worried about her gums, about the waste and cost of all the plastic from the toothbrush heads. She felt my softening and immediately softened herself.

I noticed a tiny resistance still within me and heard it in my words, the way I was explaining my behavior to her. My words didn't fully match the ache in my heart. I know instinctively that whenever I am explaining or justifying my behavior, I'm not fully owning it— not fully opening to the pain of the whole situation, the pain the other person may be experiencing, and the pain I am experiencing. Apologizing alongside an explanation or justification of the behavior is not a full recognition of the pain my actions have caused in another and in myself.

I was met with her sweetness and the innocence of her voice as she explained another aspect of the human realm to her service dog. "Wilder! Being disrespectful hurts people's hearts!" The purity, the innocence permeating her words, permeating her very being, dissolved any residue of resistance in me. I was now ready to fully own the violence of the unnecessary consequence and the heartache that resulted from that violence. I held Saachi tenderly as I told her that she had done nothing wrong. "Saachi, I am so sorry that I hurt your heart. I was harsh. That is why you said STOP. I should have listened. You did nothing wrong. This all happened because of my harshness, and my disrespect, not yours."

Lying in bed, Saachi continued to talk animatedly with Wilder about how disrespect hurts people's hearts. I returned to her room several times, my heart still aching, recognizing that we were both processing the residual energy in our own ways. Each time I returned to her room, I rubbed her back gently, telling her she had not been disrespectful, that I *wanted* her to tell me to stop whenever I spoke with harshness, that I was sorry I had hurt her heart.

Contraction and separation, when acted out or discharged externally, cause suffering and pain, not only within the target of our words or actions, but also in ourselves. Contraction and separation are the same. When we allow our hearts to open to the pain our contraction has caused in the other or in ourselves, a healing of the wound of separation takes place. The illusion of separation dissolves. This healing is a return to Love, to recognition of our Oneness with the very object of our illusion of separation. The pain itself is the doorway Home. In truth, the tenderness of pain is not separate from Love. All is One. All is born of Love.

When my attention has honed in on a thought or idea that is causing some contraction or suffering, I pull out an old tool to loosen it up, like Byron Katie's "The Work." Or if I'm experiencing a persistent emotion and accompanying physical sensation, I might intentionally bring my attention to the sensation, as in Vipassana. The difference now is that these tools show up in the moment. There is no longer an ongoing Project of Me, or an idea that there is a "me" that needs to be worked on. I am well aware of tendencies and reactions in my system, but instead of needing to change or fix them, I hold them with an appreciation for the sweetness of being human.

All of my quirks and tendencies allow for there to be a "me"—the experience of being in this realm as an individual human being. There is a preciousness and a miraculous quality that comes with being able to experience "me." There is no longer any seeking of Love, Truth, awe and wonder or the vortex or force or energy. It's all just happening and all experience is equally significant—the gift of living as an individual on this planet—in whatever form these experiences take.

Over time, my experience of life has become fuller. The profound and pervasive sense of neutrality has been enriched with more warmth and aliveness. My being now leans into the experience of being human. No longer driven by spiritual longing, I sometimes find myself in a state of wonder, as if I am discovering how humans and animals and plants and the whole world work. I am astonished by the diverse and myriad aspects of this realm.

I have been aware for many years of Saachi's wonder and delight in this realm. Each day, each moment, she seems to be discovering the world anew—as if she has just arrived here and is astonished by all that she is witnessing. Saachi shares her observations and discoveries frequently throughout the day with her dog Wilder. I often listen in to their conversations as she gives voice to her many discoveries with great excitement and astonishment and, at other times, she simply explains to him in very practical ways how the world works.

"Wilder! Those geese are full of mischief! Listen to them! They are having an argument!"

"Wilder! That computer has EMF's! Those EMF's can hurt you, Wilder!"

"Wilder, kind words nourish the soul, and mean words hurt your heart. See, Wilder, if you use mean words, they hurt people's hearts."

"Wilder, this can opener is very dangerous. It can cut you. You have to be very careful when you use it."

"Wilder! This is how you eat with a spoon. See, you put it in your hand, then you put food in it and then you put it in your mouth."

"See, Wilder, when it rains, those clouds are letting go of their water."

"Look, Wilder! That tree is waving at us!" (as she waves back)

"Wilder, we can NOT turn on the stove. It is too dangerous! It could blow up! We have to wait until we are older."

As my own sense of wonder about this world grows, I recognize even more the beauty and purity of Saachi's wonder. Most of us lose our innate sense of wonder as children, as we become more and more identified with our individual self. Saachi's wonder about the world has never faded. Her spirit is fresh, experiencing everything for the first time. Just as she often does not have the ability to filter out sensory information that may not be useful or may be overwhelming, she does not have the ability to desensitize herself to the newness and freshness and wonder of life itself.

• • •

In January 2020, I began to sense a shift, as if a river was trying to move through my chest from behind me. For many years I'd thought I would someday write a book and I began to feel that it was now time, that I was pregnant with something. I also sensed that I would need to create time and space for the river to flow through, and that this would mean taking time off from my work as a psychiatrist. Although I experienced some fear about the financial repercussions of not having an income, there was a knowing that this was what was to happen, and the decision and actions taken towards this were accompanied by the neutrality and matter-of-factness that were now familiar to me. In February, I gave a two-month notice at work, with plans to begin this new phase of my life on April 1, 2020.

I couldn't know then that the world would be turned upside down by a pandemic in the weeks before my leave began. By April 1st, Saachi's school had shifted to online teaching. Online and virtual learning were challenging for Saachi and my plans to write were quickly set aside as I supported Saachi with academics and the basics of daily life, as did so many other parents around the world. Because Saachi is immunosuppressed, we were very careful with COVID precautions. She didn't get together with other relatives or friends or go into public places. Our lives slowed down—suddenly and significantly.

Instead of rushing off to school, therapies, and soccer practice, we took long barefoot walks on the beach, stopping to marvel at the beautiful patterns in the sand, or a piece of driftwood, or a large jellyfish. Saachi learned to self-start on her bike. The golf course nearby was undergoing a big renovation and we went for countless bike rides along the meandering paths, calling out to the geese and turtles as we rode by. We clapped for first responders and caregivers every night on our front porch. We discovered night-time walks, looking up at the moon and stars and planets and clouds. We delighted in our neighborhood. We glanced nosily in neighbors' windows and giggled when we saw that one neighbor, who normally seemed quite serious, often watched "The Three Stooges" or "The Flintstones" in the evenings. The simplicity and quiet in our lives made room for so much more delight and wonder.

When other students returned to in-person learning during the pandemic, Saachi continued her schooling from home because of her immunosuppression. I picked up books from the library for her. She quickly became very attached to a book about global warming and began carrying it around with her all day, to the point where it was interfering with mealtimes and her ability to do her school work. I made a few rules about her book, like needing to set it aside while eating, doing work, and sleeping. Her awareness of and concern about global warming filled many of our conversations. During this time, Saachi also rediscovered her many flower and bow barrettes from her younger years, and began putting them in her hair... all of them, every day, and all at once, until her whole head was piled high with the colorful hair clips. To this day, her attachment to the global warming book and her daily ritual of decorating her hair with an enormous bouquet of flowers persist.

I began looking for a babysitter who was being as careful as we were with Covid precautions in order to create some time and space for writing. Saachi was participating in a virtual weekly dance class, and Saachi's dance teacher happened to have a sister who was returning home to Charleston from college, where she was studying to be a pediatric occupational therapist, because she was immunosuppressed. Saachi and I had been isolated for some time and Lila was a breath of fresh air for both of us.

And so this book was born.

• • •

Life has come full circle. I not only came back to Charleston, but finally I came home to myself. My life is full, but permeated with a simplicity, richness, and depth. An underlying river of effortlessness flows through my life even as I take part in and take care of the many things that arise. Often, I experience a sense of wonder and awe, overcome by the miracle of having been born into a human body, the miracle of being able to experience this realm as an individual point of consciousness.

The profound emptiness that followed the dissolution of the heaviness and contractions of the past has shifted into a sense of spaciousness, an openness in which compassion, and joy, and gratitude, are frequent visitors. Occasionally, sadness or frustration arise. I experience them as flavors of energy, no better or worse than any other emotion or state, just visiting and moving through this particular human being. They move through, without sticking, with nothing to stick to.

Delight, and a lightness of being, show up often, a sense of dancing through the web of life. I am not "enlightened" or "awakened," and I haven't "arrived" anywhere, except right here, where I always was and always will be. I no longer have a road map, no path or guiding principles, and nowhere to get to. Somewhere along the way all of that disappeared. I'm aware of the river of life carrying me, and you, and all other beings. Even as I experience life as "me," I am also you and the space that holds us and is us. Sometimes, the attention zooms into the "me," and other times it expands out to the space of All Oneness and I am me and you and the space simultaneously. I'm no longer trying to be one or the other.

I find myself continuing to lean into the human experience, with what feels like a wave of creation and manifestation in the world. When I sense something is trying to come through or be birthed, I listen, and throw seeds out to see what takes. I take the steps that appear internally or externally, going through the motions, seeing what blooms, without a feeling of attachment to the outcome. There is a natural cycle to the experience of life as the wave and life as the ocean. The wave is always part of and born of the ocean, whether it knows it or not.

Epilogue

We are all just walking each other Home.
—Ram Dass

My family still believes I will go to hell. They pray for me. Nowadays, I'm happy for their prayers, and sometimes give them my own prayer requests. Our relationships have a richness and depth that wasn't possible before I had made the journey through my own pain and fear and into my heart. Our shared love is in the foreground, their beliefs and thoughts barely appearing on my radar now that the contraction and stickiness of my fear and pain are no longer present to make them seem real.

A few months after my final goodbye with Satvata, I started putting into words what I knew to be true about Saachi's spirit and about others with autism. I was well aware that traditional medicine and Western society in general had a very limited understanding of individuals with a diagnosis of autism. These deeply aware and awake beings are perceived primarily through the lens of their symptoms and the disease paradigm of medicine, not their depth of being. A vision came through me of an organization and a place that would be dedicated to opening others to the hearts and spirits of autistic individuals. I felt like a mouthpiece for what was coming through, offering this deeper understanding and recognition to the world as a pathway to their own hearts, to Love Itself.

Out of this vision, a 501c3 non-profit organization, Living Darshan, was born. I was still adjusting to the equanimity I was experiencing in my life and the manifestation of Darshan seemed to highlight that neutrality. I didn't feel a sense of mission or any desire for Darshan to "succeed," and no fear that it would not. I simply took each next step as it appeared. Sometimes, the next step came in a download of information—the very detailed vision and structure of Darshan, wording for the website, and details about the plans for the buildings and grounds. Later downloads included detailed plans for hosting an annual autism conference in Charleston. Other times, the next step was more practical, like organizing volunteers for a community event, or responding to emails, or looking at land that might serve as the center.

Mindy, Wilder, Kathy, Saachi's friend Joanie, Saachi,
and Cindy representing Darshan at an event

The first benefit for Living Darshan was held pre-pandemic on March 13, 2019 in Charleston. Over five hundred people came together for kirtan with Krishna Das. The heartfelt outpouring of love and support touched us all deeply and marked the birth of Darshan into the world.

The foundation of Living Darshan (www.livingdarshan.org)—the deeper understanding of autism as an expression of spirit—came from my personal experience with Saachi and others on the spectrum. Saachi and other autistic individuals are exquisitely sensitive, vibrating at a higher frequency than most of the world. With their sensitivity comes a lack of boundaries and a merger with their environment. They operate from the frequency of love and oneness. Most of the world, including the world of traditional medicine, views autism through a limited and superficial lens: autism as a disease—a set of symptoms that needs to be treated. I knew from first-hand experience that most therapies were primarily designed to get rid of symptoms and to make individuals with autism more like the rest of us. In my journey with Saachi, I discovered that *she* was often my guide and that I had so much to learn from her, even as I supported her in learning how to navigate this world.

Darshan gives voice to the spirit of individuals on the spectrum. It is helping to make space for this deeper aspect of autism in the world, and offers the possibility of autism as a spiritual path. In awakening our spirits to the spirits of autistic individuals, we are awakening to Love Itself—the Love that we all are. For those of us on this journey of autism, it is a profound pathway to Love.

There are many paths Home to Truth and Love, each one returning to the Source, each river returning to the Ocean of what we Are. I bow to the beauty and pain and miracle of your own unique journey, to the preciousness of you, and I bow to what you Are, to what we all Are, to the Heart of all hearts. I bow to your heart, to the miracle of you, to the miracle of us, to the miracle of Life and to the miracle of Love.

ACKNOWLEDGMENTS

Saachi—You make my heart sing. Thank you for coming into this world, for shining your bright light, and for being my daughter and my teacher. I am the luckiest mom in the world!

Parvati—You are an angel who flew into my life, and on your wings this book was born. Thank you for your wisdom, kindness, clarity, and love as you walked me through the book birthing process. I have often wondered how I got so lucky to have you as my editor. Maharajji certainly intervened. To also have the gifts of your friendship and guidance is the biggest blessing of all.

Kathy—Your purity and goodness of heart have been with me since I entered the world. Your heartfelt support for sharing my story, even with our unique individual perspectives, is a testament to the unconditional love that you are. Thank you, Lord, and thank you, Buddha, for the precious gift of my sister's presence in my life!

Mom—Thank you for bringing me into the world and for your unwavering love and friendship all these years. You are a living example of gratitude, generosity, joy, and surrender. Thank you for being my friend, my teacher, and my mom. I love you.

Dad— Your love and your steadfastness remain with me, right here in my heart. You taught me patience, being deliberate, and taking my time. Our shared humor and our delight in human uniquenesses and quirks have shaped who I am. I hope your spirit is soaring, Dad. I love you.

Scott—Your tender heart touches mine deeply, my dear brother. Thank you for your eternal enthusiasm and your joy—and as Saachi is saying now, for being "Uncle Scoot."

Kevin—Thank you for instilling in me a love of books all those years ago when you taught me to read, for being my big brother, and for our special connection. I am in awe of your perseverance through thick and thin.

Ed—You are a treasure in my life. Thank you, for your rock-solid, ever-present support, and for the depth that we share. Seeing your heart so touched by purity, innocence, and beauty cracks mine wide open.

Eli, Ruby and Sophia—I love each of you to the moon and back.

Muffy—The deep connection that was forged when we shared our dark nights of the soul laid the foundation for the depth and breadth that we now share. It is a joy to watch the flowers bloom from the fertile heart-soil that came from having moved through the darkness. Thank you for your gentle, loving input with the manuscript each step of the way, and for the depth of your compassion and integrity. I am grateful for you, my heart-sister.

Maryma—You dove in head first into this giant project, all from the infinite well of generosity and brilliance of spirit, heart, and mind that you are. Your edits were spot-on, and brought the manuscript to a different level. Thank you for your clarity, for never mincing any words, and for your enormous heart.

Amita—You are an angel that came to all of us from another realm. Your gentleness, your kindness and your always unconditional love have inextricably seeped into my heart. For you to have come into my life is one of the greatest blessings in my life.

Duke—Your integrity and your determination and perseverance as you followed the inner call paved the way for so many, and your laughter continues to ring through us all. Thank you for being in my life.

Christy—Thank you for walking arm-in-arm with me through thick and thin all of these years. We have shared everything from heartache, laughter, silliness, and everything in between—often through voice mails. To have the wide-open space to share everything human and to always be met with love is such a gift. I am in awe of your generosity, your kindness, and the brilliance of your spirit.

Victoria—My soul-sister. To share this human journey and the connection beyond is an unspeakable gift. I am grateful for your love and the depth of your seeing. Thank you for coming into my life, for being in Saachi's life and for seeing her so deeply.

Tom—Thank you for being a beacon of integrity and intention, for being a force of such good in the world, and for walking this journey of life with me, my soul-brother. I am so touched by the connection Saachi and you share.

Sierra—You became part of our family the moment we met you. Your kindness, your patience, and your steadfast love and presence with Saachi are true gifts in our lives. Thank you for your support on every level—spiritual, psychological, practical, technical, artistic, and so much more.

Bubbie—Thank you for landing in our lives all those years ago, for your steadfast love and friendship, and for the heart of pure service you bring into the world.

Suzanne—Who would have thought those many years ago in Prague that our budding friendship would take us here? Your support and enthusiasm not only for this book, but for everything, has been a real blessing. Your courage, your enthusiasm, your perseverance through thick and thin, and your bright spirit are an inspiration to me.

Soul Sister group—Amita, Vicky, Cindy, Melodia, Ramita, Paula, and Sally—I bow to each of you with a full heart.

Kimsey—I love that we just drop into our shared love regardless of how long it's been since we last spoke. Our connection is a clear demonstration that love and friendship are much deeper than time spent together or talking.

Billy—Your support, down-to-earth wisdom, and friendship ever since we re-met on the beach a lifetime ago is always with me, and I am grateful. Thank you for always being there for me.

Toni—What a joy to know you and to share our hearts and ideas for bringing a deeper understanding of autism into the world. I treasure you.

Mary—I am so grateful to share our autism journey together. Thank you for our sweet friendship and for all of your support.

Ms. Schrimsher, Martha, Miss Frasier, and *Mrs. Kraft*—Thank you for seeing Saachi's spirit from Day 1, for loving her so deeply, and for giving her the love and space to Be. You have laid the foundation for the rest of her life, and for this I am eternally grateful.

Nancy and *Sarah, our extended Fam*—Y'all are just the best. Saachi and I love you to pieces. Thank you for the gift of Surfer's Healing each year, and for your love all year round.

Vicky—I'm not sure how I got so lucky to have you in my life, and to walk together all these years on our journeys. I love you.

Michael and *Annie*—You swooped into my life during a time of true despair, walked with me through that dark time, in the midst of the desert of medical school, and then stuck around as dear friends and colleagues. Thank you for coming into my life and into my heart, where you remain always.

Guy Shahar—What a joy to meet you so serendipitously! Thank you for your purity and sensitivity of heart, and for your presence and work in the world.

Emily Soccorsy—You are a true visionary and creator. I am grateful for the time you spent with me and the creative energy you shared in exploring book titles.

Izzy—You bring an ocean of love to so many families and so many beaches around the world every year. To experience the space of unconditional love, where our loved ones on the spectrum have the space to fully be as they are, is a gift beyond words.

Suzy Miller—Your depth of seeing and hearing all of the beautiful, aware, sensitive beings on the spectrum opened my own eyes and heart. Thank you for what you are doing in the world, and thank you for being a tremendous source of love during my dark night of the soul.

Anna Lembke—Your depth of insight, your compassion and your ability to share these so fully are a tremendous force of healing in the world. Thank you for your openness and for all of your support with the book.

Individuals on the spectrum—I bow to each of your beautiful, exquisitely sensitive hearts and spirits, and am deeply grateful for the collective shift into a more sensitive, open and loving way of being that you are forging in the world. Thank you for your sacrifice, for your willingness to be here in a realm that vibrates at a much grosser frequency than the subtlety of where you reside. You are paving the way for all of us.

Darshan Team—Victoria, Shelly, Becky, McCall, Maureen, Paul— You are the wheels that make Darshan turn. Thank you for your dedication and for making it possible for Darshan to be a mouthpiece for a deeper understanding of autism in the world.

To all of my *patients*—Thank you for the gift of sharing your hearts with me. I am honored to be here with you. I bow to the beauty of your spirits, and to the living example you each are of this dance of life, of every single thing that arises being a doorway to our hearts.

Neem Karoli Baba, Ram Dass, Nisargadatta, Ramana Maharshi, KD, Eckhart Tolle, Adyashanti, Tara Brach, Jack Kornfield, Byron Katie, Sharon Salzburg, Joseph Goldstein and all other beacons of light—I bow to you in gratitude. Thank you for opening the way, and for shining your lights so brightly for all of us.

Dr. Melinda Edwards is a physician in Charleston, South Carolina, providing psychiatric care for underserved adults. She attended the Medical University of South Carolina and completed her residency in psychiatry at Stanford Medical Center. She has studied complementary and alternative medicine with Andrew Weil, MD, researched the effects of MDMA on PTSD with Michael Mithoefer, MD, and is a columnist for Autism Parenting Magazine.

As a child of medical missionaries, Melinda grew up in a Mayan Indian village in Guatemala, Central America. Early in life she experienced an inner pull to a deeper truth. Her journey has taken her through various spiritual practices, including meditation retreats, guidance from spiritual teachers, travel to India, and living in spiritual communities. Her quest led to the ongoing discovery of the sacred in all. Inspired by her journey with her daughter Saachi, Dr. Edwards founded the 501c3 nonprofit organization Living Darshan to foster a deeper understanding of autism in the world.

For more information, visit
www.melindaedwardsmd.com
www.livingdarshan.org